Philosophy of Mind: An Introduction

B

Philosophy of Mind:
An Introduction

George Graham

BLACKWELL
Oxford UK & Cambridge USA

First published 1993
Reprinted 1993, 1996

Blackwell Publishers Ltd
108 Cowley Road
Oxford OX4 1JF
UK

Blackwell Publishers Inc.
238 Main Street
Cambridge, Massachusetts 02142
USA

British Library Cataloguing in Publication Data

A CIP catalogue record for this book is available from the British Library.

Library of Congress Cataloging-in-Publication Data

Graham, George, 1945–
Philosophy of mind : an introduction / George Graham.
p.   cm.
Includes bibliographical references and index.
ISBN 0–631–17955–0.—ISBN 0–631–17956–9 (pbk.)
1. Philosophy of mind.   I. Title.
BD418.3.G73   1993
128'.2—dc20   92–26972
                                                            CIP

Typeset in 11 on 13 pt Imprint
by Graphicraft Typesetters Ltd, Hong Kong
Printed in Great Britain by T.J. Press Ltd, Padstow, Cornwall

This book is printed on acid-free paper.

Contents

Preface

For you will do me much greater good by putting an end to ignorance
of my psyche than if you put an end to an affliction of my body.

Plato, *Hippias Minor*

This is a book to begin with: to begin the philosophy of mind. It
tries to make the main ideas of the subject available to readers
with little or no previous exposure to philosophy. It is primarily
intended for undergraduate students and the inquisitive general
reader.

Each chapter addresses topics which are distinguishable from
the topics addressed in other chapters. So someone who is interested in whether persons can survive bodily death could read
the second chapter without reading the first, whereas someone
who is curious about Materialism could turn immediately to the
seventh chapter for a self-enclosed guide to the rudiments of that
doctrine. While the chapters stand alone, however, the book can
be read from front to back. The first chapter provides a working
definition of philosophy of mind as well as a representative discussion of a topic within the subject. This is the question of
whether knowledge of conscious experience is essentially subjective or first-personal.

The book is then divided into seven core chapters, each of which
deals with a specific family of topics central to the subject. Both
the choice of topics and their treatment is influenced by current
philosophic research and activity. The current influence is perhaps most clearly shown in the organization of the second to
fifth chapters which directly mirrors contemporary concern with

the attribution of mind to others: the disembodied, other human beings, nonhuman animals, sophisticated computers and God. This is followed by discussions of rational action, Materialism and supervenience, freedom and personhood and the issues and debates which these topics have inspired. The ninth and final chapter applies philosophy of mind to ethical debate over animal liberation. It employs theses about animal consciousness to sup- port critical moves in the debate.

Several important figures in past and current philosophy of mind are discussed, although this is not an intellectual history text. My own positions and preferences are present, occasionally visibly in certain remarks, always invisibly in underlying editorial decisions, but this is not a personal philosophy of mind. I try to let positions and arguments speak for themselves. I also try to maintain contact with puzzlement and perplexity about the mind. The mind/body problem, for example, may be made genuinely interesting to novices when bound up with questions of survival of bodily death (as attempted in the second chapter) and of mental illness and suicidal depression (as attempted in the seventh). It is less interest- ing, perhaps even uninteresting, if people simply walk through the Philosopher's Museum of Mind/Body 'Isms' (Materialism, Dualism, etc.) without the partner of perplexity.

To offer an uncluttered text, most of the notes and references are provided at the end of each chapter. Readers interested in additional readings may consult 'A philosophy of mind bookshelf' at the back of the book.

The book was first conceived while I was a Tennent Caledonian Fellow in the Centre for Philosophy and Public Affairs at the University of St Andrews in Scotland. It evolved from conception to completeness back in my own department, reinforced by the advice and support of near and distant colleagues.

I have been the beneficiary of generous and insightful help from many philosophers. So I want to recognize my debt and express my appreciation to: James Anderson, William Bechtel, Owen Flanagan, Max Hocutt, Terry Horgan, Harold Kincaid, Gareth Matthews and G. Lynn Stephens. Special thanks are in order to James Rachels, who helped with an encouraging reading of the first draft, and to Robert Kane, J. Christopher Maloney and Bruce Waller, who read drafts, commented in detail and offered astute suggestions and enthusiastic support.

K. Richard Garrett has done far more than just read and comment on the chapters. He has also guided and influenced my thinking and pedagogy for more than two decades.

Finally, my deepest debt is to my wife, Patricia. I dedicate this book to her, a slender token of appreciation for her efforts on its and my behalf. My good thoughts would be lost without her.

1

What is Philosophy of Mind?

In reading this book you are using your mind. When you ponder this page your mind is at work. As you sit in your chair you are having experiences. When you see the colour of the book cover you are having a visual experience. When you notice the sounds in the next room you are having an auditory experience. Your mind enables you to read, ponder, see and hear.

Now think for a minute of what it would be like if the world, our Earth, was mindless. What if the world was devoid of experience and thought? At the very least, a mindless world would be, to borrow a phrase of the poet John Keats, a wide quietness, 'with buds, and bells, and stars without a name'. It would be a world in which nothing was named, in which nothing was either thought of or experienced, for there would be no one. There certainly would be no you and me.

Fortunately, the world is not mindless. Indeed, it is thickly populated with minds. In the world, moreover, minds not only name but are named. They are named by type, such as The Human Mind or The Animal Mind, and by individual, such as My Mind, Your Mind and the Minds of Charles Dickens and Emily Dickinson. Indeed, minds are not just named, they are studied and examined in science, novel and verse as well as philosophy.

The purpose of this book is to introduce the area of philosophy which studies mind: the philosophy of mind. I write for those coming to philosophy of mind for the first time.

1.1   Beginning Definitions, Elementary Ideas

What is philosophy of mind? Philosophy of mind is the area of philosophy which strives for comprehensive and systematic understanding of that which thinks and experiences, namely the mind. It tries to understand what mind is, what it does and how to uncover it.

Although philosophy of mind is a single subject, it has many parts or aspects. The aspects serve as bases for the chapters to follow. Meanwhile, one can learn something about the subject before reading the book by looking at various concepts used in the preceding definition. Let us look first at 'philosophy', then at 'mind'; then, we shall return to the complete expression 'philosophy of mind'.

Philosophy is the subject or academic discipline which attempts to comprehensively and systematically understand the most fundamental areas of human experience. These include mind as well as religion, science, art, language and morality, among others. The key words are 'comprehensive' and 'systematic'. Comprehensiveness and systematicity help to distinguish philosophy from other subjects of intellectual and theoretical endeavour such as, for examples, physics and history.

Comprehensiveness has two dimensions. One is breadth; the other is depth. Breadth? Physics studies matter in motion but not belief in God. History studies the recorded memory of humankind but not the difference between right and wrong. Philosophy studies (among many other things) belief in God and the difference between right and wrong as well as, for example, the central features of physics and history. So philosophy covers a lot of ground It covers more ground – in a systematic manner – than any other discipline. In covering a lot of ground philosophy possesses breadth.

What of depth? Philosophy penetrates beneath the ground which it covers. It tries to get to the core. Sometimes, in fact, a philosopher will argue that something close to the heart of another mode of inquiry, such as science, should be rejected or replaced. This typifies the drive for depth. Philosophy may recommend or urge changes in other disciplines, because it probes deeply into the foundations of those disciplines. To take a brief illustration, most psychologists probably agree with Susan Blakemore, a psychologist at the University of Bristol, that after the death of our physical body 'there will be no more experience; no more self'.[1] Philosophers, however, may challenge psychologists to re-examine the belief in non-survival. A philosopher may argue, rightly or wrongly, that a probing analysis of experimental and clinical data together with what is known of other areas of human experience shows that the self or mind can survive. The self is not necessarily snuffed out when the body dies.

I do not mean to convey the impression that philosophy contradicts established convictions of scientists and psychologists. Many philosophers share Blakemore's scepticism about survival. What I am concerned with here is philosophy's comprehensiveness and, in particular, its drive for depth. Philosophy attempts to penetrate even if this means challenging doctrines of other disciplines.

Thus far we have considered the comprehensiveness of philosophy. What of systematicity? The simplest way to describe systematicity, which states the basic idea but does not attempt to clarify it very much, is this: in aiming to be systematic philosophy strives to be both consistent and coherent. It aims for ideas or theses which are free of contradiction (that's consistency) and which stand in relationships of mutual reinforcement and support (that's coherence).

The elements of systematicity, mainly consistency and coherence, sound very abstract, and in truth they are difficult to describe with precision. At the same time, philosophy requires consistency and coherence. Anything less is unsystematic and unacceptable. To illustrate, consider the following three philosophic claims about mind, brain and death.

C1 The mind is one and the same as the brain; mind and brain are identical.
C2 The mind survives bodily death.
C3 The brain fails to survive bodily death.

C1, C2 and C3 cannot each be true; thus, they are inconsistent. It is not possible for the mind to survive while the brain, if mind is one and the same as brain, fails to survive. Compare with the following: I am one and the same as George Graham. Then, I cannot travel to Scotland while George Graham journeys to China. If we are one and the same, then whatever I do George must do, for he is me.

What can be done to rescue or achieve systematicity? In the case at hand, one option is to subtract C1 and then add C4:

C4 The mind is *not* one and the same as the brain. Mind and brain are distinct.

C2, C3 and C4 are consistent. Each member of the set can be true. This is not to say that each really is true. However, it is to claim that the set is free of contradiction. C2, C3 and C4 even support or cohere with one another. If, for example, mind is not one and the same as brain, then something is true of the mind which is not true of the brain. What is that something? C2 and C3 offer a possible answer. 'The mind survives bodily death whereas the brain does not survive.' C2 and C3 thus reinforce or support C4. They help to explain why C4 might be true. So, C2, C3 and C4 stand not only in consistent but coherent or mutually supportive relationships.

Unfortunately perhaps, as Gilbert Harman, a philosophy professor at Princeton University, is fond of pointing out in another context, there are no fixed rules which reveal how to achieve consistency and coherence.[2] The search for systematicity suggests that something in C1, C2 and C3 must go. But what? Should we substitute C4 for C1? Should we abandon the C2 conviction that the mind survives? How about the C3 claim that the brain fails to survive? Either alternative produces a consistent and coherent set of theses or claims. However, even without strict guidelines for systematicity, it is clear that a philosophy which is neither consistent nor coherent fails to be systematic. Philosophies can be unacceptable on a number of different grounds. Failure to be systematic is one of them.

I hasten to add that if two distinguishing features of philosophy are comprehensiveness and systematicity, these are not the sole distinguishing features. Philosophy is different from other subjects such as physics and history not merely because it systematically covers more ground, but because of its method and motive. Physics, for example, relies on mathematics and laboratory experiments; philosophy doesn't rely on mathematics or experiments.

History rests on the record of the past; philosophy doesn't rest on the past. There isn't even reliance on the great thinkers of the past, philosophers like Plato (427–347 BC) and Descartes (1596–1650), despite appreciation for their ideas. The heart of philosophic method is reason and argumentation. The motivation or source – the reason people do philosophy – consists of features of the world and human experience which people naturally find worrisome, perplexing and puzzling, such as the mind. 'What is the relation between mind and brain?' 'Does mind survive bodily death?' 'Is mind nothing over and above brain?' True, perplexity and puzzlement also motivate disciplines like physics or history, but in other subjects human puzzlement is more limited than in philosophy. In physics, it is confined to the physical world, whereas in history it is focused on the recorded past. Philosophy, like human intelligence itself, is first and last driven by *expansive* puzzlement and perplexity. The topics of philosophy cover the total spectrum of basic human concerns. Hence, when I contend that philosophy aims for comprehensive and systematic understanding, I don't mean that only comprehensiveness and systematicity distinguish it from other subjects. My statement represents the bare bud of philosophy. It does not reveal how philosophers try to achieve that understanding (the method) or what stimulates or motivates it (the motive).

We have just learned something about the nature of philosophy. We have learned that it is both systematic and comprehensive; and we have learned something about the nature of these features. What of mind?

Before offering a definition, let's consider an instance of what may be called mind at work. Suppose you are cracking walnuts with a nutcracker, and the cracker misses the shell of a walnut and you squeeze its pivoted jaws on your thumb. What happens? First there will be pain. Then probably anger. Then eventually the belief that you made an imprudent mistake. All three – the pain, anger, and belief – are activities of mind or events which take place in or because of mind. A mindless creature could not feel pain, be angry or believe that it had made a mistake. This is not to say that only creatures who feel pain, get angry and believe they make mistakes have minds. Nevertheless, such events or capacities are possible only for minded creatures.

Ponder the pain. You squeeze your thumb in a nutcracker. You feel pain. Pain is among the clearest examples of mental events philosophers and others classify as 'sensations'. In particular, pain is a bodily sensation, since, as in pain produced by squeezing your thumb, the pain seems to the person in pain to occur in a part or region of the body, in this case the thumb.

Consider the example of anger. You get angry at yourself for squeezing your thumb. Anger is among the clearest examples of mental events philosophers classify as 'emotions' or 'emotional feelings'. In particular, anger is a directed emotion, because, as in anger over squeezing your thumb, it is aimed or directed at something which is its source or cause, for instance, squeezing your thumb.

Consider the example of belief. You believe you made an imprudent mistake. Belief is among the clearest examples of mental events philosophers and others classify as 'thoughts' or (more technically) 'propositional attitudes' (which expression will be explained shortly). In particular, belief is a thought or attitude with specific content since, as in the belief in your own imprudence, belief has content or character to it; it is *about* something. In the example at hand, the belief is about yourself as imprudent thumb squeezer, not about yourself as curious reader of this book, although you are reading this book and probably have beliefs about yourself with that content as well.

A fact to notice about thoughts with content is that the same content can occur in different types or sorts of thought. So, to illustrate, I can believe that I made a mistake, I can remember that I made a mistake or I can fear that I made a mistake. In each example, there is the same content, viz. that I made a mistake; but the content occurs in different types of thought or attitude: believing, remembering and fearing respectively. Furthermore, since content can be expressed in the form of a proposition or statement, such as 'I made a mistake', philosophers refer to thoughts with content as 'propositional attitudes.' The attitude may be interpreted as an attitude towards a proposition: believing that *I made a mistake*, fearing that *I made a mistake* and so on.

It should also be noted that sensations and emotional feelings are among the clearest examples of mental events which normally, typically, perhaps even necessarily occur in consciousness and which are consciously experienced. By contrast, propositional attitudes are among the clearest examples of mental events which may not occur in consciousness. Think of the difference, for example, between your belief (when not planning a tour) that Radio City Music Hall is in New York City, and the sensation of pain or the feeling of anger on squeezing your thumb in a nut-cracker. The belief may be non-conscious. You may have it when asleep, unconscious and unaware. It is part of your memory store of background information. By contrast, the pain lashed into consciousness with anger resounding immediately thereafter. It would be hard or even impossible to imagine having *this* pain and being *that* angry while asleep or unconscious.

Let us label conscious mental events or activities 'experiences' (for emphasis 'conscious experiences'). Let us reserve 'thoughts' for attitudes such as belief which possess content and of which we can be unaware. Thoughts can be conscious or non-conscious. They can be experiences or non-experiences. Experiences, by contrast, are conscious.

Defining mind is not easy. But it is not impossible. By using the concepts of thought and experience, I propose the following definition.

Mind is that which thinks and experiences. Mindless creatures neither think nor experience. Since you and I are minded, or have minds of our own, we think and experience.

Now back to the definition of philosophy of mind introduced several paragraphs ago. What is philosophy of mind? *Philosophy of mind is the area of philosophy which strives for comprehensive and systematic understanding of that which thinks and experiences, namely the mind.*

Our definition of the subject gives us, among other things, a picture of the terrain to be covered in this book. The book will portray how philosophy aims comprehensively and systematically to understand mind. We will explore from a philosophic vantage point what mind is and does, and how to uncover it.

Before we start, with a brief example below of a problem in philosophy of mind, I should mention one thing that philosophy of mind is not. Philosophy of mind is not psychology. Psychology is science; philosophy is not science. Furthermore, rarely does psychology support theses in philosophy of mind in a direct or immediate way.

A psychologist may be either friend or foe, for example, of the thesis that mind is brain. However, philosophy of mind has traditionally given and received assistance in the development of psychology. Philosophic arguments advance and enrich psychology, while facts and lessons from psychology make philosophy more coherent and trustworthy.

1.2 Colour in Black and White

Have you ever tried to describe to another person what some conscious experience of yours is like? One day a friend of mine tried to describe for me what his migraine headaches are like. 'They feel *awful*, positively *dreadful*!' he reported, evincing the sad and sorry character of his headaches. I tried to understand them in terms of my own luckily undramatic history of aches and pains. I complained that some of my headaches have to be quieted by double doses of aspirin. However, he was insulted by my complaint. 'You obviously don't know what mine *feel* like', he protested. 'If yours are relieved by aspirin, yours are very different from my own. Mine are dreadful; *nothing* relieves them.'

Apparently some of his headaches are nothing like my headaches. The raw feel of his headaches seemed to elude me. But why? Why did his describing his headaches do so little to communicate their character to me? A natural, intuitive explanation for this sort of phenomenon goes as follows:

> Experience is the necessary educator; a description of experience is no substitute for experience. The very feel of a conscious experience eludes us unless we have had the experience ourselves. In the headache case, I can grasp the character of migraine only by having a migraine myself. Since I have never had a migraine, I do not know what the headaches are like.

Whatever merits this explanation – which I shall call the *experience explanation* – has in accounting for my friend's frustration, as an interpretation of the character of conscious experience it is incompatible with an objection advanced by several philosophers fond of physical science. The objection goes as follows:

The experience explanation neglects an important additional way in which to discover what conscious experience is like: through natural science. Physical, chemical and biological science can describe consciousness and thus what the experience of migraine is like. You don't have to *have* a migraine. Science can describe it for you.

Imagine, then, that I, having located the most advanced neuroscientific texts on migraine, open one of these texts. Will I find there a description of the character of migraines through which I can grasp, as the migraine sufferer did not help me to grasp, what migraine is like?

That is the hope of some scientifically-minded philosophers. I shall call it the *optimistic science position*. According to the optimistic position, to know each and every physical scientific fact about conscious experience is to know, among other things, what experience is like. Still, is the optimistic science position reasonable? Will it survive critical reflection? One trouble with the position is that we can outline an opposing (what I shall call) *pessimistic science position* in a plausible fashion, according to which even if we know the physics, chemistry and biology of consciousness, we still will not know what consciousness is like. This is because consciousness is subjective or first-personal: we need to *be* conscious before we can know what consciousness is like. No amount of impersonal physical scientific information about migraine is sufficient to communicate what the headache is like.

To see how the pessimistic science position may be developed, let us consider one of the most famous defences of the position in recent philosophy of mind. This is the so-called Knowledge Argument of the Australian philosopher Frank Jackson.[3] Jackson's argument is provocative and much has been written about it. I shall spend only a brief moment with it. The topic it raises – the character of conscious experience – is discussed again in the eighth and ninth chapters.

Jackson defends the pessimistic position with a direct, vivid story, which focuses on the visual experience of colour rather than the experience of migraine. It goes roughly like this:

Imagine Mary, a brilliant natural/physical scientist, who has spent her entire life cloistered within a strictly controlled room which displays only various shades of black, white and grey. Mary nevertheless (through black and white television and colourless books) has become the world's greatest expert on the physics, chemistry and biology of the visual experience of colour. She knows everything that can ever be known – physically, chemically and biologically – about colour perception. For example, she knows (assuming for the sake of illustration that the following claim is true) that all colour experiences are the product of the interplay of three retinal cones. Each experience of a particular type of colour or shade is produced by unique ratios of activity in the cones. And she knows everything else physical science can grasp about colour experience. If physical science can uncover a colour fact, Mary knows it.

Jackson believes that the two sets of phenomena – colour experience and everything there is to know of the physics/chemistry/biology of colour experience – are stuck together in a gappy or incomplete manner. The physical sciences cannot capture everything there is to know about conscious experience. For instance, there are some facts about colour experience which escape Mary's scientific understanding. To continue:

In knowing every physical scientific fact about colour experience does Mary know everything there is to know about it? Consider what would happen if Mary were suddenly released from her black and white chamber and shown a ripe red tomato for the first time. Mary would discover something she did not know before. She would learn the 'what it is like' of red colour experience. The knowledge or fact she gains on release she did not possess in the chamber. But since she already knew the physical science of colour experience, the 'what it is like' of the experience is something which cannot be known by physical science.

Spelled out schematically, Jackson's argument looks like this:

1 Prior to release Mary knows everything about the physics, chemistry, and biology of colour experience. She knows

every physical scientific fact about the visual experience of colour.
2 Prior to her release there is at least one fact about colour experience which Mary does not know, for she learns this fact only upon release. This is what it is like to see red.
3 So, there are some facts about colour experience which cannot be known by physical science.

If Jackson is right, then the 'what it is like' of *any* conscious experience – not just of colour – cannot be revealed by physical science. This is because analogous Mary stories can be told for sensations of migraine, perceptual experiences of heat, sound, taste and so on. Virtually any sort of conscious experience cannot be completely comprehended by physical science.

Consider the following variation:

> Imagine Harry, a brilliant neuroscientist, who has spent his entire life in an environment in which he has never suffered a migraine. Harry nevertheless, through books, has become the world's foremost expert on migraine headaches.

The variation can be abbreviated since details are obvious. What the variation boils down to is as follows:

1* Prior to experiencing migraine Harry knows whatever can be known from physical science about migraine.
2* Prior to migraine experience there is at least one fact about migraines which Harry does not know. This is what migraines are like.
3* So, there are some facts about migraines which cannot be known by physical science.

Jackson's knowledge argument has not gone uncontested by philosophers who are enthusiastic fans of physical science and believe that physical science leaves *nothing* out.[4] For them, everything there is to know about the world is contained in completed physical science. However, if we consider the Jacksonian argument for a moment, without considering the surrounding debate, it forms a crisp and at first sight eminently plausible defence of the pessimistic position.

First, Jackson keeps the argument or story *simple*. He introduces enough assumptions or premises to make the conclusion appealing or plausible, but not so many that readers fail to recognize his reasoning. True, critics protest that Jackson's assumptions are insufficient to warrant the conclusion. However, most often, the development of a philosophical argument or position must pass through more than one step or stage. Jackson's argument is intended for the first stage. At the first stage, the aim is not to anticipate criticism; it is to state an argument in a straightforward and direct manner.

Second, Jackson clearly and obviously exhibits his premises – or at least they were easy for us to reconstruct – so that they can be carefully scrutinized and subjected to criticism. As a general philosophic rule, first-stage arguments should be presented with *obviousness*. What is crucial in the argument should stand out for everyone to see, sympathizers and critics alike.

Jackson's argument is both simple and obvious. But is the argument sound? Should we agree that science cannot tell us what consciousness is like? Do you just have to *have* a colour experience to know what the visual experience of colour is like?

Jackson's argument is controversial. But at this point, it merely is first stage. It defines the position from which discussion and disagreement takes place. How does one advance beyond that stage? Suppose Mary emerges from the room as follows:

> Mary takes one look at the apple and says: 'The books I had in that room were absolutely wonderful. I knew exactly what looking at red is like. I have discovered nothing new by perceiving the apple. I appreciate that it is difficult for you outsiders to imagine how I could have learned of red visual experience in a colourless environment, but of course unlike you I know absolutely everything physical science can reveal about colour experience. Your knowledge of the physical science of colour is pitiably puny compared to mine. So of course it's tough for you to imagine how I could have known of what looking at red is like. But I am not in the least surprised.'

Jackson would be surprised; indeed, he would be both dumbfounded and sceptical. He would suppose that it just can't be done.

But why not? Why can't Mary know all that there is to know about the experience of colour beforehand? The next step for Jackson or any friend of the pessimistic position is to explain why even though Mary knows a lot – everything physical science can reveal about colour experience – as long as she is cloistered in a black-and-white-and-grey room she cannot know what the visual experience of red (colour) is like. That fact is hidden from her.

I will not follow Jackson's further steps here. Our discussion of Jackson offers a mere slice of the debate surrounding the knowledge argument. If after reading this first chapter, you decide to advance through successive chapters, you will notice how much more there is to say about topics in the philosophy of mind than I say about Jackson's argument. Such information, new reader, will more than suffice for a bright red migraine!

NOTES

1 Susan Blakemore, 'Minds, brains and death', in *Frontiers of Science*, ed. A. Scott (Basil Blackwell, Oxford, 1990), pp.48–9.
2 Gilbert Harman, *Change in View*, (MIT, Cambridge, MA., 1986).
3 See Frank Jackson, 'Epiphenomenal qualia', *The Philosophical Quarterly*, 32 (1982), pp.127–36; 'What Mary didn't know', *The Journal of Philosophy*, LXXXIII, 5 (1986), pp.291–5.
4 See, for instance, Paul Churchland, 'Reduction, qualia and the direct introspection of brain states', in *A Neurocomputational Perspective: The Nature of Mind and the Structure of Science* (MIT, Cambridge, MA., 1989), pp.61–6; David Lewis, 'What experience teaches', in *Mind an Cognition*, ed. W. Lycan (Basil Blackwell, Oxford, 1990), pp.499–519; Michael Tye, 'The subjective qualities of experience', *Mind*, 95 (1986), pp.1–17; Robert Van Gulick, 'Understanding the phenomenal mind: are we all just armadillos?', in *Consciousness: A Mind & Language Reader*, ed. M. Davies and G. Humphreys (Basil Blackwell, Oxford, 1992).

2

Life After Death

At some point, everyone who reads this book will be dead. Must that mean that we also will have ceased to exist? Is life after death possible? Or is it absolutely out of the question?

Some people abhor the fact that they will cease to exist: that they will 'die' in the sense of being snuffed out or extinguished. Miguel De Unamuno in *The Tragic Sense of Life* says, 'I do not want to die – no; I neither want to die nor do I want to want to die; I want to live for ever and ever.' Unamuno's sentiments are shared by the great Russian novelist, Leo Tolstoy, in *A Confession*. Tolstoy says that life would be utterly empty and meaningless if we cease to exist at death: 'Today or tomorrow sickness and death will come (they had come already) to those I love or to me; nothing will remain but stench and worms. Sooner or later my affairs whatever they may be, will be forgotten, and shall not exist. Then why go on making any effort?'

In this chapter we shall discuss the major philosophical questions concerning whether life after death is possible. These include questions about personal identity as well as about the possibility of disembodied personal existence. Such questions surround a great many people's religious beliefs and they are by no means 'academic' questions of concern only to philosophers. One important religious tradition which has attended to them is Christianity.

2.1 Christianity and the Problem of Survival

In November 1976, Jimmy Carter, then candidate for President of the United States, spoke in a much-publicized interview in

Playboy magazine. The interview revealed Carter's attitudes toward adultery, as one expects in *Playboy*, but it also contained a revealing remark about Carter's freedom from fear of death.

Playboy: You don't fear death. Why not?
Carter: It's part of my religious belief. I just look at death as not a threat. It's inevitable, and I have an assurance of eternal life. There is no feeling on my part that I *have* to be President, or that I *have* to live, or that I'm immune to danger. It's just that the termination of my physical life is relatively insignificant in my concept of over-all existence. I don't say that in a mysterious way: I recognize the possibility of assassination. But I guess everybody recognizes the possibility of other forms of death – automobile accidents, airplane accidents, cancer. I just don't worry.

Carter's relaxed and candid expression of religious faith certainly appears normal and even healthy. Indeed, it is usual among Christian believers, and Carter is a Christian, to believe in everlasting life after death. According to Christianity, individual persons continue to exist subsequent to bodily death; and they persist permanently. Once people come into existence, they never go out of existence. Death fails to annihilate.

Why do Christians believe that people never go out of existence? Surely the reason is not that our bodies do not die and decay. Obviously the human body (including brain) dies and rots. There is a deeper reason why persons are regarded as having a capacity for everlasting existence. In Christian thinking, person and body can be separated and once separated the person can survive without the body. Indeed, a person can survive without material embodiment of any kind. Hence, just because the body dies does not mean that the person extinguishes. Then an extremely powerful or omnipotent God exists who ensures that the person does not extinguish after bodily death. Apart from God's intervention death would destroy the person. As Iranaeus, a Bishop of Lyons in Gaul in the second century, writes: 'Our survival forever comes from his greatness, not from our nature.'[1] With God's intercession, personal survival is guaranteed independent of bodily death.

What is or would be involved in surviving bodily death? First, since the person survives, whatever makes the person the person he or she is – namely, his or her personal identity – must be present after death. If the survival of something, anything, means the survival of me, then 'the survivor' counts as George Graham. According to this first condition, which I shall call the *identity condition*, the survival of something non-identical with me (such as the survival of my children or ashes) cannot count as the survival of me. Second, there must be psychological awareness or recognition of personal survival after death. Carter expects in post-mortem life to recognize that he has survived. This awareness can be ensured, at least in part, by consciousness of who one is and the presence of true memories about pre-mortem life. For instance, Carter may remember having been President of the United States and his former life in Georgia. According to this second condition, which I shall call the *recognition condition*, if something unaware of survival survives, 'the survivor' fails to count as a surviving person. Personal survival requires recognition of personal survival.

Within Christianity the identity and recognition conditions are interconnected. The recognition condition means that pre-mortem and post-mortem life are linked by the memory and self-awareness of the person. Hence, the person's mind or that which recognizes and remembers must survive. Christianity then identifies personal identity with the mind. On the Christian conception, what makes me *me* is my mind, including my capacities for memory and self-awareness. Post-mortem survival essentially is psychological survival.

There is considerable room for variation here. We do not find a single understanding of personal survival within Christianity. But traditionally there have been two main approaches to the topic. Although both assume that the person survives if the mind survives, both also presuppose that the mind or person is reunited with the body. The term used to refer to reunion is 're-embodiment'.[2] The term used to refer to a person or mind capable of disembodiment is 'soul'.

(1) The first approach to understanding survival relies on introducing a distinction between the complete or full person and the incomplete or truncated person. It holds that a complete person is a union of both mind or soul and body, whereas an incomplete person is just the mind. Hence, people who survive bodily death bodilessly are incomplete persons and require re-

embodiment to be full persons. I can survive partially without my body; but absent embodiment I am not altogether myself.

The philosopher Daniel Dennett has noted that what one is *asked* to imagine, what one *can* imagine and what one *really does* imagine may be three distinct things. It is not clear whether we *can* imagine existing in disembodied form, but let us try imaginatively to enter the alleged possibility for a moment. You now have, I presume, a body. However, because a disembodied person would be immaterial, if you were disembodied, existing only as soul or mind, you would not have a leg to stand on, nor lips to kiss, nor smile to shine. Arguably, you would also lack the five senses: sight, hearing, smell, taste and touch. This is because you would lack the organs (eyes, ears, etc.) which, arguably, make perceptual sensation (sight, hearing and so on) possible.

Mentioning candidate deprivations of the disembodied is not meant to imply that the capacities which require embodiment are absolutely essential to you or for your survival. Blind people live without sight; amputees persist without legs. But it is to point out that according to the first option you are incomplete if disembodied. You persist through disembodiment; but disembodiment, according to the first option, is truncated.

Let me add one extended personal note. To me it is not surprising that many Christians look forward to the Resurrection. The term 'resurrection' refers to the divine reconstitution of the embodied person. 'Resurrection', with a capital 'R', refers to the Second Coming of Christ and to the general resurrection which is supposed to accompany it.

Disembodied existence is unappealing to many Christians. They expect to exist for a time apart from the body, merely as souls; but soul existence may seem unattractively lean and barren. Taking a walk, kissing one's lover, singing sacred music: these sorts of enjoyable activities would be impossible. Indeed, the Apostle Paul holds that the body with which a person is reunited on Resurrection will actually be a spectacularly improved version of the pre-mortem body. 'It is sown in dishonour, it is raised in glory; it is sown in weakness, it is raised in power' (1 Corinthians 15:43).

Surely reconstitution of the body in exactly the same condition as before death would be pointless, for it would quickly rot and disintegrate. On Paul's account, then, resurrection is no mere reunion; rather, it is bodily reunion plus enrichment of the body's health and power. Christians expect to experience the body as 'raised in glory'. Just how glorified?

The Reverend Billy Graham, popular evangelist and television personality, describes glorification as follows:

The body that lies in the grave has been neglected. It may be worn out with age, abused by disease, or broken by accident, but in the resurrection that body is raised in glory! It will be free of all infirmities. . . Those who are burned or maimed in wars will be whole. Old people will be young and virtuous.[3]

Graham speaks for a large number of Christians who feel that there is not only little or nothing desirable in disembodiment, but little or nothing desirable in regaining the body if it remains subject to the same infirmities as before death.

(2)   The second approach to survival interprets persons in exclusively spiritual or immaterial terms. According to the second approach, the human body is not essential to the (whole) person; the body is utterly and absolutely dispensable. The full person in complete powers can survive purely mentally.

The second approach is more problematic, from a philosophic point of view, than the first. It is difficult to explain how a person – a sighted, hearing, talking person – can survive permanent loss of embodiment. (Temporary disembodiment is also problematic. The topic of disembodiment will be examined in detail later in the chapter.) Within Christianity, belief in the more dramatic form of personal survival represented by the second approach is less popular than belief in the first, viz. reunion in order to recover full personhood. The first is the more traditional Christian option. Nothing in the second approach, however, is meant to deny reunion. Even if reunion is not necessary for full survival, it might be essential for other post-mortem purposes, including divine reward or punishment. A disembodied person may be unable to reap the joys of heaven or suffer the torments of hell.

In any case, let's welcome back Carter. It is easy to appreciate what Carter as a Christian expects if we remember the identity and recognition conditions. When viewed from the perspective of someone who pictures death as the end of personal existence, life can seem dangerous and fragile, fraught with the threat of annihilation. From Carter's Christian perspective, however, things look very different. He expects to survive bodily death and to realize that he has survived. He expects to remember his Presidency and former residence in Georgia. Before death, he will not feel frustrated and upset (at least for himself) whenever he thinks that he may be assassinated. He will not deem his death a personal annihilation.

Thus far we have seen that there is widespread agreement among many people (Christians are the example employed here) that personal life does not terminate at death. Persons survive (although perhaps only with God's help) the rot and disintegration of their bodies. But if the anticipation of disembodied afterlife is reasonable or justifiable there must be argument for it. Only if strong, coherent reasons can be given for the prospect of post-mortem disembodied survival is it reasonable to believe with Carter and others in personal persistence beyond the grave.

What of disembodied survival? Can a person exist without material embodiment? René Descartes (1596–1650) is famous as an advocate of *substance dualism* (also known in his honour as *Cartesian dualism*). The main idea behind substance Dualism is that bodies are material and disintegrate, but they can be separated from minds which do not. Souls or minds are independent of the physical world and have the potential to last forever. In the words of philosopher Richard Watson, 'The theological demand that human souls be immortal drives Descartes to his dualism of kinds of substances'.[4]

Maybe Descartes is right. Perhaps minds (souls) survive intact; no doubt bodies do not. However, leaving Descartes' main idea aside, the arguments he provides for the independence of mind from body are vulnerable to serious criticism. We will examine one of those arguments (the so-called 'first argument for dualism') in the seventh chapter. Like other critics, we will find the argument weak and insufficient.

Is there argument for disembodied survival which does not involve a conceptual journey through Cartesian dualism? Can we look elsewhere for warrant that disembodied survival is possible?

The hypothesis that minds or disembodied persons can survive would actually be best confirmed if it could be shown that people actually do survive.

Consider the following analogy: Suppose someone asks, 'Can Great Blue Herons survive winters in Alaska?' Friends of the Audubon Society know perfectly well that they can. While most Great Blue Herons migrate south in the autumn, a few remain in Alaska during the winter. The actual presence of Herons in Alaska in the winter confirms that wintry Alaska survival is possible.

In general, if we know that something really does happen, then we know that it can happen. In thinking about disembodied survival, is there anything which shows that it occurs?

2.2 The After-Death Experience

St John of the Cross, a Christian poet and mystic of the late sixteenth century, once remarked that 'God is want to enlighten and spiritualize [persons]... by means of certain supernatural visions.'[5]

What reason can be given for counting post-mortem survival possible? Why should anyone suppose that he or she can survive bodilessly or immaterially, if only for a time, beyond the grave? Perhaps the answer lies, as John mentions in the above quote, in experiences or visions, whether supplied by God or not. Experiences or visions may reveal the actual occurrence of disembodied survival.

Let us begin by looking at a sort of case which appears to show that people do survive without a body. The type of case is a so-called 'after-death out-of-body experience' (or 'near-death experience' depending upon one's favoured interpretation of the time of death) in which a person purports to have left their body at or near death and returned. The example I am about to discuss is a fictional composite adapted from reports of individuals who actually claim to have had after-death out-of-body experiences. These reports have been widely publicized in the media and popular press. They have also been studied by physicians such as Elisabeth Kübler-Ross and Michael Sabom.[6]

Gloria G., at the age of only 39, had been diagnosed as having brain cancer and struck with the bombshell that she had only a few weeks to live. Her sole and slim chance for survival was if she submitted to a dangerous neurosurgical operation to remove the tumour. She did. This is how she reported the operation after recovery.

As I was lying on the table I heard the doctors pronounce the operation a failure and pronounce me dead. I then remember them frantically trying to resuscitate me. But what I recall, which seems funny in retrospect, is that while they were trying to bring me back to life, I was just floating up near the ceiling. It was a weird feeling because I was up there and this body was below. I could see them trying to get my heart started. From where I was looking I seemed to float higher, above an enormous fluorescent operating room light... and it was quite dirty above the light. Then I seemed to wander up through the floors of the hospital. I saw plainly, for instance, a young man who had been injured in an automobile accident crying with a woman, perhaps his wife or mother, at the news that he would lose a leg. Then everything began to get dark: I passed through what seemed to be a spiralling tunnel – long, very narrow, and dark – until I seemed to come to a place illuminated by an immensely bright light. Not an artificial light; more inviting and warm like the sun. Then suddenly, and this was the weirdest sensation of all, the light revealed wonderfully beautiful and spacious surroundings – flowers, trees. A tremendous peace overcame me. My grandmother, who had died nine years before, was there. I couldn't see her – for she seemed behind me – but I could feel her presence and hear her voice. She spoke in a combination of English and Hungarian, as she had while alive. I don't recall literally speaking to her, but I seemed to communicate without making noise. She told me that I was not going to remain with her at that time. That I would visit later. I pleaded with her to let me stay because I was beginning to feel an indescribable joy. But then I was thrust back into my body. I don't know how or why. My next recollection is of the nurse standing near me in the recovery room.

Gloria's after-death experience as reported by her has four important features:

1 She experienced herself leaving and living out of her body.
2 She experienced herself witnessing from 'out of her body' her body.
3 She experienced herself capable of moving around her body's immediate physical surroundings.

4 She experienced herself encountering completely different
   'other- worldly' surroundings and returning to her body from
   those surroundings.

When all these four features are present, we have the clearest
and most typical description of after-death out-of-body experience.
And while it is common after the experience (itself apparently
uncommon) for the person to report feelings of happiness and joy
and to report meeting departed relatives and friends, sometimes
people report no such feelings or meetings. Some individuals undergo much discomfort.

British philosopher A.J. Ayer expressed how astonished he was
to have an after/near-death experience, but how equally anxious he
was not to savour it. During the experience he seemed to emerge
into a bright red light which was distressingly painful. Having
'returned' to his body he was dismayed at the prospect of having
to die and perhaps experience the harsh light again. In an article
which appeared in the *National Review* in 1988, he wrote: 'My
recent experiences have slightly weakened my conviction that my
genuine death, which is due fairly soon, will be the end of me,
though I continue to hope that it will be.' Ayer was an atheist. In a
lead- in to the article written by editors of the *Review*, they ask,
'What happens when the world's most prominent atheist dies? A
first-hand account.'

Doubtlessly, people (philosophers and non-philosophers alike)
have after-death out-of-body experiences. The problem is how to
understand and explain them. Just because a person has an experience does not mean that the experience is trustworthy or reliable.
Under the influence of alcohol, for instance, I may complain of the
pink elephant visually experienced astride my computer. Although
the huge creature appears terribly real to me, no beast straddles
the machine.

Are there good reasons to doubt the reliability of after-death
experience? It is tempting to dismiss the experience as unveridical
or untrustworthy – as illusion.

In the history of the psychology of religion, unsympathetic
readings of religious experiences and visions enjoy considerable
currency. Sigmund Freud (1856–1939) in *The Future of an
Illusion* (1927) depicts religious beliefs as 'illusions, fulfilments of

the oldest, strongest and most urgent wishes of mankind.' God, for example, for Freud, 'is nothing other than an exalted father' whom we invent so as to bury ourselves in perpetual infancy, trying to protect ourselves – in our own mind – against the cruel and bitter forces of nature. Under the influence of doubts, hopes and fears we believe in God, but no Supreme Being answers to the belief. God does not exist.

Perhaps after-death experiences can be explained as Freudian projections, fuelled by false hope for survival and sparked by traumatic experience (e.g. surgery). However, while the projection hypothesis may cover certain cases, at least some experiences are tough to explain in the projectionist manner. Some subjects of after-death experience report no religious feelings or strong religious or anti-religious hopes or fears prior to the experience. One investigator of after-death experience claims that nearly a third of his subjects were agnostic and gave no indication of anxiety about death.

Perhaps after-death experience can be explained in terms of physical conditions of the traumatized subject: as a form of delirium caused by over-medication or oxygen deprivation. Again, while this sort of explanation may bear on some cases, it seems irrelevant to others. As claimed by Ian Wilson in his book *The After Death Experience*, '[T]here are many instances of [such] experiences in which the patient received no form of drugs or other medication.'[7] What about oxygen deprivation or, more exactly, the condition of 'hypoxia', which is a delirium caused by diminishing oxygen supply to the brain at the beginning of the death process? According to a Columbia University physician reported by Wilson, the typical experience of hypoxia is sluggishness, irritability and poor memory recall, 'a far cry from the euphoria and clarity so consistently reported in near-death experiences' (p.128). One subject of an after-death experience was recorded as having normal blood-oxygen and carbon-dioxide levels at the reported time of his experience.[8]

Other facts seem to support a sympathetic reading of the experience. Some survivors of after-death experience report alleged information about physical surroundings near their body which they could not have discovered if restricted to the body's location. Recall Gloria's purported recollections of dirt on the operating theatre lights and of the accident victim in the hospital room. Others sometimes claim to encounter people after death whom they did not previously learn had died, but who actually had died. Isn't this information which could only have been available to them out-of-body? In the world of the disembodied? It seems so.

Still suspicion persists. Another source of scepticism is that there are distinctively 'Christian' visions in the after-death experience and these clash with the visions of people in other religions. Christians, for example, often report the bright light as Jesus, Hindus as Hindu deities. Presumably one and the same light cannot be both Jesus and Vishnu. An unsympathetic interpretation of this divergence would be that Christians experience dying in terms of Christian images, which seem to them to require leaving their body but which in fact leave them absolutely embodied. A Hindu expecting reincarnation makes the same rash inference in their own terms. They never really leave their body; they merely feel as if they do. There are, however, striking similarities in the experiences of people from different religions (viz. the four typical features mentioned above) and data from the reports of young children who have had after- (or near-) death experiences seem to confirm a pre- or non-cultural bedrock of commonality within such occurrences. Perhaps descriptions of Jesus or a Hindu deity are misguided attempts within the experience, or memory of it, to describe leaving the body in culturally familiar terms, rather than a genuine clash in what really is experienced. A sympathetic view is that people from different cultures actually do leave their bodies, but descriptively go out on an imaginary limb. Under cultural influence they conceptualize and report things they really do not observe. A bright light is seen; radiant Jesus or luxuriant Vishnu is not.

Where does this leave the possibility of disembodied existence? I confess that my own dispositions about the significance of after-death experience are elusive. At times I am prepared to argue that the experience cannot be dismissed out of hand. Scepticism enjoys no prior plausibility. Reports of the experience should be treated like reports of any other alleged observation and subjected to unbiased scrutiny. After-death experience is not the obvious result of projection, drugs, oxygen deprivation or anything else of a contrary nature. So disembodied survival may well be possible.

One should keep an open mind and let the evidence speak for itself.

At other times I am disposed to allow scepticism prior control and then I find myself saying that disembodied survival is impossible. It is too dissonant with the rest of our experience. It is the proverbial pink elephant sadly astride a dying machine.

Part of the puzzle of understanding out-of-body cases is the difficulty of finding independent confirmation. In the experience I described above of Gloria G., a fictional composite drawn from real life, she claims to have seen dirt above the surgical light. Perhaps while Gloria herself did not see *that* dirt, her general knowledge of hospitals and lights led her to expect dirt in certain spots, such as above the light. Reports of surroundings may stem from background knowledge rather than disembodied acquisition of information. The same suspicion may attach to Gloria's 'recollection' of the accident victim; just the sort of scene one expects to confront in a hospital.

It would help in assessing the significance of after-death experience if investigators followed up survivor reports by trying to fit them together with evidence obtained or checked by other means. The credibility of Gloria's claim to acquire out-of-body information depends on her lack of relevant background knowledge. Did she possess such background knowledge? If the answer is no, then provided there really was dirt above the light, her claim gains in warrant. Similarly, subjects who provide indications of bodily surroundings should have their observations confirmed. Is there a young male accident victim in the hospital whose leg will be amputated? These claims to information should be treated like parts of a jigsaw puzzle that, taken in isolation, offer no evidence of anything except the active imagination of the reporter, but when glued together with warranted hypotheses about background knowledge and other relevant evidence could produce the confirmation needed to justify a sympathetic interpretation of after-death reports.

Alas, with few anecdotal exceptions whose significance is ambiguous, the jigsaw approach has not been taken by investigators. Investigators tend to be impressed by the vividness, sincerity and occasional detail of reports, but do not track the facts claimed to be witnessed outside the body but present in physical surroundings.

Perhaps no one can travel with Gloria through her luminous forest, but someone should walk upstairs to the second floor to learn if a mother's son must lose his leg.

I turn now to my thinking in moments of more dismissive scepticism and here I find myself pessimistic about whether the jigsaw approach will warrant anything except saying that sympathizers of the experience are cursed with an unhealthy superabundance of sentimentality and credulity.

2.3 Dissent from After Death

Imagination may tempt us into believing that disembodied personal existence is possible. We have all, I suspect, imagined ourselves losing or being stripped of various physical features or characteristics: hair, feet, arms. If we can think of someone whose every physical characteristic is stripped, the possibility of disembodied survival seems ensured.

Philosophers worry, however, whether a person can be stripped of physical attributes without therein squeezing to a vanishing point and altogether ceasing to exist. Many philosophers deny that disembodied existence is possible. Three arguments for the impossibility of disembodiment have been proposed:

(1) The first points out that stories of after-death experience implicitly violate the assumption that the person is disembodied. Suppose, in the case described by Gloria, someone allegedly passes through a tunnel and into a luminous forest. What is more unintelligible than a disembodied person moving *through* space? Could something immaterial be *in* a tunnel? A forest? How could someone 'see' a bright light without eyes or 'hear' a grandmother's voice without ears? The stories are at odds with the idea that people truly are out-of-body, for they are framed in physical language: of passage, seeing, hearing and so on. Such terms make it sound like the person is embodied, albeit perhaps not in the former body.

(2) The second line of argument is to point out that advocates of disembodied personal existence need to explain how people can

interact − see, hear, communicate with − each other in a dis-embodied condition or world. Supposedly, people are expected to commune with others after death, just as, for example, Gloria claims she interacted with her grandmother. However, once stripped of the body, there may be no coherent or truly intelligible way to interact with other people. One benefit or function of the body is that it enables us to see and observe other people. But how is communion accomplished while disembodied?

Jimmy Carter's nemesis during the 1980 US Iranian crisis, Ayatollah Khomeini, is (or was) bearded; Carter is clean-shaven. Any confusion between Carter and Khomeini can be resolved by reference to their physical features. We would refuse to recognize Khomeini as Carter in part because the Ayatollah sports a beard. After death, how would we be able to recognize these two former political leaders?

Interaction is unalloyedly mysterious in a disembodied world. It may be enticing to believe in disembodied interaction, but isn't the truth harsher? Physical communion is the only communion there is; without embodiment interaction is impossible.

(3) The third, related, and most subtle line of argument rests on the idea of *personal identity*. The identity of a person distin-guishes or picks out the person from other persons from whom otherwise he or she is indistinguishable. My identity is what makes me me; your identity is what makes you you. Without the first, I could not exist; without the second, you could not exist.

Persons can be distinguished in a variety of ways: by finger-prints, personality profiles, parents, birthmarks and so on. Some modes or manners of distinguishing are coarse-grained; others are fine-grained. A mode is coarse-grained when it leaves room for other people to be confused with the person in question; a mode is fine-grained when it leaves no room for confusion. When there is no confusion and the mode of distinguishability is fine-grained, then the person has been picked out by reference to their personal identity, that is, by reference to what makes them them as opposed to someone else. For instance, suppose you distinguish me by reference to my parents. Reference to my parents serves to divide me from you since we have different parents. However, it fails to divide me from my brother since he and I have the same parents. So picking people out by reference to parents is coarse-grained. It distinguishes me from you but not from my brother. It fails to pick me out by reference to what makes me me as opposed to him: it fails to capture my identity.

What about the mental or psychological characteristics of people? Do they offer coarse-grained or fine-grained distinctions among persons?

The answer is coarse-grained. Any mental or psychological characteristic of a person can be shared by someone else. Since it can be shared by someone else, it does not permit fine-grained distinctions between people. For example, if I am sad, you, too, could be sad. If I want to read a book, you also could want to read a book. If you are afraid of flying, I also could harbour the fear. Fear of flying is not what makes me me and you you.

Choose your favourite psychological characteristic and someone else may well be discovered with the very same characteristic. So psychological characteristics provide only coarse-grained ways of distinguishing persons. What, then, distinguishes people in a fine-grained manner? What serves to specify me by reference to my identity? What makes me me?

Christians may oppose the answer, but one attractive answer is the body. The body seems to afford fine-grained distinctions among people. You and I may share in sadness and fear; while my brother shares my parents. But no one else shares my body – at least, at one and the same time as me.[9] My body serves to divide me from other people. It makes me me.

True, there is no simple rule for how the body distinguishes the person. This is partly because the concept of personal identity is not a cleanly-carved concept. It is loosely textured and there is plenty of room for analysing it and the role of the body in personal identity in different ways.

Most philosophers agree that personal identity has two main elements. One part consists of persons *at any one time* being divisible or distinguishable from each other. For instance, we refuse to call Carter 'Khomeini' because Carter is clean-shaven, whereas the Ayatollah is bearded. The other part consists in being able to say that persons have *their own histories*. For instance, the person interviewed by *Playboy* and who was candidate for President in 1976 now lives in Georgia and lectures about peanuts and world peace. Carter's history is different from that of Khomeini; Khomeini's history includes living in Iran.

Divisibility or distinguishability at any one time – provided there is just one person per body and no doubts about his history – is unperplexing. People are divided just by virtue of distinct embodiments. However, personal history is deeply perplexing.

Personal history's deep perplexity stems from the fact that bodies and persons exhibit distinguishable histories. The histories of bodies do not necessarily coincide with personal histories. Bodies rot and decay; whereas if Christianity is right, persons do not. If Christianity is wrong and death is extinction, then persons cease utterly to exist often long before their (former) bodies cease to exist. Either way the history of a body is not necessarily the history of a person. The two may overlap, for a personal biological lifetime, but they are not identical.

Consider the beginning of life. A body comes into existence at conception, but does the person? No less a Christian than St Thomas Aquinas (1225–74) argued that the human fetus is not a person until several weeks after conception. For Thomas people begin to exist *after* bodies enter existence. We may disagree with the venerable saint, but the point is that argument is needed. Personal history can be distinct from bodily history.

If the history of a body is not necessarily the history of a person, then the body cannot be used in any simple or straightforward way as the fine-grained basis for distinctions among persons. You may legitimately ask whether the history of my body is the history of *me*. Still, many philosophers wish to claim that the fundamental idea of using the body to pick out people in a fine-grained manner is sound and correct. My identity depends on my body. It depends on my body at least in the following sense: *without a body which is mine I am nothing at all*. If deprived of embodiment, I could not exist.

2.4 Glorifying the Afterlife

If deprived of embodiment, I could not exist. There is no easy way to defend this non-existence thesis, but let us return to the case of Gloria for help.

A common feature of our everyday discourse about ourselves and about other people is the practice of identifying people by reference to their bodies and the locations of their bodies. Examples are legion:

Albert believes that Filbert is in Siberia.
My aunt sees me sitting next to my uncle.
I think I will walk in the park this afternoon.

In these, and a host of other examples, the identification of a person via the body is natural and useful. In addition, normally, there is general inter-subjective agreement about these identifications. If you wish to find me this afternoon, come to the park; at supper look for me next to my uncle; if Albert is right Filbert is now chilly and isolated.

No doubt there is lots of room to debate the significance of the practice of identifying people by reference to their bodies. But among the many topics of debate, one stands out. Concern with whether personal existence is possible without the body has been a major focus of debate. One line of argument defends the thesis that the identity of people evaporates in a disembodied afterlife.

Suppose, for example, we discover on another operating table an exact psychological likeness of Gloria G. Suppose this likeness perfectly like Gloria; thought for thought, feeling for feeling, attitude for attitude. For illustration, just as Gloria fears flying and loves oranges, so the likeness fears flying and loves oranges. And just as Gloria calls herself 'Gloria', so the likeness calls herself 'Gloria'. For convenience, however, we shall refer to the likeness as 'Floria'.

If we return for a moment to Gloria's after-death experience, suppose, remarkably, that at the exact same moment and in the exact same words, Floria also reports an after-death experience. Just as Gloria reports passing through a tunnel and perceiving flowers and trees, Floria reports passing through a tunnel and perceiving flowers and trees. Nothing in the reports, not even the grandmother descriptions, is different.

Who *really* had an after-death experience? Who *really* passed through? Who interacted with a grandmother? Neither? Both? One but not the other? Which one?

How should we answer these questions? What is really at stake here is the issue of what determines the identities of Gloria and Floria. Those with sympathies for disembodied survival must suppose that no matter how much alike Gloria and Floria are psychologically – and despite the fact that after death they are disembodied – *something* distinguishes them. But what can this be? If we grant that Gloria and Floria are absolutely alike mentally, we end up with no way to distinguish them. Floria so completely and fully matches Gloria over the stretch of time of the (alleged) after-death experiences that there is no way to differentiate between them. By contrast, as long as persons are embodied, personal identity is maintained or preserved. No matter the mental match between Gloria and Floria, while they rest on separate tables, they are distinct persons.

The problem is not that disembodied people are hard to identify. The problem is that there is *no person* to identify. In outline, the argument goes like this: Psychological characteristics are coarse-grained; so what makes me me and you you cannot be specified in terms of psychological characteristics alone. Hence, to specify what makes me me and you you reference must be made to our bodies – we can't be identified in a way that is independent of our embodiment. However, disembodied survival requires that people be specified independent of embodiment. But since they can't, people cannot survive.

It must be admitted that the case of Gloria and Floria may strike some readers as just bizarre. Can we suppose that two people are psychologically indistinguishable? But let me add one word of clarification. We must take care not to confuse the question of whether any two *actual* people are psychologically alike with whether any two people *can* be psychologically alike. In advancing the case of the two (alleged) out-of-body experiences, I intend it to illustrate the implications of the idea that psychological characteristics provide only coarse-grained distinctions among people. Anyone with the slightest knowledge of human behaviour knows that if you search long and hard enough you will distinguish people psychologically. But it does not follow from the fact that actual people are psychologically distinguishable that what makes us us consists in psychological characteristics. That would be like claiming that since some of my psychological characteristics are different from some of your psychological characteristics, that

those which differ are part of my identity. Yet they are not part of
my identity. For we surely want to allow that you could eventually
share mine – *without becoming me*.

2.5 Solace and Annihilation

I am not absolutely sure where the above reflections leave the topic
of whether life after death is possible – supposing that this requires at least temporary non-physical survival. As I mentioned at
the outset, my own attitudes are elusive. One should attend to the
empirical evidence, and it is quite possible that scepticism about
survival will be displaced by the jigsaw puzzle approach to after-
death experience. If the best explanation of the experience (or of
anything else for that matter) refers to disembodied survival, then
we should endorse the conclusion that life after death is possible
and that persons can persist without embodiment, even if the
problems associated with formulating a conception of disembodied
survival are formidable.

Of course, one should also attend to the power of argument. The
great unanswered question which advocates of survival must face is
whether (and how) disembodied people can preserve their identities. Under disembodied conditions, personal identity appears
abolished. Advocates must make disembodied survival seem possible.

Or must they? The insistence that believers in survival must
explain how survival is possible would be resisted by some Christians. Some Christians countenance the omission of *any* obligation
to explain.

'But', says perhaps a wishful gentleman, an earnest man, who would
gladly do something for his eternal happiness, 'could you not inform me
what an eternal happiness is, briefly, clearly and definitely. Could you not
describe it "while I shave". . .'[10]

Hardly. The quote is an ironic quip from the trenchant nineteenth-
century Christian philosopher, Søren Kierkegaard, who adds that
you cannot seek information about life after death 'in a textbook
of geography'. Kierkegaard warns in another context, 'Thou can

well conceive how abhorrent it is to God that people want to wipe his mouth with formulas.'[11] Was Kierkegaard thinking of formulas like 'no me without my body'? Or 'if deprived of embodiment we are snuffed out'?

For the devout Christian St Paul's example is often cited as something to emulate. Paul urges that life after death from the viewpoint of pre-mortem life must always remain a huge mystery. So we should not try to plumb its depths or describe its possibility. He says, 'No eye has seen, no ear has heard, no mind has conceived what God has prepared for those who love him' (1 Corinthians 2:9). For Paul, God not man decides whether there is life after death; and God successfully divines how survival is possible. Such, Paul suggests, is the theological virtue of faith that it permits trust in God to supersede the bounds of human conceivability.

Although Paul's example may be worth emulating by the religious sympathizer, his admonition to trust in God may offend the non-Christian or (more generally) anti-religious person. Tough- minded atheists resist any temptation to believe let alone trust in God. For them, if you want to discover the truth about survival, there is only one way this can be done, namely, by weighing up the evidence and arguments – not by believing in God and letting it end in that.

What can we say from the point of view of the person who believes that life altogether ends in death; there is no disembodied post-mortem survival? Philosophers have proposed an immense range of attitudes appropriate in the face of death understood as annihilation. The major division is between those, like Unamuno, who centre upon abhorrence and fear, and those who deny that death should be feared. For them, fear of death is an unworthy and undignified attitude for a reasonable and courageous person. One philosopher writes: 'A free man, that is to say, a man who lives according to. . . reason alone, is not led by the fear of death. . . [H]is wisdom is a meditation upon life.'[12]

People vary considerably in their ability to meditate upon a life which permanently ends in death and it is hard to do this without sounding like someone who fondles the morose. So I ask poets how to do it and am reminded of Swinburne's haunting, gentle and courageous meditation *In the Garden of Proserpine*:

From too much love of living,
    From hope and fear set free,
We thank our brief thanksgiving
    Whatever gods may be
That no life lives for ever;
    That dead men rise up never;
That even the weariest river
    Winds somewhere safe to sea.

Should a person want to cling to life *forever*? Swinburne's message is resonant: If we have done all we can to live, death marks the point when we should feel we have lived *enough*.

NOTES

1 Quoted in Stephen T. Davis's fine article 'Christian belief in resurrection of the body', *New Scholasticism*, LXII (1988), p.74. An instructive comparison of Christian attitudes towards death may be found by contrasting Billy Graham, *Facing Death* (Word, Texas, 1987) with Milton M. Gatch, *Death: Meaning and Mortality in Christian Thought and Contemporary Culture* (Seabury, New York, 1969).

2 I will not address questions about how the post-mortem body can be one and the same as the pre-mortem, original body. Within Christianity the fundamental idea – or, should I say, one of the fundamental ideas – has been that God collects the ultimate material components of the body, which may have been scattered since death, and omnipotently remakes it a human body, rejoining it with the mind. Since the very same matter composes the body, the body is the very same body as the pre-mortem body. This is a fascinating and controversial idea but one which I cannot explore here. As will be evident, I wish to examine how the person – on the traditional Christian view – is supposed to survive while disembodied.

3 Billy Graham, *Facing Death*, p.251.

4 Richard Watson, 'What moves the mind: an excursion in Cartesian dualism', *American Philosophical Quarterly*, 19 (1982), p.73.

5 As quoted in Anthony Kenny, 'Mystical experience: St John of the Cross', in *Reason and Religion* (Basil Blackwell, Oxford, 1987), p.88. Brackets added by me.

6 See Ian Wilson, *The After Death Experience* (Morrow, New York, 1987) as well as the books cited in note 8.

7 Ibid., p.130.

8 Ibid., p.128. Wilson is less a direct investigator of after-death experience than a reporter of the research of others. Among the investigators whom Wilson most frequently cites are Raymond Moody, *Life after Life* (Mockingbird,

Georgia, 1975); Kenneth Ring, *Heading Toward Omega: In Search of the Meaning of the Near-Death Experience* (Morrow, New York, 1984); and Michael Sabom, *Recollections of Death: A Medical Investigation* (Harper & Row, New York, 1982).

9 Really? No one? See Kathleen Wilkes, *Real People* (Oxford University Press, Oxford, 1988).

10 Søren Kierkegaard, *Concluding Unscientific Postscript*, tr. W. Lowrie (Princeton University Press, Princeton, 1968), p.351.

11 Søren Kierkegaard, *Attack upon 'Christendom'*, tr. W. Lowrie (Princeton University Press, Princeton, 1968), p.153.

12 Benedict de Spinoza, *Ethics*, tr. W.H. White and A.H. Sterling (Oxford University Press, Oxford, 1930), p.235.

3

The Problem of Other Minds

This chapter courts scandal. As students of philosophy quickly discover, more than occasionally the claims and denials of philosophers run foul of common sense. Some philosophers say that the external world does not exist or that every event which has occurred will occur again or that involuntary euthanasia is morally defensible; I could add to the list. Therein lies flirtation with scandal.

Fortunately, there is no scandal unless you make a certain background assumption. You must assume that the way people ordinarily think is the way that they should think. You must assume that common sense and truth are in harmony. If you do not, then there is nothing scandalous in someone defending involuntary euthanasia or the unreality of the external world, no matter how strange such claims may be. There is even nothing scandalous in denying that other minds – thinkers other than yourself – exist. It may sound odd to deny other minds and it would certainly amuse if vigorously debated in public. However, from a philosophic point of view, what matters is how well the claim stands up to examination and analysis, not whether it squares with common sense.

Of course, the vast majority of philosophers do not deny the existence of other minds. In fact, denial is more often encountered in imaginary example than actual advocacy. My purpose in this chapter is to make the rudiments of the denial available to the reader, and to explore its implications for philosophy of mind. Before turning to this task, let me set the stage by briefly describing our own imaginary example.

3.1   The Loneliness of Scepticism

Imagine the following. Thomas Doubting is a student. More accurately, he is a philosophy student with, as one of his teachers graciously puts it, a mind all of his own.

Thomas is reading this book in the university library. The library is filled with dozens of other people. However, Thomas is convinced that he is alone, for he believes that others are mentally vacuous automatons, or robots, completely mind-like in behaviour, but whose behaviour arises from something other than states of mind. Indeed, Thomas is convinced that he possesses the only genuine mind in the whole wide world. When he travels outside the library, he denies the presence of other minds wherever he goes.

Thomas's convictions are as simple as they are startling. One mind exists: his. No other mind exists.

It is tempting to dismiss Thomas on the grounds that his denial contradicts common sense. According to common sense, the library is filled with other minds, other persons. Imagine, for example, that your husband or wife is sitting next to Thomas. However, lest we dismiss Thomas as scandalous, crazy or absurd, let us remind ourselves that each of us has felt at least some of the scepticism or doubt about the minds of others which infects Thomas. Some scepticism about other minds is familiar to everyone.

How much do you really know about another's mind? You watch what others do and the sounds they make. You notice how they respond to their environment – what things attract them and what things repel them. None of this, however, reveals their thought and experience with the immediacy or directness with which your own mind is revealed to you or Thomas's mind is revealed to him. If you believe anything about the minds of others, it is on the basis of observing them and by drawing inferences from what you observe. From bodily damage and moaning, you infer that they are in pain. From smiles and laughter, you infer happiness. From gazing at books in the library, you infer reading. From the complex and appropriate manipulation of book pages, library cards, entrance and exit doors, you infer beliefs. But you can't crawl inside others' heads to confirm that what you suppose they experience they actually do experience. You can't peer into their minds.

So a problem emerges: What justifies or warrants the sorts of inferences cited and beliefs held, when all that is obviously and directly revealed is another's public behavior? Is your spouse reading a book or planning a divorce? Is your husband or wife studying calculus or pondering the dissolution of marital bonds?

The difference – indeed, the seeming gulf – which separates the access you have to your own mind from the inferences you make about others can produce heartache in personal life. Does your spouse really wish to remain married? Apparently yes. But suppose your spouse hungers to be liberated from what he or she secretly thinks of as 'the shackles of wedlock'. You can only surmise or infer on the basis of evidence: on the basis of what your mate says and does. The fact that you cannot get inside another's mind seems to preclude access to feelings or thoughts which would decisively settle the presence of a desire to divorce. Accordingly, the inaccessibility of other minds may pose personal problems. You may, for example, remain married, sadly later to learn that your spouse really wished to divorce and now is having a tempestuous affair. Scepticism has a foothold in this sort of interpersonal misfortune. Observation suggested to you that your spouse wanted marriage. The affair, alas, shows that you were wrong. You feel like a fool.

Of course, Thomas's scepticism explodes far beyond the interpersonal scepticism of doubting whether your spouse wishes to remain married. Thomas is sceptical about your spouse's mind full stop, as well as about the minds of everyone else. Thomas is no minor sceptic; Doubting is Big Time. Therein lies the potential for scandal. Although Thomas shares in familiar scepticism, he does so only because he raises scepticism to an uncommonsensical degree.

To Thomas you are not merely unwarranted in believing in your spouse's desire to remain married. You are unwarranted in believing in other minds. In describing Thomas's scepticism, therefore, it is important to distinguish between the denial of *particular* ascriptions of beliefs, desires and other states of mind ('Your wife really wants divorce, not marriage') and the *general* denial of other minds ('Your wife is a mentally vacuous automaton and so is everyone else'). Thomas embraces the second denial.

The *problem of other minds* is the problem of how to defend our common sense belief in other minds against the general denial of other minds. How can we show that this belief is warranted and that wholesale scepticism about other minds is wrong? How should one decide whether something other than oneself – a denizen of the library – is really a thinking, conscious being and not an automaton devoid of genuine mentality?

Philosophers have been struggling with the problem of other minds at least since Descartes in the seventeenth century. Descartes believed that there is a realm of mind distinct, and for him separable, from that of the behaving body upon which the mind acts. Cartesian dualism of mind/body is not just a means of dividing the universe into two domains (the mental and the physical), it also gives primary warrant to the mind. We *know* that we have minds or at least I know that I have a mind. I experience it within myself. According to Descartes, my own mind is what I primarily am and know best. But what about others? Couldn't they just be mindless physical bodies going through the motions?

Partly because of the influence of Descartes in the history of philosophy of mind and partly because of the desire to avoid scandalizing common sense, there is no shortage of attempts to defend belief in other minds and to show that the belief is warranted. So, luckily, if one is uncomfortable with scepticism about other minds, philosophers offer several reasons for asserting that belief in other minds is warranted.

3.2 How Not to Solve the Problem of Other Minds

Let us start with reasons which fail, although from which important lessons may be extracted.

(1) There are four sorts of reasons or arguments by philosophers designed to show that belief in other minds is warranted. I shall begin with the simplest, which is also the least intuitive and appealing.
What you directly observe is all there is. We find out about the minds of others only through observing what they say and do: through observing their public behaviour. Being restricted to public behaviour, however, is not a liability. It is an asset, since minds just are what people say and do. Pain is moaning. Happiness

is smiling. If we could subtract behaviour from mind we would have nothing left over. So, there is no problem of whether belief in the existence of other minds is warranted. If you observe what another says and does, since saying and doing is mind, you are amply warranted in believing that the person is minded.

To illustrate. Suppose I see a young man at the beach with a deep cut on his knee. The cut is bleeding profusely; he is bent over clutching his knee with his hands. He looks pale and tense, and has beads of sweat on his brow. He also moans and groans.

I believe that the young man is in pain. Am I warranted in believing this? If 'what I directly observe is all there is', I am richly warranted, for such pain behaviour is pain. Indeed, there is no superior reason. To observe the behaviour is to witness the pain. To ask whether he is in pain is about as ridiculous as asking, for instance, whether a father is a male parent. Fatherhood is male parenthood; pain behaviour is pain.

The claim that only outward appearances matter, the 'what you directly observe is all there is' argument, has been dubbed by philosophers 'logical behaviourism' or 'peripheralism'. This is because its basic idea is that outward or peripheral bodily behaviour (including speech and sounds) constitutes mind. Logically or conceptually speaking, the two are equivalent.

Today there are not many logical behaviourists. There are two objections to the position; the first is that logical behaviourism misunderstands the nature of mind. Mind is not overt; it is internal, 'in the head'. A person can be entirely stripped of the capacity to behave – to speak, to do – by being given a paralytic drug or perhaps by having his brain removed from his body and placed in a vat. However, he still may think and experience. Indeed, he may suffer psychological torment in paralysis, perhaps because of total restriction in bodily behaviour.

The second objection is that there are insurmountable difficulties specifying the behaviour which allegedly constitutes thought and experience. Falling off a cliff is behaviour but not mind; it just is physics. Whereas, according to logical behaviourism, moaning is both behaviour and mind; it is pain. So some behaviour is mind, whereas other behaviour is not. But which is which? Why is moaning mind but falling physics? How can one tell when behaviour witnessed is mind observed?

Which act or behaviour is believing that it will rain? Staying indoors? Grasping an umbrella? Walking Aunt Tilda home? What behaviour constitutes anger over foolishly smashing your thumb with a hammer? Screaming at the manufacturer? Throwing the hammer against the wall? Crying and going to bed? Even experiences, such as pain, which seem to have typical or natural expressions in behaviour, such as moaning and grasping the injured part of the body, can have atypical, unnatural manifestations. A stoic in pain tells jokes and plays the violin. A suffering saint sends money to the poor. Appearances also deceive. The moaning actor on stage is merely pretending, not truly in pain.

Of course, the second difficulty is connected with the first. Since mind is inner and behaviour outer, the outside may not reveal or express the inside. Appearances both confuse and deceive. Stoics suppress; professional actors merely simulate pain.

The 'what you directly observe is all there is' argument does not solve the problem of other minds. It magnifies the problem by reminding us, unintentionally, that mind is not directly or straightforwardly revealed in behaviour. For behaviour to reveal mind, the right sorts of things must happen *inside* a person. Moaning reveals pain only if the person genuinely is in pain. Doubting should be unmoved by peripheralism.

(2)   The second argument is both more challenging and more difficult to describe with precision. It says that knowledge of one's own mind presupposes warranted belief in other minds.

A humbling disclosure about self-revelation. The problem of other minds arises because it seems that I can be aware of the existence of my own mind without being warranted in believing in other minds. But this appearance is an illusion, since knowledge of one's own mind presupposes warranted beliefs in other minds. To grasp myself is already to apprehend others. Hence, there is no problem of other minds. Since I know my own mind, I am warranted in believing in other minds.

Although this argument has been offered by a number of philosophers (for example, there are claims for it in Ludwig Wittgenstein's *Philosophical Investigations* and in writings of various philosophers influenced by him such as P.F. Strawson[1]), it is 'more often encountered in the oral tradition than in published writings', as American philosopher Alvin Plantinga has noted.[2] Like much that is oral it metamorphoses in successive retelling. This is unfortunate, for the plain truth is that the disclosure is hard to assess without its clarification and explanation. We should try to assess it, however, for the disclosure would solve the problem of other minds if correct.

First, it is important to note what is *not* disclosed by the second argument. The main idea is not that knowing one's own mind sometimes depends on knowing others. Surely, self-knowledge is sometimes dependent on knowing others. Consider a humorous sort of case. A man under hypnosis is given a post-hypnotic suggestion to the effect that he must stand on a chair after coming out of the trance. Later, when fully conscious, he gives some completely bizarre motivation for his behaviour. He says, for example, 'There are tiny gremlins crawling around on the floor', during which he climbs onto a chair. He doesn't know his own mind, for the real motivation for climbing onto the chair is to satisfy the demands of the hypnotist. We say, 'You intend to do what the hypnotist wants.' He says, 'I want to avoid stepping on small creatures.' He is wrong. His unconscious thoughts are not directly revealed to him. If he wishes knowledge of his own mind, he does best to ask outside observers. He does best to assume that we have minds of our own and can tell him what is happening inside his own head.

The problem of other minds can hardly be resolved by appreciating that some thoughts are not conscious and that other minds (friends, therapists) may need to help us uncover unconscious motives, for the problem of other minds is generated by thoughts and feelings which are conscious and directly observed. Access to our own conscious experience and thought seems to require absolutely no support from others. All mental phenomena that are in consciousness, in experience, to adopt the phrase of the influential German philosopher Franz Brentano (1838–1917), are 'immediately evident'.[3] The immediacy or directness of conscious thought and experience creates the gulf between knowledge of ourselves and inference to others. Our convictions about our own experience seem to wear their warrant on the sleeves of our own awareness. Recall, for example, some typical experience of being in pain and then ask yourself, 'Could I have an experience *like this* and not realize it?' There is neither need nor temptation to survey the opinions of friends or therapists here; there is the immediacy of pain.

The humbling disclosure is not about need for outside help in revealing the unconscious. The disclosure is much more bold. It is that knowledge of one's own *conscious* thought and experience depends on apprehending other minds. Only if I recognize other minds can I consciously apprehend my own. Is this true? As I mentioned above, no philosopher has offered a definitive formulation and defence of the disclosure. Wittgenstein's (1889–1951) signs of the disclosure, for example, are difficult to interpret. He claims that everything we know of our own experience has its source in a social context. But his defence of this claim consists in one of the most famous, controversial and yet obscure arguments in twentieth-century philosophy, the so-called 'Private language' Argument. So I shall try to develop a defense which is representative of typical defences without, I trust, lapsing into obscurity. The defense will be Wittgensteinean in spirit if not letter. It runs as follows:

1   If scepticism about other minds is correct, then I know my own mind but am not warranted in believing in other minds.
2   I cannot know my own mind without applying Mind concepts to myself. If, for example, I think of myself as angry, then I self-ascribe Anger. When I feel in pain, then I conceptualize my experience as Pain.
3   I cannot apply Mind concepts to myself without apprehending or realizing that they apply equally to others. I cannot self-ascribe without other-ascribing. If, for example, I possess the concept Anger and apply it to myself, I must realize that others, too, experience the very same emotion.
4   Therefore, to know my own mind is to realize that others are minded, too. It is to have warranted belief in other minds.
5   I know my own mind.
6   So, scepticism about other minds is incorrect. I am warranted in believing in other minds.

The preceding argument may seem discouragingly long and complicated. Yet the heart of the argument is easy to penetrate.

The argument combines the knowledge which I have of my own mind together with a thesis about Mind concepts into an attempted solution to the problem of other minds. To illustrate, suppose I see a person with a nail stuck in his foot groaning and writhing on the floor. If, so the argument goes, I apply the concept Pain to myself, when, for example, I am in pain, then I must appreciate that it applies to the person with the nail in his foot as well. If Pain applies to me, it applies to him. He has pain of his own.

Two features of the argument are worthy of pause. The first concerns the difference between having a concept of something and lacking it. If I have a concept of something, then and only then can I classify it; without concepts, I cannot classify. For instance, if I believe that Descartes is a great philosopher, I classify Descartes as a great philosopher. The classification 'great philosopher' depends upon my having the concepts Great and Philosopher. Without these concepts, I could not believe 'Descartes is a great philosopher'.

The idea behind premise 2 is that in knowing my own mind I apply concepts of Mind, Pain, Anger and so on, to myself. I classify this experience as anger, that experience as pain, and classify myself as minded. Meanwhile, the gist of premise 3 is that self-application presupposes other-application. Classification bridges over the potential warrant gulf which separates self from other. Concepts used in my own case must be used in the case of others. Mind concepts are, as it were, public or social concepts rather than private concepts.

The second feature of the argument concerns the fact that the argument cuts against common sense. Ordinarily, we suppose that self-awareness affords me an inside or superior look at myself, whereas I possess only an outside or inferior look at others. I immediately grasp my own pain, but I infer pain in another. However, if the humbling disclosure is sound, observing other minds is most unlike what we ordinarily suppose. According to the argument, the outer demotes the superior and independent warrant position of the inner. I know my own pain only if I have prior or simultaneous grasp of pain in others. I must grasp the pain of the other, so to speak, before or as I conceptualize myself in pain.

The humbling disclosure sounds like an argument which is too good to be true. Simply to self-ascribe Mind concepts is to be apprised of other minds. Frankly, it is too good to be true. The argument has two serious flaws.

In the first place, the requirement of applying concepts to others as or before I self-ascribe has an expensive price tag. Applying concepts to others goes hand in hand with observing behaviour (presumably the only access we have to other minds); and, thus, advocates of the disclosure have difficulty avoiding *some* form of logical behaviourism. They have difficulty avoiding some form of the thesis that 'pain' means *pain behaviour*, 'anger' means *angry behaviour*, and so on. Perhaps this is what Wittgenstein means when he says, metaphorically, 'The human body is the best picture of the human soul'. To witness the body is to perceive the mind. But if that is what Wittgenstein means, he is mistaken. Mind is something inner and not behavioural. Behaviour may be the best or only inter-subjective evidence of another's mind, but it is not mind itself.

There is a second problem. Premise 3 commits a type of reasoning error which philosophers call 'begging the question'. We may characterize the mistake in different ways. But the heart of the error is that premise 3 assumes what needs to be proven. In particular, it assumes that Mind concepts cannot self-apply without other-applying. It presupposes that when I classify my experience as anger or pain I must appreciate that others, too, such as the writhing person with the nail in his foot, have experiences which should be classified in the same way.

Philosophers are displeased when questions are begged. Questions should be answered, not begged. Critical solutions should be defended, not assumed. Anything less isn't comprehensive; anything less lacks depth. Isn't it conceivable that my concept Pain just does not apply to others? Isn't it possible that I have private Mind concepts which enable me to know my mind without applying those concepts to others? Isn't it possible that the writhing of the nailed person arises from something other than pain? Sceptics argue that this is exactly why we are unwarranted in believing in other minds. We don't know whether others employ terms such as 'pain' and 'anger' in the way that we employ them, that is, for certain sorts of conscious feelings, since we cannot check by having another's feelings. The writhing person may be a mentally empty robot. Pain may mean one thing to me, nothing whatsoever to the denizens of Thomas's library.

Examples help. Imagine a person who has for some reason been held captive all his life, alone in a small, bare, windowless room containing a dictionary which rests on a table. The prisoner spends most of his waking hours turning pages in the dictionary, not understanding that it is a dictionary, of course, but turning pages. Sadly, the volume falls off the table and smashes his toe. He knows that he is in pain: he feels dreadful, awful. However, since the prisoner has not been outside the room, he does not appreciate such things as that there exist *other* minds. So his concept of pain does not require him to apply it to others. The dictionary contains concepts which apply to others, but the 'dictionary' in his head operates in a language – a private language – utterly his own.

The painful prisoner is of course a far-fetched case, which may be impossible in practice. Still, it seems that such a case is perfectly imaginable. If scepticism is correct, our *normal* situation with respect to pain ultimately is like that of the prisoner. Just as the prisoner is painfully aware without being apprised of other minds, so we are painfully aware without good and sufficient reason to believe in other minds. Pain self-applies to me without my being justified in believing in other minds.

The disclosure begs the question. It hides an unproven assumption as well as a commitment to logical behaviourism. Doubting should be unrelieved by Wittgenstein.

(3)   Bertrand Russell (1872–1970) is the most celebrated philosopher in twentieth-century Anglo-American philosophy, famous not just as a philosopher but as an influential player in the intellectual life of England and the United States. When Russell in *Human Knowledge: Its Scope and Limits* discusses the problem of other minds, he embraces a third attempt to solve the problem. It is referred to as the *argument from analogy*. It goes roughly like this:
Argument from analogy. I know that I think and experience; in short, that I am minded. I observe that I am similar to others: others have similar bodies and exhibit similar sorts of behaviour in similar sorts of situations to me. So I am entitled to infer that others are minded like me.

On Russell's view, first I am familiar with my own mind because it is immediately evident; then, I justifiably bridge the gap to other minds 'in proportion as their bodily behaviour resembles my own'. Another celebrated English-speaking philosopher and actually Russell's godfather, J.S. Mill (1806–73) wrote fifty years before the publication of *Human Knowledge*:

I conclude that other human beings have feelings like me, because, first, they have bodies like me, which I know in my own case, to be the antecedent condition of feelings; and because, secondly, they exhibit the acts, and other outward signs, which in my own case I know by experience to be caused by feelings.[4]

Mill, too, embraced the argument from analogy for other minds. Indeed, the historical popularity of the analogy argument with philosophers has been widespread. However, the consensus among contemporary philosophers is that the analogy argument is weak. Why? Here, briefly, are two influential criticisms.

Parochialism The analogy argument for other minds may be perfectly natural and appealing when others are like me, but what of cases in which the others are dissimilar in anatomy and behaviour? To take an obvious if controversial illustration, if the God of Christianity exists, presumably he is minded. However, presumably he is most unlike us in circumstance, behaviour and body. He might even be without a body (chapter 5 discusses the mind of God). For other examples: Various abnormal humans (e.g. schizophrenics), animals (dogs) and aliens (martians) are also bypassed by the argument from analogy. Each is disanalogous from us in obvious and potentially critical ways; so, neither is readily understood as minded if warrant is restricted to analogy.

Consider two examples from the animal kingdom. Pigeons learn to peck a lighted key to avoid electric shock. A hungry hamster will dig, rear or scrabble to acquire food. Why? Perhaps the answer, even though I am built like neither pigeon nor hamster, and even though I don't peck or scrabble, is that they believe that these activities will, respectively, avoid shock and secure food. I don't look or act like them; I am neither winged nor prone to peck. So what grounds do I have for saying that they have beliefs and minds? Perhaps the answer involves our individual dissimilarities.

I find it hard to grasp why they peck and scrabble without supposing them to believe that such behaviour secures goals or ends. Marked differences in body types and behaviour patterns, to the point of very little analogy, may block or discourage analogical inference, yet the differences may prod me to picture certain creatures as minded.

Feeble base The analogy argument represents my warrant for other minds as resting on strictly one case viz. me. However, just because every case of similar behaviour, and so on, is accompanied by pain in me does not warrant me in believing that it is accompanied by pain in others. This would be like supposing that all bears are white merely on the basis of observing a single bear (polar bear) or that all people in Scotland are Grahams just on the basis of discovering one Graham from Aberdeen. Paul Churchland writes: 'It may well be wondered whether our robust confidence in the existence of other minds can possibly be accounted for and exhausted by such a feeble argument. Surely, one wants to object, my belief that you are conscious is better founded than *that*.'[5]

It is the great irony of the argument from analogy that it is used to argue that I am not unique, that others are minded, whereas one of its outstanding problems is that merely one case – my unique case perhaps – is insufficient to warrant the conclusion that others are minded. The reason that we should not accept analogy arguments based on one case is that we should not, at least without supplementary argument, assume that our own case is typical. Just as a polar bear is not a typical bear, perhaps being minded is not typical of creatures who look and act like me.

Today most philosophers recognize the failure of the three arguments we have examined. There are not many logical behaviourists; those sympathetic to the humbling disclosure have tried to reformulate the disclosure without presupposing that Mind concepts are behaviouristic concepts; and those friendly to the argument from analogy have revised the argument so that it is virtually indistinguishable from the fourth argument we will now examine.

Fourth argument? Examining three arguments has required patience, especially since none has produced satisfactory warrant for belief in other minds. It is tempting to abandon patience and to endorse a 'quick fix' solution to the problem of other minds.

Quick fixes purport to require little or no argument. There are quick-fixes on the philosophical market. Here's one:

Warrant by telepathy (WT). One person can become aware of the thoughts or experiences of another in a direct or telepathic way which does not involve inference or the observation of behaviour. One person can immediately experience another's mind by exercising telepathic powers.

WT attempts to settle the question of other minds not by argument but by invoking special power to bridge the gap between self and other. However, WT is infected with difficulties. First, not everyone claims to be blessed with telepathic powers; I certainly do not. But we all wish for warrant in believing in other minds. Second, if people were telepathic this would not so much solve the problem of other minds as relocate it. Suppose I am telepathic. How do I know that what I experience is the mind of another? For instance, suppose I somehow experience *your* pain. How do I know that it is *your* pain? Arguably, if I experience pain, *my* experience is painful. So what makes it your and not my pain which I experience? Finally, in the history of psychology, claims for telepathic powers have a history of failure, of being replaced by better explanations and more sensible claims. Hence, it is most unlikely that people are telepathic.

The temptation to quick-fix we must admit. Yet we should not yield to it. Philosophy requires patience. So, let us turn to a fourth attempt to solve the problem of other minds. Happily, the fourth argument succeeds. Patience pays with a solution to the problem of other minds.

3.3 How to Solve the Problem of Other Minds

The fourth and currently most favoured attempt to solve the problem of other minds is a version of what is known as *inference to the best explanation*.[6] The argument has several versions, each suggesting the same general point.

Best explanation. I am directly familiar with my own conscious thoughts and experiences; so, I am amply warranted in believing that I am minded. Moreover, there are certain phenomena which I must explain if I am to satisfactorily understand the world.

Specifically, I must explain the behaviour of other apparent minds (people, animals and so forth). I see others moan, shelve library books, hammer nails and peck keys and I need to explain why they say and do these things. I need to account for their behaviour. The proposition or hypothesis that others, like me, are minded provides the best explanation of their behaviour. Therefore, I am warranted in believing in the existence of other minds.

One of the most powerful warrants for accepting a proposition or hypothesis is that the hypothesis explains something (some datum or phenomenon) better than any available (and otherwise acceptable) alternative hypothesis. For instance, suppose I hold up a piece of wire and ask, 'Why does this wire conduct electricity?' Consider the following two explanations:

A1   Because it's made of copper and copper conducts electricity.
A2   Because I bought it at Sam's Electrical Supply Store and whatever Sam sells conducts electricity.

Even though A2 is plausible as explanation, A1 is a much better explanation than A2. The superiority of A1 to A2 as explanation is good and sufficient reason for believing A1 rather than A2. In the same way, according to best explanation, in observing the behaviour of others, we should prefer the best explanation of behaviour.

Suppose I point to a man whose hand has just been cut and who is moaning, and ask 'Why is he moaning?' Consider the following two explanations:

A3   Because he is in pain and pain causes moaning.
A4   Because he is a mindless robot and cut hands in mindless robots cause moaning.

Again, we would not hesitate to say that A3 is a better explanation than A4. Again, the superiority of A3 to A4 as explanation is good and sufficient reason for holding A3 rather than A4. Thus is born the idea that belief in other minds is warranted by providing the best explanation of behaviour. The picture is this. If I consider explanations which do not invoke the idea that others are minded, and compare them with explanation which does, explanation in terms of other minds is best. Since it is best, I am warranted in believing in other minds.

The idea that explanation in terms of other minds is best, is intuitively plausible in the light of cases like Thomas's library dwellers. Picture the dwellers again. They walk adroitly about the library; they place books appropriately on shelves; when they lock themselves in the reading room, they unlock the door before they exit; when they slam the door on their foot they moan; and so on. Suppose we ask why the dwellers behave in these ways. One explanation is that they are mindless robots which have been programmed or designed to act in such fashions. Another explanation is that they are minded. They walk adroitly about the library, because they *see* where they are going and *want* not to bump into shelves and walls; they place books appropriately on shelves, because they *wish* to place books where they *know* the books belong; and so forth.

In comparing and contrasting robot and mind explanations, mind-explanation emerges as superior especially once it is realized that robot-explanation will be immensely complicated and difficult to construct. A fan of robot-explanation, such as Thomas, must describe robots in robot terms; he must identify their design or program as well as the origin of the design or program. He must also explain why everyone else but him is mindless although he behaves exactly as they do in the library and possesses an anatomically similar body. The advocate of the other minds explanation faces no such tasks. Other minds explanation is natural and simple; indeed, it is part of common sense. Not only do I explain others' behaviour in terms of reference to (their) minds, but I commonly explain my own behaviour by reference to my own mental activity. Plus, unlike Thomas, since I believe in other minds, I do not have to explain why I am minded while others are unminded, although they resemble me in other respects.

3.4 Other Minds and the Best Explanation Argument

To many philosophers the best explanation argument is the key to warranted belief in other minds. What are its virtues? I have already mentioned some, but let us look at four main virtues in more organized detail.

(1)   The argument avoids both problems connected with the argument from analogy. Marked differences between myself and others may discourage analogical inference, but if believing that dissimilar others (animals, aliens and so forth) are minded best accounts for their behaviour, then the differences are not truly important. Others are analogous to me in being minded even if, unlike me, they are winged, schizophrenic martians who are prone to peck. Likewise, the warrant for belief in other minds depends on its explanatory power and this is not in any way impaired by the fact that there is only one mind (my own) of which I have direct observation. All that matters is the relative explanatory strength of the other minds idea as compared with competing non-minds hypotheses. This is not in any sense to deny the essentially inferential step to other minds, nor to endorse claims about the ease of knowing oneself. Self-knowledge is vexing and difficult. It just is to say that as long as we can better explain another's behaviour by attributing mind than by not attributing mind, we are warranted in believing in other minds.

(2)   The argument accounts for the popularity and appeal of the analogical argument. In many situations (say, the fanciful library example) others closely resemble me. They look similar, act similar and occupy similar circumstances to me. Now it is clear that if they don't possess minds, I must explain how they can emulate or simulate me, as it were, without being minded like me. Why do they act like I do when I am in pain if they themselves are pain free? The task is not just to explain their behaviour but to explain their behaviour *plus* my uniqueness. Of course this chore is avoided if I hold that they, like me, are minded.

When there are genuine analogies between myself and others, the best explanation argument urges me to understand others in ways analogous to those in which I understand myself. Just as I painfully moan, they painfully moan.

(3)   Our pre-philosophic, common sense view of mind is that mind causes behaviour. Minds are responsible for behaviour. I moan because I am in pain. I throw the hammer against the wall because I am angry. I grab an umbrella from the closet because I believe that it will rain.

The fact that we often can successfully predict what others will do or say next, by attributing minds to them, suggests that explanation by attribution of other minds is generally accurate. We can anticipate the future behaviour of others by ascribing minds to them. 'He believes it is raining, so he will grab an umbrella from the closet.' 'He will moan because he is in pain.'

(4)   For several years one of the most active areas of psychological science has been the psychology of conceptual development. The psychology of conceptual development is the study of how people acquire and use concepts. One of the most deeply entrenched hypotheses in the psychology of conceptual development is the idea that very young children cannot make sense of others without believing in other minds. The behaviour of others is enigmatic to them unless they believe in other minds. Some psychologists even try to identify when children begin to believe in other minds. Alison Gopnik, a psychologist working in this area, writes: 'Clearly, at least from the age of five, [a child's] notion of belief is not solipsistic.'[7] Gopnik means that a five-year old conceives of not only herself as minded but others as minded. She does not merely self-ascribe Mind concepts; she other-ascribes them.

Other psychologists implicate absence of belief in other minds in various childhood deficiencies and impairments such as autism. Autistic children fail to enter into satisfying relationships with other people. Perhaps, as Alan Leslie speculates in a recent paper, this is because autism tragically strikes at their ability to believe in other minds. Autistic children fail to treat others as having feelings and experiences distinct from their own.[8] Somehow or for some reason, the autistic child does not fully or genuinely believe in other minds.

Evidence from developmental psychology does not directly support the best explanation argument. However, developmental evidence does suggest that the hypothesis of other minds should be virtually irresistible. In childhood as well as adult life, we make sense of others by attributing minds to them. The best explanation argument codifies this practice into an argument that belief in other minds is warranted because of its explanatory power and success.

Imagine what it would be like to believe that others are mindless. When one person spoke to another, there would be no presumption that he was saying anything intelligible or meaningful. No mind would be at work. So if another says, 'I wonder if Thomas was an autistic child?' he hasn't asked a meaningful question. The meaning of the question, and its answer, depend on the fact that when people use the words 'I', 'wonder', and so forth they are minded: they use 'I' *intending to refer* to themselves, 'wonder' *intentionally* connotes wonder, 'child' is *deliberately* deployed to denote a child and so forth. Mindless speech is indistinguishable from mere noise, from blibble blabble.

Within Thomas's library, if the denizens really are mindless, there would be no reason to assume that the building deserved to be classified as a library or merited holding books. Social institutions like libraries (and universities) and artifacts like books presuppose minds engaged with them. Books are read, not robotically eyeballed. Libraries are places where subjects of thought and experience – minds – study and do research, not empty-headed ambling. In fact, there is no building libraries unless real minds properly design and construct them. Imagine, for example, what it would be like to describe how creatures construct libraries without presupposing that building behaviour is under the guidance of minds. The intricate patterns of architectural design and construction activity would seem inscrutable without presupposing minds at work.

Many philosophers have remarked that without believing in other minds it is virtually impossible to identify or describe the behaviour of others, let alone explain why behaviour occurs. Mind is implicated in intelligent speech, social institutions, creation and use of artifacts and a host of other sorts of activities. Whereas if we believe in other minds, we avoid the difficult task of disbelieving. Speech turns out to be speech (meaningful, not just noise); books turn out to be books (read, not just eyeballed); libraries turn out to be libraries. Belief in other minds is childhood wisdom in knowing the best explanation of otherwise baffling and senseless behaviour.

Are there difficulties with the argument? Are there reasons to suspect that it is incorrect? Certainly there are questions which need to be addressed. In the first chapter, I mentioned that philosophy is comprehensive. Unanswered questions spoil comprehensiveness.

One question is what to include in other minds explanation. Does the attribution of mind have assumptions built into it? One assumption which many philosophers say is packed into the idea of mind is that mind is rational. A completely and totally irrational mind – especially one responsible for intelligent behaviour – is a contradiction in terms. Another question is whether explanation of behaviour in terms of mind deserves to be called a 'theory' (albeit an implicit theory when possessed by children and ordinary folk) which should be tested and confirmed like theories in science. A third question is how to select from among competing other-mind explanations of behaviour the very best. Andy takes Melville's *Moby Dick* out of the library. Why? Does he want to read about whales? Or does he wish to impress Annie with his taste in literature? Or both? What is the very best explanation among the best? It is beyond the scope of this chapter to discuss these questions. I mention them simply to note that although the best explanation argument is favoured among contemporary philosophers, questions need to be addressed in its comprehensive and systematic development.

Absent developments, is it possible to quarrel with the undeveloped version of the argument presented above? Is it possible to object to the argument?

At the heart of the best explanation approach is a certain background assumption about explanation: where we have behaviour **B**, and explanatory hypotheses or proposals **P** and **P***, we should endorse **P** rather than **P*** if **P** offers the best of the two explanations of **B** (and provided that **P** and **P*** are otherwise satisfactory or acceptable[9]). To take a simple illustration, where we have another's moaning, and propositions that the moaner is in pain or that the moaner is not in pain, if the proposition that the moaner is in pain better accounts for the moaning, we should infer that the moaner is in pain.

Some philosophers worry that at present we do not know enough about best explanation to use this idea to warrant belief in other minds. The very idea of best explanation, of **P** being better than **P***, to adopt the purple prose of Alvin Plantinga (*God and Other Minds*, p.269), 'is still a black and boundless mystery'.

The worry is potentially ambiguous. It can be interpreted as a worry about two different things. One is whether warrant for belief in other minds should hinge on other minds being best explanation; and the other is whether we know enough about best explanation to say that *any* explanation of *any* phenomenon from electrical conductivity to moaning is best.

On the second interpretation, the worry is misplaced. We know enough about best explanation to know when certain explanations are best even if at the present time we do not comprehensively and systematically understand explanatory bestness. For example, one criterion for best explanation is that the explanation indicates why what is explained could have been expected to occur. This amounts to saying that an explanation is a potential prediction and that the best explanation offers the best potential prediction. After I wrap wire around the battery terminal and it conducts electricity, the conductivity is explained by its being copper; prior to wrapping, the wire could have been predicted to conduct because it is copper. After I moan, my moaning is explained in terms of the sensation of pain. But prior to moaning, the behaviour could have been predicted on the basis of pain. 'Graham was in pain, so he did moan.' 'Graham is in pain, so he will moan.'

Although at present we cannot completely and exactly specify the elements of best explanation, nevertheless we know enough about explanation to know, very often, when an explanation is best – best from an available pool of otherwise acceptable explanations. So, for instance, if reference to other minds best predicts, this is one good reason for claiming that explanation by reference to other minds is best.

On the first reading, the worry may be more troublesome. Again, suppose we have behaviour **B**, and explanations **P** and **P***. Suppose **P** refers to minds; **P*** does not. Suppose **P*** refers only to, say, the electrochemistry of the brain. Now suppose the following puzzling phenomenon takes place: **P*** seems the *best* explanation. Suppose, for example, that I best predict whether another will moan on the assumption that moaning is caused by another's brain states and not on the assumption that moaning is produced by pain.

If competition is genuine and not bogus, explanation by reference to other-minds can in theory be defeated by explanation without reference to minds. If or when this happens (and it may never happen of course), would this mean that we lose warrant for believing in other minds? Yes it would.

Some philosophers find the vulnerability of competition and the risk of lost warrant too dear a price to pay to endorse the best explanation account. They claim that the best explanation argument leads to trouble, for it represents warrant for belief in other minds as hinging on the success of other-minds explanation. Whereas, they contend, warrant exists prior to and independent of explanatory success.

To understand this anxiety more clearly, let us illustrate it my means of a brief, concrete historical example.

Nothing shows how to refute an other-minds explanation of a particular sort of behaviour better than the medical history of Dr Samuel Johnson (1709–84). Johnson was a respected poet, playwright, and biographer. He edited the greatest of all folios of the works of Shakespeare, and composed the first great dictionary of the English language. But throughout his life, Johnson exhibited spasms, tics, jerks and obsessive mannerisms. According to Johnson's contemporaries, these movements were regarded as the idiosyncracies of his genius. Because Johnson thought and felt oddly, he acted oddly. But over two hundred years after his death, we know better. Johnson, it seems, was a victim of Tourette's Syndrome, a neurological movement disorder, which had nothing directly to do with his genius. His spasms were not mind caused ('psychogenic' in technical clinical jargon); instead, they were purposeless, involuntary contractions of his muscles, necessitated, at least according to the best and most popular hypothesis to date, by chemical abnormalities in the brain.

Johnson's fate has a philosophic moral. Once belief in other minds is accepted as the hypothesis which explains behaviour, something *may* come along and refute it. In the case of Johnson's tics, evidently it did: reference to Tourette's Syndrome and to understanding the Syndrome in neurochemical rather than psychological terms.[10]

Thus, there is risk in holding that belief in other minds is warranted just when attribution of mind best explains behaviour. The attribution may be refuted. But what sort of risk is it? Is wholesale defeat of the assumption that others are minded a serious possibility? Is our overall sense that others are minded likely to be defeated by competing non-minds explanation?

Surely not. Consider just one person: Johnson. Reference to

Tourette's Syndrome defeats reference to Johnson's genius in explaining his tics. But there is much more to Johnson than tics; there are plays, poetry, dictionaries and Shakespeare. Suppose it is true that, say, Johnson's tics were produced by chemical disorder. It does not follow from this that we can explain his plays, poetry and editing of Shakespeare without reference to Johnson's mind – his imagination, sense of language, feeling for Shakespeare. It is grossly unlikely that we can explain Johnson's behaviour in writing plays and other creative and intelligent activity without referring to his thought and experience. Chemistry can account for tics, but it barely scratches the surface of creative genius.[11]

True, in certain behavioural instances (such as Johnson's tics) attribution of mind should be challenged and can be eliminated. Non-minds explanation should be preferred to other-minds explanation. In others, however, such as building libraries, writing books, speaking and so on, reference to mind seems ineliminable. Johnson had his wits about him in writing plays, even if his tics were mindless.

Scepticism about other minds is sometimes attacked for being in the grip of an overly simple or narrow picture of how belief in other minds can be warranted. The idea develops that since access to other minds is indirect, belief in other minds is unwarranted. The best explanation argument breaks the grip of the simple picture. It challenges the sceptic to account for the behaviour of others without presupposing the existence of other minds. Impotent scepticism creates no scandal. Explanatory warrant is strong enough to preserve our common sense conviction in other minds.

NOTES

1 P.F. Strawson, 'Persons' in *Individuals* (Methuen, London, 1964), pp.87–116.

2 A. Plantinga, *God and Other Minds* (Cornell, New York, 1967), p.199.

3 F. Brentano, *Psychology from an Empirical Standpoint* (Open Court, 1946), pp.182–3.

4 J.S. Mill, *An Examination of Sir William Hamilton's Philosophy*, 6th edn (Longman's, Green & Co., Inc., New York, 1889), p.243.

5 Paul Churchland, *Matter and Consciousness* (MIT, Cambridge, MA., 1984), p.69.

6   See, for example, Robert Pargetter, 'The scientific inference to other minds',
    Australasian Journal of Philosophy, 62 (1984), pp.158–63.
7   Alison Gopnik, 'Developing the idea of intentionality: children's theories of
    mind', *Canadian Journal of Philosophy*, 20 (1990), pp.108–9.
8   Alan Leslie, 'Some implications of pretence for mechanisms underlying the
    child's theory of mind', in *Developing Theories of Mind*, eds. D. Olson,
    J. Astington and P. Harris (Cambridge University Press, Cambridge, 1988),
    pp.19–46.
9   The topic of best explanation is not without its own internal subtleties, inde-
    pendent of the problem of other minds. For instance, suppose the only avail-
    able explanations of a phenomenon are weak or unacceptable, but one is best
    among the weak. This certainly does not warrant endorsing the best. Thus,
    to be warranted in accepting the best available, the availables must not be
    unacceptable. Subtleties of the kind just mentioned lie beyond the scope of
    this book. Except for the remarks of the next few paragraphs, I bypass them.
10 On Johnson I am indebted to Harold L. Klawans, 'The eye of the beholder',
    in *Toscanini's Fumble and Other Tales of Clinical Neurology* (Contemporary
    Books, New York, 1988), pp.87–91.
11 For more detailed discussion of the relationship between mind explanation
    and non-mind explanation, see the seventh and eighth chapters.

4

Belief in Animals

4.1 The Mental Community

Who or what has a mind? Which creatures or beings deserve to be counted as card-carrying members of the community of mind? Philosophers answer this question in different ways. Some – 'panpsychists' – go to extremes of tolerance. Everything is minded, including volcanoes, viruses, thermostats and thermometers. Others– 'psychological chauvinists' – go to extremes of intolerance. Nothing but humans have minds. All else is mindless.

I shall assume that the truth lies somewhere in the middle: in neither panpsychism nor chauvinism. Humans do but viruses do not have minds, while various other creatures or beings likewise have minds. But where in the middle? Which creatures or beings? Some philosophers say that God has a mind; others ascribe minds to computers; many of course contend that nonhuman animals have minds; while some philosophers hold each of these positions.

Philosophers are sometimes bewildered when confronted with the possibility of nonhuman minds. There are two sources of bewilderment: (1) the complex variety of mental states and activities in the human case; (2) fear of slipping into crude anthropomorphism. Crude anthropomorphism, the view that nonhumans may be characterized in absolutely literal human psychological terms, is an intellectual dead end.[1]

A little reflection reveals serious flaws in crude anthropomorphism. The flaws are visible when we consider examples like these:

1 Primitive peoples invest trees and other natural objects with human minds as part of an explanation of the objects' behaviour.

Plants grow because they 'want' sunlight; clouds burst because they are 'angry'. Primitives see human personalities everywhere. Science displaces crude anthropomorphic explanations with superior non-anthropomorphic explanations. Clouds burst because of barometric pressure; plants grow because of sunlight and nutrients in the soil.

2 Young children invest dolls and other toys with human hungers, fears and tears. As children grow they outgrow these attributions.

3 Some religions invest God with human or human-like traits. In Christianity, for example, God is pictured as a loving, knowing, faithful parent even though he is also supposed to be radically other – perfect, incorporeal, timeless. This tension between the picturing of a human-like God and his radical otherness makes for the intriguing theological project of explaining how God can be both human-like and not human. It is commonly recognized that crude anthropomorphism, speaking of God's jealousy, envy, cowardice and tears should be avoided; although, it is hoped, other ways of referring to God as, for example, loving and knowing can be given analogical extensions or legitimate meanings when applied to him.

Thoughtful advocates of minds in animals, computers or God recognize that crude anthropomorphism must be avoided and fear heading into it. Mental terms and mind concepts must be given, or otherwise possess, extended or merely similar (not identical) meanings if applied to nonhumans. If mind concepts apply to God, computers or animals, as well as to human persons, they do not apply univocally, with the exact same meaning in each sort of case. The mind, for example, of a perfectly knowing and loving God is not the same sort of mind as the mind of an imperfect human person. So talk of God's mind is not just like talk of your or my mind. If God loves, he doesn't crave kisses.

As for the first source of bewilderment, the immense variety of human mental phenomena makes consideration of nonhuman minds truly complex and difficult. Think of the diverse phenomena of human mental life: perceptual experiences, memories, dreams, beliefs, desires, bodily sensations, decisions, emotions, self-awareness. We have and lead complex mental lives. Do

animals share all of it? Some of it? What about computers? It may
be thought that computers share some (memory) but not the spicy
or dramatic parts (sensations, feelings) or the truly intelligent
parts (belief, reason). Or perhaps mental concepts which apply
to humans are mere metaphors when applied to computers.
Computers really do not remember or believe. It is sheer poetry to
speak of computer thought and machine recall.

In face of the bewildering variety of human mental states and
activities we must restrict the range of discussion in both this and
the next chapter. In these chapters I will focus primarily on *belief*
in nonhumans. I will begin by considering whether animals possess beliefs and related attitudes. Then, in chapter 5, I will turn
to beliefs and related attitudes in computers as well as God. The
purpose of these discussions is not only to explore the possibility
of nonhuman minds but to illuminate the various mental phenomena themselves. Selected themes in recent philosophy of mind will
wind their way through the discussion. One of the most important
will be Intentionality.

4.2   Optimism about Animal Belief

David Hume (1711–76), the great Scottish philosopher of the
eighteenth century, might well be called 'philosophy's majestic
sceptic'. Hume was unyielding in the application of sceptical
doubts to our most popular notions of causality, mind, selfhood
and divinity.[2] Yet there was at least one notion which Hume could
not doubt, one proposition he did not question:

Next to the ridicule of denying an evident truth, is that of taking much
pains to defend it; and no truth appears to me more evident, than that
beasts are endowed with thought and reason as well as men. The
arguments are in this case so obvious, that they never escape the most
stupid and ignorant.[3]

Nonhuman animals, or 'beasts' as Hume called them, have
minds. Hume's principal 'obvious' argument went like this. If a
person behaves intelligently, we believe that he or she has a mind;
so, if an animal behaves intelligently, we should believe that it, too,

has a mind. Meanwhile, many animals behave intelligently. So, we should believe that they have minds. Hume's examples include 'a dog, that avoids fire and precipices, that shuns strangers, and caresses his master' and 'a bird, that chooses with such care and nicety the place and materials of her nest' where she sits upon her eggs taking precautions of 'the most delicate proportion'.[4]

The details in Hume's reasoning may be expressed as follows. We explain and predict the behaviour of fellow human beings who shun fires and protect their young by ascribing states of mind to them; so, we should explain comparable behaviour of the dog and bird in the following parallel way. The dog is *fearful* on *seeing* the fire; the bird *wants* to protect her eggs and *believes* that she can do this by building a strong nest and guarding it. Other terms may be used, perhaps less sophisticated psychological concepts should be employed; but we must ascribe mind in some way if we want to account for the animals' behaviour, just as we must attribute mind to explain comparable human behaviour.

The age of close scientific inspection of animals had not dawned, so when Hume said that animals are minded, he did not intend this as precise designation of where on the ladder of evolution or scale of intelligent behaviour to draw the line between creatures with minds and those without. If, for example, we consider how the primitive little flatworm, *Planaria*, behaves, then we probably should avoid attributing mind to it. Planarian behaviour seems to lack the intelligence required to reveal a mind at work. Its moving parts are capable only of a narrow range of stereotyped movements and its sensory receptors are so simple that it cannot register the direction from which stimuli come. However, cats, dogs, birds, dolphins, chimpanzees and a host of other sorts of animals qualify by Hume's criterion.

Nor did Hume explicitly delineate the standard by which intelligence in behaviour should be defined. Hume seemed to presuppose the unproblematic standard to be, roughly, the capacity for appropriate and flexible responses to a variety of environmental changes or events. Thus, if a dog shuns strangers but caresses its master or a bird chooses appropriate elements for a nest, these behaviours are sufficiently intelligent to reveal 'the reasonings of beasts'.[5] Striking additional examples, which Hume might have mentioned had he been familiar with the contemporary animal

psychology literature, include accounts of co-ordinated co-
operative hunting behaviour among lions and the versatility with
which domesticated chimpanzees can learn and employ elements
of American Sign Language for the Deaf.[6]

Today most philosophers recognize the truth of Hume's thesis.
There are not many who deny that animals are minded. However,
there are denials. We will examine in detail one such denial. Then
we will extract a critical moral from this examination which helps
in understanding animal minds.

4.3 Pessimism about Animal Belief

Writing in the academic journal *Dialectica* in 1982, Donald
Davidson recounts the following story due originally to the philosopher Norman Malcolm:

Suppose your dog is chasing the neighbour's cat. The latter runs full tilt
toward the oak tree, but suddenly swerves at the last moment and dis-
appears up a nearby maple. The dog doesn't see this manoeuvre and on
arriving at the oak tree he rears up his hind feet, paws at the trunk as if
trying to scale it and barks excitedly into the branches above. We who
observe this whole episode from a window say, 'He thinks that the cat
went up the tree'.[7]

However, to believe that the cat it was chasing has gone up a
certain oak tree, says Davidson,

the dog must believe, under some description of the tree, that the cat
went up that tree. But what kind of description would suit the dog? For
example, can the dog believe of an object that it is a tree? This would
seem impossible unless we suppose that the dog has many... beliefs
about trees: that they are growing things, that they need soil and water,
that they have leaves or needles, that they burn. There is no fixed list of
things someone with the concept of tree must believe, but without many
[such] beliefs, there would be no reason to identify a belief as a belief
about a tree, much less an oak tree. Similar considerations apply to the
dog's supposed thinking about the cat.[8]

Davidson's idea is that the topic of animal belief is not so simple
as Hume and others contend. His claim is that only if animals

possess many beliefs which are themselves presupposed by the beliefs ascribed to them, do they truly possess the beliefs ascribed. However, animals do not possess the presupposed beliefs, for they are conceptually and cognitively impoverished. Genuine belief, therefore, escapes them.

Suppose, for instance, we say of the dog that it believes that the cat has run up the tree. According to Davidson, the dog can believe such a thing only if it also believes related things such as that trees need soil and water, that they have leaves or needles and that they burn. However, since the dog does not believe these things, it does not believe that the cat has run up the tree. The dog may act *as if* it believes that the cat has run up the tree. But it does not really believe it. It is a nominal or apparent believer, but it is not a true or genuine believer.

To make Davidson's argument clearer, consider an (imaginary) related human case, due to the philosopher Stephen Stich.[9] Mrs T. has grown old and now suffers from a serious neural disorder evidenced by an unusual memory loss. As a youngster, she was shocked and greatly impressed by news of the assassination of President McKinley. Expectedly, when questioned about McKinley, she says that he was assassinated. However, so serious is her disorder that she seems to recall nothing else about the man or event. If, for example, asked whether McKinley is dead, she replies that she does not know. If asked whether the Vice President took office after the assassination, she asks 'Vice President? What's a vice president?' In brief, she has no, or virtually no, grasp of either assassination or presidency, although she plainly insists that McKinley was assassinated. How are we to understand this?

Does Mrs T. believe that McKinley was assassinated? Is there a state of her mind which deserves to be called *the belief that McKinley was assassinated*? The question provokes two responses, depending upon which criterion or standard is used for the presence (or absence) of a particular belief.

Job criterion. One criterion for belief presence is that a belief is a particular behavioural job done by the mind. A belief is a mental state or attitude which performs a job. If the job is performed, the belief is present; if the job is not performed, the belief is absent. To take a simple illustration, in saying of a person, Smith, that Smith believes that it will rain today, we are attributing to Smith the psychological state which performs the job of leading Smith to wear a raincoat. If Smith wears a raincoat, Smith believes that it will rain today. If, on the other hand, he sports a sun visor, he believes that it will be sunny. By the job criterion, Mrs T. believes that McKinley was assassinated, for she says 'McKinley was assassinated'. If she disbelieved, she would not assert that he was assassinated.

Network criterion. Another criterion or standard for the presence of a particular belief is that a belief is a network state in the mind with links or cross-references to other states of mind. A belief is a mental state or attitude positioned in a total scheme or network of beliefs and other states of mind. Only if the scheme is present is the belief present. For example, in saying of Smith that Smith believes that it will rain today, we are saying that he also believes such things as that rain is wet, that he should wear a raincoat if he wishes to keep dry, that driving conditions may be hazardous and so on. If Smith's supposed belief that it will rain today is not part of such a network, then it should not be classified as the belief that it will rain today. By the network criterion, Mrs T. fails to believe that McKinley was assassinated because she sincerely confesses not to know whether McKinley is dead. Her understanding of assassination is too conceptually impoverished to permit her alleged McKinley belief to count as *the belief that McKinley was assassinated*.

An analogy will help in understanding the network criterion. Imagine a baseball game with a full count on the batter. What is the significance of the next pitch? If another 'ball' is thrown, the batter walks freely to first base; if a 'strike' is thrown, however, the batter strikes out. The meaning of the next pitch, whether it walks or strikes out the batter, depends on the pitches before it. Likewise, whether the pitch ends the game (last batter, last inning) or merely retires the batter depends on its location in the game. The pitch is positional. Its character is a function of its position in the scheme or network of the game. By the network criterion, the same is true of belief. Mrs T. has no, or almost no, understanding of assassination, for her alleged belief that McKinley was assassinated is not positioned so that she also believes that he is dead. But if a person does not realize that assassination constitutes death, how can he or she believe that someone has been assassinated? Beliefs, like strikes, occur in a total scheme. A belief unconnected with belief in death does not count as belief in assassination. Analogously, strikes do not strike out unless two strikes on the same batter precede them. Perhaps Mrs T. merely recollects the words of a newspaper headline. Why does she assert 'McKinley was assassinated'? Perhaps she echoes the headline without genuinely believing that McKinley was assassinated.

The moral to be extracted from the digression about Mrs T. is that Mrs T. is just a special instance of the situation of the dog in Malcolm's story. (For convenience now, let's refer to the dog as 'Phaedeux', pronounced 'Fido'.) Davidson adopts a network criterion for the presence of belief. The presence of a thought, he says, 'cannot be divorced from its place in the. . . network of other thoughts.'[10] Davidson contends that the network criterion leads to nothing less than the complete rejection of animal belief. If we accept that beliefs must occur in networks, we must reject, Davidson says, that animals believe.

Consider Phaedeux again. Suppose we entertain the hypothesis that Phaedeux believes that the cat has run up the tree. What should we expect Phaedeux to believe of trees if the hypothesis is correct and he really believes that the cat has run up the tree? Does he believe that trees are growing things, that they need soil and water, that they have leaves or needles? This seems unlikely, says Davidson. For what should we expect him to believe of e.g. water, if he believes that trees need water? That water is composed of chemicals? That it evaporates? This also seems unlikely. Failing to have such beliefs, the dog doesn't believe that the cat has run up the tree. His 'tree beliefs' are not positioned in a suitable network to count as tree beliefs. Dogs simply are not conceptually sophisticated enough to believe things which they must believe if they *really* believe that the cat has run up the tree. Indeed, dogs are not conceptually sophisticated enough to possess beliefs at all, for the Davidsonian argument may be repeated with necessary changes for beliefs about cats, bones and anything else which dogs allegedly believe. Similarly, it may be reiterated for any and all nonhuman animals. Our temptation to attribute beliefs to 'beasts' is undermined by their conceptual poverty.

Davidson's argument, then, may be formalized like this:

D1   A creature can have a belief only if the belief is positioned in
      a network of beliefs.
D2   Animals lack belief networks.
D3   Hence, animals lack beliefs.

Does this argument succeed in establishing that animals lack
beliefs? It is, in my judgement at least, the best effort by a philosopher to demonstrate that animals lack beliefs. But there are two
ways in which to criticize it. The second criticism works, although
the first fails entirely.

The first criticism is directed at D1. Since D1 is the network
criterion of belief presence, one might try to defend a job criterion.
One might argue that the belief that the cat ran up the tree is present just in case Phaedeux does such things as bark at the branches
and paw at the trunk. The dog's behaving in such a fashion is the
handiwork of believing that the cat is up the tree. Since the job is
performed, contrary to Davidson the belief is present.

Alas, the job criterion is narrow in the extreme. Do I wear a
raincoat just if I believe it will rain today? Whether I wear a raincoat is determined not just by whether I believe that it will rain,
but in conjunction with various other attitudes, such as the desire
to keep dry, wishes with respect to alternate ways of keeping dry,
beliefs about the water repellant properties of the coat and so on.
Furthermore, even if I do not wear a raincoat, I may still believe
that it will rain today. Suppose I wish to get soaked. Or suppose I
am ignorant of the water repellant properties of the raincoat and
believe that nothing can protect me. Thus, my behaviour is not a job
performed by a particular belief. The job criterion is too restric-
tive. Beliefs do not perform jobs all alone by their particular selves.

We can appreciate the excessive narrowness in the job criterion
even with respect to animals. Does Phaedeux paw at the trunk and
bark at the branches just because he believes that the cat has run
up the tree? Whether he paws and barks seems determined not
just by whether he believes that the cat has run up the tree, but
rather in conjunction with the desire to capture the cat, beliefs
about whether barking will scare the cat out of the tree and so on
and so forth. Again, even if Phaedeux does not bark and paw, he
still may believe that the cat is up the tree. Suppose he believes
that barking and pawing is fruitless. The cat isn't going to climb

out of the tree. Phaedeux trots away, though convinced that the cat has run up the tree. Even in the case of animals the job criterion is too narrow a standard for the presence of belief.

Most contemporary philosophers of mind favour the network criterion. A typical recent statement is the following. 'What I do is not just a function of a single psychological state but rather of the total psychological "field" at the moment.'[11] The network criterion admits into the picture the way in which surrounding beliefs and other states of mind – networks or fields – influence behaviour. If I wear a raincoat, this is not merely because I believe that it will rain but because I want to keep dry and believe that the raincoat is water repellant. The belief that it will rain does not by itself perform the job of leading me to wear the raincoat. Other states of mind are included in the picture. Similarly, the belief that the cat has run up the tree does not alone perform the job of leading Phaedeux to paw and bark. Other states of mind must be mentioned in the story.

In addition to trying to defend the job criterion, which is seriously defective, there is a second criticism to be made of Davidson's rejection of animal belief. This second criticism is successful. It attacks D2.

Suppose Phaedeux's belief that the cat has run up the tree is somehow connected with other beliefs about both tree and cat. Assume that the network criterion is true. It does not follow that we should insist on the complement of beliefs which Davidson requires the dog to possess, that is, that Phaedeux must believe that the tree has leaves or needles, and so on. Belief networks occur along something like a continuous or floating scale. Think of my belief that Horowitz was a better classical pianist than Rubinstein. My competence in answering questions about piano skill is negligible when compared with my colleagues in the music department. Surely, however, I do believe that Horowitz was a better pianist than Rubinstein, and so might they. The musicologists and I share the same belief but in varying ways or different degrees, where the ways or degrees are determined by our conceptual sophistication and the sophistication of our different belief networks. In me the belief that Horowitz was a better pianist than Rubinstein does not rest in the same belief network as it does in the musicologists.

Analogously, Phaedeux may believe that the cat has run up the tree, although he has no notions of the value of soil and water or of whether the tree has leaves or needles and burns. Phaedeux conceives of the tree with his own stock of concepts. However we ultimately describe his belief network or conceptual stock, it does not need to be very similar to ours.

Recognizing that belief networks occur in scales does not help Mrs T., but it helps animals, for it shows that Davidson's attempt to undermine the case for animal belief is at best severely strained, at worst fails. Mrs T. isn't helped, because if her 'McKinley assassination' belief is so conceptually impoverished that she does not even know whether the poor fellow is dead, then it is absurd to suggest that she believes that McKinley was assassinated. Her belief is off the assassination scale. On the other hand, we may be perfectly justified in ascribing beliefs to animals. Ascribing beliefs to animals, as Hume noted, can help to account for their behavior: why the pawing? Why this tree? Phaedeux's pawing at this tree is accounted for by his belief that the cat has run up it and desire to catch the cat. To employ the language of chapter 3, when the ascription of beliefs to animals best explains behaviour, animals believe.

True, human beliefs may be deeply embedded in complex networks. However, we should not insist on similar networks for animals, just as, I hope, my colleagues in the music department will admit that I believe that Horowitz was a better pianist than Rubinstein without insisting that my network is similar to theirs. I believe that Horowitz was a better pianist than Rubinstein, although I cannot tell an arpeggio from a cadenza. Phaedeux believes that the cat has run up the tree, although he cannot distinguish oak from pine, or burnt leaves from crisp autumn foliage.

It is also worth noting that some animals may fail to have beliefs because they lack belief networks. The flatworm, rigid in its movements, displays no recognition of the direction of stimulation. In a dish of water brightly illuminated at one end and dark at the other, a set of flatworms will eventually assemble in the shade. But what conducts the flatworm into the shade? Beliefs about effective movements, the source of light, the merits of tightly knotted curls as opposed to the occasional loop as it gravitates towards darkness? Hardly. Its meandering and almost random trail as it drifts into the shade is feeble warrant for attributing conceptual stock. Flatworm behaviour is too feckless and unintelligent to evidence a network of beliefs.

Neither Mrs T. nor the flatworm draw succour from the network criterion. Meanwhile, Phaedeux is unthreatened by Davidson's attack on animal belief. The dog, I believe, believes.

4.4 The Challenge of Animal Belief

The denial that animals are minded has had advocates in the history of philosophy, although it has not been popular. Davidson is a thinker of importance who supports the denial. Descartes (1596–1650) is another philosopher who denies animal minds. However, as demerits of various denials have surfaced, philosophers have extracted from the debate an important challenge to advocates of animal belief.

The challenge is noted by David Armstrong in his *Belief, Truth, and Knowledge*, and has since been discussed by several philosophers, including John Heil.[12] *If we want to say that animals believe something, we must be able to say what*. It is intellectually irresponsible to suppose that we can explain animal behaviour by ascribing beliefs if we cannot say what it is that animals believe. We must be able to identify the content of animal beliefs – the 'what' – if we ascribe beliefs to them.

The challenge of identifying animal beliefs is complicated by three factors. First, if beliefs occur in networks, how do we non-arbitrarily characterize networks of animal beliefs? How do we discover animals' stocks of concepts? If we wish, for example, to attribute to Phaedeux the belief that the cat has run up the tree, which sorts of concepts or beliefs does he have of cats and trees? When Phaedeux fixes his gaze on something across the lawn, 'we may wonder', notes John Heil, 'whether it is best to describe him as seeing Tabby, as seeing a cat, a furry grey animal, or a foe.'[13]

Second, there is a general and related feature of beliefs as well as of other propositional attitudes, such as desires and fears, which stands in the way of any simple or facile response to the challenge. We can describe a particular belief as a belief only if we

acknowledge that it is embedded in the believer's attitudinal point
of view or conceptual perspective. This feature of belief – point-of-
view embeddedness or fusion – is simply the logical recognition of
the *aboutness* of belief. The dog's belief that the cat has run up the
tree is about the cat (and the tree). Your belief that the book you
are now reading is an introduction to philosophy of mind is about
the book. Of course, just because you see yourself as reading an
introduction to philosophy of mind does not mean you also believe
that you are reading a best seller, even if the book is (I hope!) a
best seller. Likewise, just because Phaedeux believes that the cat
has run up the tree does not mean he also believes that Tabby has
run up the tree, although the cat is Tabby. From the point of view
of you and your belief network, the book is just an introduction to
philosophy of mind. Fused to the dog's stock, Tabby is a nameless
cat. Phaedeux does not appreciate that 'Tabby' is her name.

The same goes for desires, wants and other attitudes with the
feature of aboutness. Each is fused to the point of view of the
person or creature who possesses the attitude. For instance, suppose Phaedeux wants to catch the cat; then if it is true that

1   The cat is Professor Malcolm's favourite pet,
we do not get the conclusion that
2   Phaedeux wants that he catch Professor Malcolm's favourite
    pet.

This is because wants, like beliefs, possess aboutness; and, since
they possess aboutness, they are fused to a point of view. Just
because Phaedeux wants the cat does not mean he wants something which he conceives as 'the professor's pet'. The concepts
Professor and Pet may not be part of his conceptual stock.

Here is one more example. Suppose you believe that your neighbour's teenage son would make a good museum curator and
suppose, unknown to you, he is the Neighbourhood Vandal. You
don't, in believing he would make a good curator, also believe that
the Neighbourhood Vandal would make a good curator, for you
don't conceive of the son as the vandal. From your angle he is
simply the generous young man next door, who spends many self-
less hours keeping a watchful and protective eye on other people's
expensive lawn statuary.

In philosophical jargon, the aboutness of belief and other attitudes is called 'Intentionality'. This is because the attitudes are pointed, as it were, outside themselves. Your belief that the son would make a good curator is about, directed at, or aimed at the son. (The word 'Intentionality' may confuse since it sounds like it identifies something voluntary, as in 'He shot the sailor intentionally'. But Intentionality should not be confused with intentional in the sense of voluntary. 'Intentionality' means aboutness. To avoid confusion I follow a convention introduced by the philosopher Daniel Dennett of beginning the word with an upper-case 'I'.) Meanwhile, the fusion of beliefs and other attitudes to points of view means, in philosophical jargon, that belief ascriptions are 'referentially opaque'. Though boy and vandal are one and the same, believing that the boy would make a good curator is not equivalent to believing that the vandal would make a good curator: you, for example, believe the one but not the other. However, no matter the jargon, a thorn by any other name would still hurt as much. In describing animal belief, the challenge is not just to describe beliefs and networks but beliefs and networks *as* points of view. It is the tree and cat as conceived, seen as, or thought of as, by the dog which must be described, along with the belief network within which the dog's conception of tree and cat is embedded.

The third factor which complicates the challenge of describing animal belief is that animals – nonhuman beasts – are mute. They don't speak or communicate in language. Or at least they don't possess languages with the grammatical devices or communicative sophistication of human language. This means that animals cannot tell us what they believe. We may, if we like, say that Phaedeux's pawing and barking at the tree tells us something; but all we mean by this is that the animal's behaviour is best explained by attributing beliefs. And we may, if we like, say that a dolphin who touches a paddle after searching its tank in Sea World Amusement Park tells her trainer that she wants a reward; but all we mean by this is that she expects a reward after touching the paddle and the trainer knows this. However, Phaedeux cannot say 'I believe that the cat has run up the tree.' Nor can he write a memorandum concerning the 'Terrible Truth about Professor Malcolm's Favourite Pet'. Nor can the dolphin protest 'I've performed my trick, so now reward me'. Neither animal can string words together; neither creature can read, write or speak.

The third factor should not be overestimated. Perhaps the most serious form of overestimation is to insist that without language animals lack beliefs. Thought requires talk. A few philosophers, including Davidson, adopt this line.[14] However if, as Hume argued, belief evidence hinges on intelligent behaviour, then it is difficult to see why this should necessitate linguistic ability. Many sorts of speechless animals appear to behave sufficiently intelligently: appropriately, flexibly. So why not classify them as true believers? On the other hand, lack of linguistic ability should not be underestimated. It may be impossible for a creature to conceptualize certain situations or engage in certain belief activity without language.

The German philosopher Gottfried Leibniz (1646–1716) surmised that animals are incapable of scientific beliefs and theories because they cannot form long chains of reasoning; and, they cannot form long chains of reasoning because they lack linguistic ability – the ability to string words together. Words permit long chains. 'The world changes and. . . men become cleverer and find hundreds of new tricks – whereas the deer and hares of our time are not becoming craftier than those of long ago.'[15] Might Phaedeux, for example, possess beliefs about the Löwenheim-Skolem Theorem? Has he the ability to endorse capitalism over socialism? These seem to be sorts of attitudes which require linguistic mastery and attendant capacities to read books, converse, participate in ideological discussion and so on.

Indeed, once we admit that animals are incapable of certain sorts of attitudes and activities without language, tantalizing theoretical possibilities emerge. Some philosophers contend that language is critical for expectations about the distant future, or memories of the distant past, or beliefs about propositions or statements. Phaedeux barks at the foot of the tree, but we feel no compulsion to credit him with the belief that the following statement is true: 'The cat is up the tree'. A belief that a statement is true obliges Phaedeux to have concepts of true or false statement. Arguably, such concepts are available only to linguistic creatures. (Caution: This is not to deny that Phaedeux believes that the cat is up the tree. It is only to deny that he believes the truth of a certain statement. Phaedeux may believe that the cat is up the tree without believing 'The statement "The cat is up the tree" is true.')

How about the distant future? What can Phaedeux do here and now to evidence the belief that next year his master will move to Siberia? So long as he remains speechless, we may never have the slightest warrant to suppose that he expects that next year his master will move to Siberia. Some thought requires talk even if thought itself is compatible with speechlessness.

Thus to sum up: Animals believe. However, the challenge to those who attribute beliefs to animals is to say what animals believe, given that they cannot tell us, beliefs occur in networks and networks are permeated with aboutness. To make the task or challenge clearer, consider two cases from the animal psychology literature in which the challenge has been acknowledged and the attempt has been made to meet it.

Clever Hans, a once famous horse, was exhibited in Berlin at the turn of this century by his trainer and owner, von Osten.[16] Hans was trained to answer questions by tapping his hoof and shaking his head, and his trainer, von Osten, claimed that Hans was able through tapping and head shaking, and a communication code which von Osten had devised, to demonstrate that he could solve arithmetic problems, read and spell many German words, tell the time and understand the calendar. Von Osten was sincerely convinced that he had a clever horse and although many observers were sceptical and some suspected fraud, no one ever discovered duplicity on the part of von Osten.

However, in 1904 sceptics started to search for unconscious and unintentional communication between Hans and his questioner. They noticed that Hans's talents retreated when either Hans could not see the questioner or the questioner himself did not know the answers. So the sceptics surmised that Hans' talents hinged not on cleverness, but on unintentional subtle motions of questioners in asking Hans questions and observing Hans 'answer'. These included head posture, nostril dilation and the raising and lowering of eyebrows. Some of these behaviours Hans believed to be 'go' signs, prompting Hans to begin tapping or shaking his head, others he took as 'stop' signs. Hans 'read' the signs; while his non-sceptical belief ascribers, including von Osten, interpreted Hans' behaviour as showing that he possessed complex beliefs, including beliefs about arithmetic, German, time and the calendar.

The sceptic's procedure is one good way to show that one set or network of belief ascriptions should be replaced with another. Essentially it involves demoting or deflating the alleged conceptual sophistication of an animal by demonstrating that a less sophisticated stock of concepts and beliefs suffices to explain its behaviour. The sceptics showed that Hans did not conceive of or possess beliefs about arithmetic, German, dates and times; beliefs about such things were not in his network or conceptual stock. From von Osten's point of view, Hans understood German. But from Hans' own perspective, he simply desired to 'go' when the questioner behaved in one manner, and 'stop' when the questioner behaved in another. He had not learned to recognize German *as* German, dates *as* dates, or arithmetic *as* arithmetic. Although he wasn't stupid, he certainly wasn't clever.

Two features of the Hans case are relevant for our purposes; and then we shall turn to another case. Both concern the challenge of describing animal beliefs. First, just as belief ascription to Hans involved ascribing a network to him, described allegedly from his own point of view, so demoting the ascriptions involved demoting the network, and replacing concepts alleged to be in the animal's stock with less sophisticated concepts. No belief was treated as isolated. Each had to be treated as part of a network: a network of beliefs about arithmetic, time and German, or (after demotion) a network about 'go' and 'stop'.

One way in which philosophers speak of belief ascription as involving whole networks is by referring to the 'holism of intentional interpretation'.[17] Belief ascription – interpreting the attitudes of another person or subject – is inherently holistic; it ascribes networks. The stop/go ascription is inimical to attributing the sophisticated network necessary for grasping German. The German network breaks down when Hans is viewed as less sophisticated in conceptual stock. Looked at the other way around, we can succeed in ascribing particular sophisticated concepts to a creature only if we presuppose that its conceptual stock is already at least partially sophisticated. If, for example, Hans has beliefs about 14 January *per se*, he must have beliefs about other days in January, other months and so on. The holism of intentional interpretation is a by-product of the network criterion of belief. Beliefs are linked together; hence, belief ascriptions are linked together.

The point I am making in the above two paragraphs is not that when *one* belief is replaced or demoted *each* and *every* other belief is discharged or deflated. Holism or network embedding is not all or nothing. You can have beliefs about months, without knowing of January. Suppose a young child is learning about months for the very first time and January has yet to be mentioned. What I am saying is that, when beliefs are replaced and demoted, those beliefs with which they are cross-linked are demoted; the network destabilizes.

A second feature of the Hans case is also relevant for our purposes. The Hans case reveals the fear expressed at the beginning of the chapter about crude anthropomorphism, but it also reveals how to respond reasonably to that fear. Sceptics worried that Hans did not believe what von Osten claimed, for although von Osten's ability to answer German questions presupposed that he understood German, Hans's ability to answer did not necessarily mean that he, too, understood German. Indeed, the doubters proved that Hans was responding to stop and go signals, not to German. His trainer's interpretation of Hans was crudely anthropomorphic.

It is all too easy to slip into crude anthropomorphism without a proper dose of caution or scepticism. A classic and still useful antidote to crude anthropomorphism has been offered by Lloyd-Morgan, an animal researcher and psychologist whose influential textbook, *An Introduction to Comparative Psychology*, was first published in 1894. 'In no case may we interpret an action as the outcome of the exercise of a higher psychical faculty, if it can be interpreted as the outcome of one which stands lower on the psychological scale.'[18]

This is sometimes referred to as Morgan's Canon. The main idea behind the Canon is that when animal behaviour can be explained by reference to either sophisticated or unsophisticated belief networks, the unsophisticated should be preferred. Why? The short answer is that observing Morgan's Canon helps to resist slippage into crude anthropomorphism. When von Osten ascribed sophisticated beliefs to Hans he projected his own human intelligence onto the horse. But Morgan's Canon chides that before endorsing human projection, one must seek to discover whether a lower or less complex belief network is sufficient to produce the same behaviour. Rudimentary conceptual stocks should always be preferred over sophisticated, human ones. The Canon fires a warning shot at crude anthropomorphic interpretation.

Let us conclude our discussion of animal beliefs by considering a second case in which the challenge of describing animal beliefs has been understood and addressed.

Partly because chimpanzees have been able to learn elements of American Sign Language for the Deaf and segments (at least) of other similar language systems, there has been a tremendous interest, not just in the scientific community but in popular culture, in the mental capacities of chimpanzees. One of the most remarkable manifestations of this interest has been the work of the psychologist Gordon Gallup. Here is one of Gallup's projects.

Gallup set out to determine if chimps have a self-concept. The main idea behind possessing a self-concept is that a creature with a self-concept can recognize or classify itself as itself. It has a sense of itself as such. If a chimp possesses a self-concept, then some of its beliefs must be described with a self-referring expression. For instance, 'That object, with that appearance is me.' To test this possibility Gallup conducted a simple experiment. He placed a large mirror next to a chimpanzee's cage, and within a few days the chimp started to use her image in the mirror as a means of exploring parts of her body which she could not see directly (e.g. by picking bits of food from between her teeth).[19] Gallup argued that the chimp seemed to recognize itself as itself and not as another chimpanzee; it seemed to possess a self-concept. If so, the use of the mirror to guide the chimp's behaviour should be explained by ascribing to the chimp beliefs with content like 'That food is between my teeth' or 'That creature, with that food between its teeth, is me'.

Gallup's claim would be resisted by certain philosophers. Immanuel Kant (1724–1804), for instance, adopted a demoting attitude towards animal self-concepts. He claimed that although animals notice and respond to conditions of their bodies, they cannot believe that they themselves are in such conditions. They lack concepts of themselves.[20] They may perceive food between their own teeth but not *as* food between their own teeth. Gallup, however, seems to have shown that Kant is wrong and that at least some beasts are equipped with self-concepts, although the jury is still out on this issue.[21] In any case, I wish to make a different point.

I am not concerned with whether chimps actually harbour self-concepts. My point is that Gallup put his hypothesis of animal belief to the test. He checked his conjecture by running a controlled experiment. It is through tests (and more generally careful observation) that, ultimately, we should be able to discover animal beliefs and meet the challenge noted by Armstrong. Animal belief is empirically researchable territory. Kant exclaimed, from his library armchair, that animals could not have self-concepts; Gallup said, from his observations, that the question is empirical. We can test the ascription of animal belief and belief networks by casting about for evidence and by designing both field and laboratory experiments to uncover animals' stocks of concepts. Does the chimpanzee believe that food bits are between her teeth? Well, does the chimpanzee behave differently towards her body now that she has looked at herself in the mirror? Does she treat her body differently than she treats the bodies of other chimps? Does she use mirrors for herself but not for others? Almost inevitably behavioural details begin to mount in favour of one set of answers rather than another. Perhaps like the rest of us on a Monday morning she thinks 'My goodness, that chump in the mirror is me'. If so, that would be belief indeed!

NOTES

1 John A. Fisher wisely argues that much conceptual confusion surrounds the fear of anthropomorphism; see his 'The myth of anthropomorphism' in *Interpretation and Explanation in the Study of Animal Behaviour*, eds. M. Bekoff and D. Jamieson (Westview, Boulder, 1990), pp.96–116.

2 This fact about Hume has not been lost on friends of the idea that animals are minded. See, for example, Bernard Rollin, 'How animals lost their minds: animal mentation and scientific ideology' in Bekoff and Jamieson, p.375.

3 David Hume, *A Treatise of Human Nature*, ed. L.A. Selby-Bigge (Oxford University Press, Oxford, 1739/1960), p.176.

4   Ibid., p.177.
5   Indeed, Hume does not use the expression 'intelligent behaviour' but speaks instead of behaviour which reveals the 'reasonings of beasts' and 'that act of mind which we call "belief".' Hume, *Treatise*, p.178.
6   D. Griffin, *Animal Thinking* (Harvard, Cambridge, MA, 1984), pp.85–7; B. Gardner & R. Gardner, 'Teaching sign-language to a chimpanzee', *Science*, 165 (1969), pp.664–72.
7   Donald Davidson, 'Rational animals', *Dialectica*, 36 (1982), pp.318–27; reprinted in *Actions and Events*, eds. E. LePore and B. McLaughlin (Basil Blackwell, Oxford, 1985), pp.473–80.
8   Ibid., p.47. Parenthesis added.
9   Stephen Stich, *From Folk Psychology to Cognitive Science*, (MIT, Cambridge, MA, 1983).
10 Donald Davidson, 'Rational animals', p.475.
11 William Alston, 'Functionalism and theological language', in *Divine Nature and Human Knowledge* (Cornell University Press, Ithaca, 1989), p.68.
12 David Armstrong, *Belief, Truth, and Knowledge*, (Cambridge University Press, Cambridge, 1973), p.25; John Heil, *Perception and Cognition*, (University of California Press, Berkeley, California, 1983), pp.176–215.
13 Heil, *Perception and Cognition*, p.189.
14 Donald Davidson, 'Thought and talk', in *Mind and Language*, ed. S. Guttenplan, (Oxford University Press, Oxford, 1975), pp.7–23.
15 G.W. Leibniz, *New Essays on Human Understanding*, tr. and ed. by P. Remnant and J. Bennett (Cambridge University Press, Cambridge, 1981), p.51.
16 For an account of the significance of the Hans case for belief ascription to animals, to which I am indebted, see Hugh Wilder, 'Interpretive cognitive ethology' in *Interpretation and Explanation in the Study of Animal Behaviour*, eds. M. Bekoff and D. Jamieson (Westview, Boulder, 1990), pp.344–68.
17 John Haugeland, 'Understanding natural language', in *Foundations of Cognitive Science*, ed. J.L. Garfield (Paragon, New York, 1990), p.399.
18 C. Lloyd-Morgan, *An Introduction to Comparative Psychology* (Walter Scott, London, 1884), p.53.
19 Gordon Gallup, 'Self-recognition in primates', *American Psychologist*, 32 (1977), pp.329–38.
20 From a letter to Marcus Herz, cited in Jonathan Bennett, 'Thoughtful brutes', *Proceedings of the American Philosophical Association*, 62 (1988), p. 207.
21 See R. Epstein, R.P. Lanza and B.F. Skinner, 'Self-awareness in the pigeon', *Science*, 212 (1980), pp.695–6; Lawrence C. Davis, 'Self-consciousness in chimps and pigeons', *Philosophical Psychology*, 2 (1989), pp.249–59; see also Bennett (note 20).

5

Belief in Computers, Suffering in God

According to Plutarch, the ancients were convinced that elephants entertain religious beliefs, since they cleanse themselves in the sea and face the rising sun with trunks lifted in supplication. But so loosely analogous is elephant behaviour to religious behaviour that Morgan's Canon should be used to demolish the conviction. Attribution of mentality should not turn on loose analogy. On what should it turn?

The present chapter is an attempt to explore two questions connected with the attribution of mind. The first is a question philosophers have been debating at least since Thomas Hobbes (1588–1679), the foremost British philosopher of the seventeenth century, although historically, it took work on artificial intelligence and the design of sophisticated computer programs to render the question deeply puzzling and problematic. This is the question of whether mechanical artifacts or machines, in particular computers, are minded. Could a computer possess a mind? Could a computer qualify as a true believer?

The second question arises from religious faith and ideas. Any normal human being will possess or be capable of numerous sorts of feelings and attitudes: dreams, hopes, ambitions, fears, desires, pains and so forth. What of God? The picture which many religious people have of God is that God, too, has a mind but that his mind is radically different from the human mind. Historically, the mind of God is pictured in many different ways, typically exemplifying some single or restricted set of attitudes or states but hardly the complement or range found in human beings. One popular conception is the Christian model of a morally benevolent and psychologically impeccable being. To be sure, there are certain religious perspectives which conceive of God as mindless, as Pure Being. However, when God is conceived as minded, his mind is no ordinary mind. The second question is: How should we conceive of the mind of God? Should there be restrictions placed on the concept of God's mind just because it is divine?

5.1   Could a Computer Believe?

Clearly, we need a grip or focus on the question of whether computers could have minds. I propose to focus on whether computers could have beliefs. This question flows naturally from the discussion of animal beliefs in the last chapter, and while it is not the only question asked of computer minds by philosophers, it is one of the most popular.

Could a computer believe? At first sight, the answer seems obvious. No. Computers are made of silicon chips rather than neuroproteins; they house dry hardware rather than wet brains. By contrast, humans and animals possess brains. One is tempted to say, for example, as the Berkeley philosopher John Searle says, 'neurons firing in specific neural architectures' – in short, brains – are necessary for belief as well as for thought and experience more generally.[1] Since computers are brainless, they are mindless. However, fans of the idea that computers could believe charge that Searle begs the question when he insists that brains are essential for belief. Searle assumes what needs to be proven. One counter-argument runs in outline form something like this: If brains are unnecessary for intelligent behaviour, and intelligent behaviour is sufficient for belief, and computers behave sufficiently intelligently, then even though computers are brainless, they believe. More generally, they possess minds of their own.

To see all this a bit more clearly, recall the discussion in chapter 4 of David Hume on animals. According to Hume, the mark of mindedness in an animal is the capacity for intelligent behaviour – not perhaps of the flatworm but of the bird or dog. Now it is commonplace knowledge that computers behave intelligently: they win chess games, perform numerical calculations and guide missiles. On this behavioural way of thinking, if computer behaviour is sufficiently intelligent, computers have minds. So misgivings about Searle's deference to brains arise. Could a computer believe? Even though its brainlessness tempts saying no, its behaviour prompts saying yes.

What are the prospects for resolving the debate between brain chauvinists like Searle and more ecumenical attributors, between those who contend that brain is essential and those who fix on behaviour?

Imagine that a creature from another planet lands in your back-yard and tells you (in perfect English) that it is going to enroll for courses at Princeton University. Then the creature dresses up like a human (suppose that otherwise it looks most unhuman and that the creature is devoid of anything which we would recognize or classify as a brain) and enrolls at Princeton. Within three months it is awarded a Ph.D. in Comparative Literature! What should you say? Should you say that brains are essential for belief or that they are inessential?

I shall call this the Case of the Ivy League Alien. In this case, most of us would think it obvious what we should say: we should say that brains are unnecessary. The alien has a mind of its own even if it lacks a brain.

The Case of the Ivy League Alien is, of course, a fictitious example; but it shows that Searle's particular and initial insistence on brains is unreasonable. The basic idea is this: If an individual's behaviour is sufficiently intelligent – if it is, for example, relevant-ly similar to human behaviour of the sort which in us warrants the attribution of belief – then there is good reason to say that it believes, even if it lacks a brain. If a human who enrolls at Princeton and is quickly awarded a Ph.D. believes, then an alien who enrolls and is quickly awarded a Ph.D. also believes. We should not say that the human believes and then deny that the alien believes. Of course, this does not prove that the brain *is* unnecessary. Perhaps brains are needed to manifest behaviour of sufficient intelligence to evidence genuine belief. Perhaps there is no way a brainless computer or alien could support what an organic brain supports: rapid progress towards a Ph.D. Or perhaps brains are essential for conscious experiences or other psycho-logical states or processes which may be necessary for belief.

It does not automatically follow that because we can imagine (or think we can imagine) an ivy league alien, the brain is inessential. We should only disallow claiming without defence that brains are necessary. The Case of the Ivy League Alien shows that defence is needed and that, absent defence, evidently a computer could believe if it was capable of sufficiently intelligent behaviour.

A second line of argument may be more convincing in denying computer belief. Again, this line is developed by Searle; and although he interlocks the second line with the first about brainlessness, strictly speaking they are distinguishable points.

Searle urges that we observe a distinction when we consider whether a computer could believe. This is a distinction between 'intrinsic' Intentionality and 'as-if' or 'observer-dependent' Intentionality. Intentionality, it will be recalled by readers of the last chapter, is a critical feature of beliefs and other attitudes. What has Intentionality is *about* something. It is directed towards something. My belief that Descartes is a great philosopher is about Descartes; your fear of flying is about flying; my love of oranges is directed at oranges. Searle's gloss 'intrinsic' refers to Intentionality which *is* (real, honest-to-goodness) Intentionality. It is the Intentionality of genuine belief and the true believer. His as-if Intentionality, by contrast, is not real Intentionality. It is Intentionality in the eye of the beholder which does not truly inhere in the subject beheld; it is the Intentionality of nominal belief, not genuine belief. To some eyes, for instance, water flowing downhill has Intentionality. A primitive cave-dwelling observer in the grips of crude anthropomorphism might ascribe beliefs and other attitudes about the hill to the water. It *tries* to flow downhill and *wants* to get to the bottom. However, of course, the water really does not try, want or believe. Its Intentionality is in the eye of the cave-dweller. Water Intentionality is as-if Intentionality.

Searle uses the distinction between as-if and intrinsic Intentionality to undermine the idea that computers could believe. His tactic, which we will examine shortly, is to argue that computers possess only as-if Intentionality. On this way of thinking, they cannot genuinely believe. Searle clarifies the distinction between as-if and intrinsic by means of illustrative examples. We will look at his most famous and provocative example, which he uses to try to undermine computer belief, in a moment. First, however, Searle's distinction is so suggestive that it is worth digressing to briefly note one of its aspects.

The reader blessed with a good memory will recall that the third chapter was sparked by scepticism about other minds. A central element in scepticism is the claim that no amount of purely behavioural evidence is sufficient to absolutely prove that another creature possesses a mind. There is always an inferential gap or step between evidence for the presence of belief (mind) and belief (mind) itself. Searle's distinction between as-if and intrinsic Intentionality is rooted in that gap. Central to his distinction is the point that there are no sure steps from behaviour to mind. And for the most part (except for logical behaviourists and disciples of Wittgenstein) those who try to tackle the problem of other minds agree. Even if we maintain (as argued in chapter 3) that belief in other minds is warranted, there is still an *inference*. No behaviour, by itself, proves beyond the shadow of doubt the presence of mind. Between behaviour and mind there is conceptual space for denying that other minds exist.

There is much more that can be said about Searle's attitude towards the relationship between behaviour and mind. But set Searle's view of mind/behaviour aside. More important, for our present purpose, is that Searle's distinction between intrinsic and as-if Intentionality enables him to build an argument against computer Intentionality and belief. The argument is built around an imaginative example, which, for reasons which will soon become obvious, is known as the *Chinese room argument*.

Chess and related examples (e.g. numerical calculation) provide well-studied cases of the intelligent behaviour of computers. But chess and such activities may be misleading. They are utterly flat or one-dimensional and, in the words of John Haugeland, 'separable from the rest of life'.[2] Hence, a chess-playing computer is more tool or toy than true believer. Although we may speak of the computer as if it has beliefs about e.g. the current board positions, and possible continuations of the game, this is too restricted and shallow a belief network to qualify a chess-playing computer as a true believer. Consider the following situation. You are playing chess with a chess-playing computer. Suppose you wonder if the computer plays Monopoly as well as chess. Alas, it doesn't. It is limited to chess, unless you load another program. It is as if a chess playing computer is a brilliant flatworm, locked in stunning stereotype. It can knock a person's socks off in chess, but it sits impotent in the face of Monopoly.

'Yes, it can play chess. But is it minded?' So goes the usual re-action to chess-playing computers. Alan Turing (1912–54), a distinguished logician and father of a lot of the modern theory of computers and computation, had another behavioural criterion for whether computers are minded. Not chess, but conversation. He proposed, in a paper which appeared in the journal *Mind* in 1950, that if a computer could communicate with a human being in such a way that the human being could not tell the difference between conversing with the computer and conversing with another human being, then it would be rather arbitrary to deny that the computer is a believer simply because it is a computer.[3] Turing argued that the capacity for linguistic conversation is a good, strong test for computer belief. Wouldn't it be impressive if a computer could speak a language, say Chinese, and engage in real dialogue? Its conversational range might manifest a thick and elaborate belief network, a stock of attitudes visible through its 'speech', concern-ing such topics as chess, Monopoly, games of all sorts – on boards, in love, politics and life. Who could deny intrinsic Intentionality of an intelligent conversationalist, even though it was brainless?

To challenge the validity of Turing's proposal that computer conversation would demonstrate computer belief, John Searle has constructed an imaginative 'thought experiment' (the example to which I referred earlier). Thought experiments are important analytical devices in the history of philosophy. They have already appeared in this book, in the forms of Mary the Superscientist and The Case of the Ivy League Alien. Classic examples include Plato's Ring of Gyges and Descartes's Evil Demon Argument. A thought experiment consists in hypothesizing certain imaginary assumptions and extracting insights from those assumptions. Plato, for instance, supposes that a person possesses a magical ring the rubbing of which enables him to become invisible and to commit undetected immoralities and misdeeds. By this device Plato explores the view, which he himself abjures, that we follow moral rules merely because we fear punishment and not because we respect morality for itself. The Ring of Gyges is a thought experiment in human moral psychology.

5.2   The Chinese Room Argument

Searle's Chinese room is a thought experiment in computer conversational psychology. It goes roughly as follows:

Imagine that a man is locked in an enclosed room with one postal slot through which symbols in a language, say Chinese, are sometimes sent in and one exit slot through which symbols can be sent out. In the centre of the room are several baskets containing various sorts of Chinese symbols. Then, if the person in the room was fluent in his native language, say English, but ignorant of the language of the symbols, and had a book of instructions written in his native language which told him to send certain Chinese symbols out when certain other symbols were sent in, it would seem to outside observers as if the person in the room understood Chinese. However, to him Chinese writing looks like meaningless squiggles; nor does the book of instructions decode their meaning, for the book, we may imagine, identifies symbols entirely by their physical shapes and does not require that the man understand any of them. The book is not a dictionary but a set of rules which tells which symbols to send back out of the exit slot. 'Take a squiggle-squaggle from basket number one and place it next to a squaggle-squiggle from basket number two; then bring both symbols to exit slot.' In following such instructions, the person seems to outside observers to answer Chinese questions and comments received at the entry slot with responses delivered at the exit slot. For example, someone outside might hand him symbols that unknown to him mean, 'Who is your favourite philosopher?' and he might after following the rule book hand back symbols that, also unknown to him, mean, 'My favourite philosopher is Donald Davidson, though I admire Martin Buber a lot.'

While unapparent to outside observers, Searle contends, it remains certain that the person in the room does not understand Chinese. He applies instructions, and he understands those instructions, but the sequences of Chinese symbols are gibberish to him. Also clear, contends Searle, is that the entire system of the room plus the person and its contents is ignorant of Chinese as well. Nothing here grasps Chinese, except those sending and receiving messages, and those who composed the instruction book. No conversational response of man or system has any intrinsic

Intentionality, or is about anything, or means anything, except as it is viewed by outside observers interacting with it.

Searle contends that the Chinese room argument hits the mark of undermining computer intrinsic Intentionality, belief and understanding. For the setup contains everything relevant to a computer. The person in the room, functioning like the central processor of a computer, manipulates physical symbols (in computer jargon 'syntax'); the instruction book is the 'computer program' for manipulating the symbols. The baskets full of symbols are the 'data base'; the small bunches that are handed in are the 'input' and the bunches then handed out are the 'output'. According to Searle the impact of the example is as follows: If the person in the room (or system) does not possess intrinsic Intentionality (does not understand Chinese) solely on the basis of following a computer program for understanding Chinese, then neither does any computer on the basis of running its program possess intrinsic Intentionality. Manipulating symbols in accordance with rules, which is the essence of computer program operation and transpires in the Chinese Room, produces mere as-if Intentionality, as-if belief, as-if Chinese understanding.

Given Searle's conclusion, there cannot be any dispute about whether passing the Turing test is sufficient for computer belief. For it is not. Far from being the product of intrinsic Intentionality, computer conversation by itself reveals nothing more than as-if Intentionality and as-if belief.

Searle first presented the Chinese room in the pages of *Behavioral and Brain Sciences* in 1980, and it has since appeared and been refined in several of his publications. It also has been subjected to a flood of comment, discussion and criticism, including 26 commentaries to the original article.[4]

Even to critics, much of what Searle says seems both right and important. He is clearly correct in his contention that the example shows that someone or something can appear to understand without genuinely understanding; or appear to converse without really conversing; or appear to believe without truly believing. In life, we may simulate characteristics or abilities we really do not possess. Behaviour can mask ignorance. Also, Searle is on to something significant in his thesis that as-if Intentionality differs from intrinsic Intentionality. Few would deny that people differ from water flowing downhill. The distinction between as-if and intrinsic Intentionality may mark the psychological divide which separates water from persons and non-believers from believers. However, we can agree that these are good points without agreeing with Searle that computers could not believe. Many philosophers continue to contend that computers, in one way or another, could believe.

The most popular anti-Searle, pro-computer belief counter-argument attacks Searle at just this point: it urges that various other possibilities, in addition to the Chinese room, are relevant to determining whether a computer could believe. Therefore, the Chinese room does not undermine computer intrinsic Intentionality.

The first counter-argument

Perhaps the person in the room (or the system of person plus room) does not understand Chinese, but more sophisticated kinds of computers with programs using discoveries about human linguistic intelligence could. What Searle's Chinese room is missing is realistic analogy to intelligent conversational behaviour. Searle's person in the room is utterly constrained by the book of instructions. He engages in strict rule-governed dialogue in which conversational questions lead to answers generated by combining symbols in slow and plodding accordance with the book; his performance is too stiff and limited to count as intelligent Chinese. If, however, the person simulated more realistic Chinese conversation, then he (or the system of which he is a part) would understand Chinese. Indeed, even if he did not realize that he understood Chinese he could understand it. For people can understand things which they are unaware that they understand. At any rate, as the distance between human conversational behaviour and the conversational behaviour displayed by the person or person-plus- room or a computer decreases, the evidence for intrinsic Intentionality, belief, and linguistic understanding in a computer increases.

The central point in the counter-argument is the contention that Searle's Chinese room is a hollow mock-up of the possibilities of a computer. It wants to defuse the Chinese room before it starts to fire. As Searle sees it, the Chinese room convinces outside observers that the person (or system) understands Chinese, but fans of the counter-argument are unconvinced. For them the behaviour of the system is too unlike a normal, human Chinese conversationalist to foil or fool serious investigators. Meanwhile, if programmers and computer scientists could just set in motion an upgraded flexible and dynamic computer, it could produce the linguistic understanding found in human beings. Such a computer could burrow into the soul of intrinsic Intentionality.

Does the counter-argument succeed? Is Searle wrong to deny that a computer could believe? The counter-argument succeeds only if computers can be upgraded. But the critic of computer belief (and friend of Searle) need not admit this. The critic can retort that computers are unlikely to be upgraded. Immensely difficult hurdles must be surmounted, so difficult, that from where we stand, it is safe to say that computers could not simulate a normal, human conversation.

We will not dwell on details, for they would take us into the esoteric interior of linguistics and artificial intelligence research. Briefly, however, ponder the up-scale standards set by human conversation.

Human speech involves several distinguishable types of abilities and capacities. Foremost is the ability to draw on relevant aspects of the actual world as the conversation changes and dictates. One example – suggested by John Tienson – will illustrate the nature of the capacity to which I refer.[5]

Recently, one of my philosophy students took a group of children for a concert at the zoo. They were all familiar with zoos, and some had attended concerts, but none of them had attended a zoo concert. Yet they were able to blend together their knowledge of zoos with their understanding of concerts. Apart from a few highly restricted mistakes, they managed intelligent ongoing conversation throughout the trip and visit. What's so impressive about this is that speakers never know what is going to be relevant next. The whole direction of conversation can shift from zoos to concerts to concerts-within-zoos to what's-for-lunch to where's-the-toilet, and so on, so that speakers must make sense of topic changes and must appropriately co-ordinate conversation to changing circumstance and conversational contour.

Because we adjust conversation so fluidly, and topical changes seem so natural and obvious, it may be difficult to appreciate how skilful is ordinary speech. However, as John Tienson has pointed out, no one has a clue about how to get computers to do it. In my own academic department, where a taste for verbal shenanigans and encyclopedic display prevails, it is a rare day that does not witness at least a hundred topical shifts before the closing siren. But none of our verbal jousting and professorial showboating makes conversation immensely difficult. Quite the contrary, topical shifts polish conversational contours, making speech lively, expressive and engaging.

Consider any Chinese room which tries to simulate merely the children at the zoo – not a philosophy department. There are virtually no limits to the zoo and concert knowledge which may be relevant to a potential comment or query at the entry slot. If the room is to match the performance of the children, the instruction book must not only be massive in size and topical scope, but it must enable the person in the room to respond appropriately and quickly to all sorts of metaphors and ambiguities, which children deal with rapidly and adroitly. What makes it especially difficult to simulate normal speech is the unpredictable and often startling way that odd little topics show up and fold in (to borrow one of Tienson's apt metaphors) as relevant:

> 'The monkeys are listening to the concert,' says the child, 'while the lions are staring at the man with the stick.'

Is 'monkey' the mammal, or a pejorative reference to the quality of attentiveness in one's classmates? Are 'lions' noisy students, or the big cats in cages? And how about 'the man with the stick'? Conductor, zoo keeper, or elderly patron with a cane?

To load an instruction book – program a computer – to comment appropriately in such a conversation would be a herculean task. Arguably, there is no realistic prospect that the Chinese room or a computer can scale up to match human conversation, even those of children. And so long as we are profoundly short of making such a computer, and ignorant of how to program the ability to respond intelligently to unpredictable changes of topic, we cannot afford to be optimistic about computer conversation. Fanciful aspirations like 'Some day a computer will speak like us' mask the enormous problems quickly accommodated by normal human speakers. It may be possible, but it just does not appear likely.

Now of course nothing I have said here comes close to a knock-down argument against computer belief and in favour of Searle. Some advocates of computer belief say that computers with the skill and versatility necessary to simulate speech are on the technological horizon. Some say the potential speakers are the so-called massively parallel distributed processing machines or connectionist systems currently being advertised as a major innovation in computer design, rather than the traditional von Neumann style digital computers (on which Searle's room seems modelled). Some claim that connectionist systems will display sufficient intelligence and versatility in behaviour to warrant the attribution of computer belief.[6] One day parallel processors will converse in Chinese about concerts at the zoo. This is a bold prediction. If it turns out to be correct, it will mean that computers have performed a marvellous feat. I, for one, will be only too pleased to concede that computers possess intrinsic Intentionality. In the meantime, however, the barrier of simulating human speech will not be easily surmounted. Similarly, the divide which separates as-if from intrinsic Intentionality will not be easily crossed. So, for now, it is a safe bet that no computer will talk its way into belief, Turing notwithstanding.

I have argued that the first counter-argument rests on a currently unwarranted expectation or hope. Parenthetically, it may be noted that Searle responds to the first counter-argument differently, by arguing that even an upgraded computer/room, a massive parallel processor, which he dubs 'the Chinese Gym', cannot possess intrinsic Intentionality. Searle insists that simulating normal conversation is insufficient evidence of intrinsic Intentionality even if it occurs. But why? The main reason seems to be Searle's scepticism about the power of *mere* behaviour to provide sufficient evidence of belief. Searle assumes that no facts about behaviour warrant attribution of belief without the possession of a brain. If the behaving subject is brainless, it is mindless. But this makes it unreasonable to attribute beliefs to the Ivy League Alien. However, again, which is more important, a Ph.D. from Princeton or brain cells? Attribution of belief to the alien seems warranted even if the alien is brainless. It thus is suspect of Searle to say that the room may be upgraded but still lack Intentionality. Better to admit that sufficient upgrading would provide ample evidence of belief but argue that computers are unlikely to be upgraded. This focuses the debate over computer belief on the nature and likelihood of upgrading rather than on allegiance to brains, an allegiance which can only be described as prejudicial and biologically biased.

The remaining criticism of Searle is much more serious and dramatic.

The second counter-argument

A small circle of contemporary philosophers of mind offers a very different reply to Searle's Chinese room argument. The second counter- argument is not designed, like the first, to evoke the concession that a computer could possess intrinsic Intentionality. Quite the contrary, the fundamental idea behind the second counter-argument is that *nothing* possesses intrinsic Intentionality. The counter-argument has been proposed by Patricia and Paul Churchland and Daniel Dennett, three of the most respected figures in recent philosophy of mind.[7] It goes as follows.

The first counter-argument contains more misunderstanding than promise. While it can reasonably be claimed that if a computer could simulate human conversation, it would possess intrinsic Intentionality *if* humans themselves possess intrinsic Intentionality, humans do not possess intrinsic Intentionality. Intrinsic Intentionality is wholly elusive, vague and mysterious; nothing has intrinsic Intentionality. It does not exist. Moreover, since intrinsic Intentionality does not exist, all Intentionality merely is as-if. A human being is just as innocent of intrinsic Intentionality as a computer. Furthermore, since as-if Intentionality is observer dependent, computer Intentionality and 'belief' is easy to demonstrate. Even a Chinese room may qualify as an as-if believer, if it fools or motivates outside observers into ascribing belief to it. Granted, Searle's Chinese room is not up to the level of human conversation. But intrinsic Intentionality does not lie at that level. It lies at no level.

The   impetus   behind   the   Churchland-Dennett   counter-argument comes from several sources, not just desire to attack Searle. The main source is scepticism about the prospects for incorporating reference to intrinsic Intentionality into the scientific and materialist picture of mind favoured by both the Churchlands and Dennett. However, the Churchlands' and Dennett's interpretation of science aside, suppose we take the Churchland-Dennett line seriously.[8] What would be some of the consequences for computer belief?

1   We would no longer have to worry about whether and when computer behaviour is sufficiently intelligent to reveal intrinsic Intentionality. This, of course, is one of the main virtues noted by both the Churchlands and Dennett. No Intentionality threshold would separate nominal believers from true believers.

2   We could decide whether computers 'believe' merely by determining whether we are fooled, tempted or otherwise led into saying that they believe. The Churchland-Dennett line suggests the following simple criterion for determining whether a computer 'believes': if it stumps external observers, it 'believes'. Hence, if, for instance, the Chinese room leads external observers who interact with it into saying that the person in the room or system understands Chinese, then the person or system 'understands' Chinese, for understanding is mere as-if or in-the-eyes-of-the observer understanding.

In spite of, or perhaps because of, its consequences philosophers by and large have rejected the Churchland-Dennett approach. We will look briefly at three reasons for rejection.

1   The approach is incompatible with common sense. Ordinarily we suppose that people do, but water does not, believe. The Churchlands and Dennett do not agree with this. For them there is no psychological threshold separating persons from water flowing downhill. On their view, there is no objective psychological difference between persons and water. Of course, water flowing downhill is not viewed by us non-cave-dwelling moderns as believing. But this is not a fact about water, it is a fact about us (observers). It reveals not a threshold between water and people but between our interpretations of water and people. We manage

without ascribing beliefs to water; we cannot manage (at least not yet) without ascribing beliefs to ourselves.

Whatever the precise impact of clashing with common sense, there is one thing we can be sure of: we have a lot to lose by running foul of common sense. Our common sense conviction that we believe is deeply entrenched in ordinary life. It plays a major role in our sense of ourselves as morally responsible agents and as parents, lovers, citizens and friends. People assume themselves to be believers, and the Churchland-Dennett alternative, strictly speaking, abandons that assumption.

2   The Churchland-Dennett reply rests on an idea which is difficult to formulate and may even be incoherent. It isn't clear to what extent the Churchlands and Dennett really offer a 'counter-argument' or 'reply'.

A counter-argument or reply is characterizable by reference to two factors: (a) a particular object or direction of the reply (in this instance, what Churchlands-Dennett talk about), and (b) its thrust or purport (what they say about it). Thus, the second counter-argument is presumably a reply *to* or *about* Searle's Chinese room argument. However, at the same time, the Churchlands and Dennett say that there is no aboutness in anything. The thrust is that nothing – neither computer, nor animal, nor human being, nor speech – possesses intrinsic Intentionality. Well, if nothing possesses intrinsic Intentionality, their counter-argument is not *about* Searle; it is all mere as-if aboutness. Hence, paradoxically, were the Churchland-Dennett reply correct, no reply (even theirs) would be a reply.

This last point may sound a bit bewildering, so let me give it a slightly different twist in presentation. If we accept the Churchlands' and Dennett's counter-argument against Searle, we lose grounds for saying that counter-arguments are counters to anything. We as outside observers may attribute Intentionality to the counter-argument, or to the Churchlands and Dennett, and certainly we do. But there is no Intentionality in either the counter-argument or its proponents, the Churchlands and Dennett, if the counter-argument is correct. The incoherence or difficulty is this: Once intrinsic Intentionality is eliminated, this sounds dangerously close to saying that the counter-argument itself isn't a counter-argument. Unless some way can be discovered to remedy this problem in formulating the counter-argument, the judgement must be that the counter-argument is defective. Absent aboutness no counter counters.

3 The Churchland-Dennett reply seems to fly in the face of the facts. These three philosophers labour heartily to defend the uncommonsensical conclusion that nothing has intrinsic Intentionality. But there are good reasons to say that intrinsic Intentionality does exist. The view that intrinsic Intentionality is *here* – there *are* genuine Intentional states – is called Intentional Realism. Intentional Realism seems like the correct view. Ask yourself, for example, what you appear to yourself to perceive or visually experience right now. Perhaps your answer is that you see a page of a book. Perhaps you are preparing a meal in your kitchen while you are reading the book. So, in addition to a page, you visually experience a stove, plates, food, kitchen table and much else.

Notice that when you seem to yourself to see the page, it appears to have certain properties or to be situated in a certain way. The page appears as shaded, as containing words about the Churchlands and Dennett, and as having a specific location relative to its environment and to yourself. The visual experience is of a page in a book which itself is on the kitchen table; all of which is in front of you. This includes a great deal of Intentionality. For ask what your experience is *about* and the following would be included: a page of a book, being on top of a kitchen table, being in front of you and so on.

Visual experiences of the above sort support the view that some things possess Intentionality intrinsically. The experiences have *aboutness* in themselves. Indeed, even when visual experiences are false or mistaken, they carry Intentionality within themselves. Your visual experience of a page has Intentionality even if the page does not exist. Perhaps you are hallucinating or dreaming. Still, the question 'What do you seem to see?' would have the same answer, 'A page of a book.' Or suppose we place you in a fake kitchen with cardboard cut-outs of a stove, table and the like, and you may still seem to yourself to be reading in a kitchen. Aboutness is in the experience even if you are not in a kitchen.

The Churchland-Dennett counter-argument interprets the Intentionality of visual experience as as-if, and thus seems deficient for this reason. Indeed, it interprets the Intentionality of all experience as as-if, and so seems flawed for that reason. We seem to hear, taste and smell birds fair and foul in feast and famine. But in each case Churchland-Dennett would say that we have got something wrong, and that our description of experience as *about* is in error. Such a claim makes a great many philosophers charge that the Churchland-Dennett line is mistaken.

Thus, the second counter-argument seems defective in three places: it violates common sense; it is difficult and perhaps even impossible to formulate; and it seems to fly in the face of experiential facts. At a brief level of analysis, at least, it is flawed.

Now back to computer belief. Could a computer believe? The following overall answer emerges. A computer could believe if its behaviour were sufficiently intelligent. However, there is nothing in well studied computer behaviour (such as chess playing) which is sufficiently intelligent to warrant attributing belief to a computer. So perhaps a computer could believe if it could engage in realistic (i.e. normal human) conversation; in essence this is Turing's Test. However, conversing realistically seems far beyond the capacity of present-day computers. From where we stand, computer conversation is over the rainbow. And *that* conclusion may mean that computer belief is well beyond the horizon of realism as well.

One last point before closing this section of the chapter. Both our discussion of animals, in the last chapter, and our discussion of computers, here in this chapter, presuppose a distinction between behaviour of sufficient intelligence to reveal or warrant attributing belief and behaviour of insufficient intelligence to reveal or warrant belief. On one side of the divide is Phaedeux (the dog of the previous chapter) and the hoped-for computer conversationalist; on the other side sits the flatworm and chess-playing computer. This distinction requires codification. I propose the following division: Behaviour which is sufficiently intelligent to reveal belief is *genuinely* intelligent; there is intelligence – a mind – directly underlying the behaviour. Behaviour which is insufficiently intelligent to reveal belief is (to borrow an idea from Searle) *at best* as-if intelligent. There is no mind directly responsible for the behaviour. In the case of the chess-playing computer, the mind is in the programmer, not within the computer.

I will take no stand here on how the distinction may be precisely delineated or even whether it should be precisely delineated. In the previous chapter, I suggested that part of the difference lies in whether a creature shows flexibility and appropriateness in behaviour. By this suggestion I mean to exclude the flatworm, whose behaviour is invariably elicited by particular stimuli, but to include children conversing during zoo concerts, who discriminate different kinds of situations and respond appropriately to topical shifts. I leave it to the reader to decide if this is a worthwhile suggestion and how it may be developed. The topic is vexing. It is tempting to exclaim: Only God knows the correct answer.

5.3   The Mind of God

God knows? No mind is further over the horizon than God's, for not only does there exist a great deal of disagreement concerning the very existence of God, but the divine mind itself, since it is God's, may be so wholly other, so totally transcendent, that no mind concepts we can form may apply to it. Perhaps we should remain silent about God's mind.

Silence about the mind of God leads to problems, however, for the conception of God as minded is deeply rooted in Christianity and other theistic religions. Communication between God and man is at the centre of the Judaeo-Christian picture of the relation between God and man. A large portion of Scriptures consists of God speaking his mind to man. Similarly essential is the idea of God as a 'personal agent' – a subject who created the world and carries out intentions, plans or purposes in his actions; a being who is capable of entering into personal relationships and acts in people's lives, bestowing his grace, offering his love. In this section of the chapter I propose to examine, albeit quickly, the topic of what sorts of mind concepts apply to God. How should we describe God's mind? A philosopher should not take shelter in silence.

First, I need to make one brief point about a central presupposition behind the discussion to follow. If there are sufficient grounds to deny that God exists, then of course no mind of God exists. A crucial premise in our discussion, which I do not defend here, is that God exists.

David Hume wrote: 'I weigh the one miracle against the other; and according to the superiority which I discover, I pronounce my decision, and always reject the greater miracle.'[9] Is it more miraculous (incredible) that God does exist or that he truly does not exist? Hume would answer that God exists; so he would reject the presupposition that God exists and not bother to examine the mind of God. However, if a reader of Humean temperament denies that God exists, there may still be interest in the discussion to follow because it enables us to examine certain connections between mental phenomena: between belief and representation, on the one hand, and love and suffering, on the other. The connections are worth exploring even if the vehicle for their discussion (viz. God) is not. So, I hope that those who share Hume's scepticism about the existence of God may still take interest in the discussion to follow.

A dilemma for St Thomas

Some of the greatest theologians and philosophers of religion have theorized about the mind of God, including St Thomas Aquinas (c.1225–74). In his masterpiece the *Summa Theologica*, St Thomas asks whether 'evils, deprivations, and defects' ever enter into the mind or thought of God. Does God think about evil? His answer is that God thinks about evil 'speculatively', but not 'practically'; that is, he knows of evil's existence, but not of what it is like to do evil or experience suffering. Evils, deprivations and defects are not part of His practice. God knows of the evil and suffering which transpire in our world, but he does not know as, say, Hitler knew evil by performing terrible misdeeds and depriving people of life and limb. And he does not know by experiencing suffering himself, as tragically happened to Hitler's victims.

What prompts Aquinas to ask his question? Why does he wonder whether and how evil enters into the divine mind? Aquinas's question is prompted by a dilemma specifically for the Christian understanding of God. The dilemma concerns the overwhelming importance to Christianity of God's knowledge, love and power, and the sort of mind the Christian God is supposed to have. Let's take a few paragraphs to present the dilemma.

According to Christianity, God is perfectly knowing. In technical jargon, he is omniscient. Being perfectly knowing means different things to different Christians, but most of the different meanings

coalesce around the following two-part idea: To be perfectly knowing is to be (1) thoroughly free of ignorance (if something is true,
God knows it; he is not ignorant of any fact or truth whatsoever)
and (2) altogether sound (He is without error or mistake; he is
free of falsehood). You and I, by contrast, are both ignorant and
mistaken at least in most matters. I don't know anything about,
say, the mating habits of dolphins or atmospheric pressure on
Venus; and I am certainly mistaken in many of my beliefs about,
say, potash and pottage. So I am imperfectly knowing. I know some
things, but I also swim in a vast sea of ignorance and error.

If God is perfectly knowing, presumably he should not be ignorant of dolphins and Venus; and he should harbour no falsehoods
about potash and pottage. Likewise, he should know of evil and
make no mistake about it. Dolphins transpire in the world; evil
does too. God should know of them both. But the question is, how
does he know about evil? If evil enters into his mind, how does it
enter?

Sadly, you and I know of evil all too often by engaging in it. Evil
enters our thoughts through intentional misdeed. We lie, cheat
and steal; we behave selfishly and ungenerously towards our fel-
lows. We know what cheating is because we cheat; we know what
it means to steal because we steal. An onlooker ignorant of
Christianity and related conceptions of God might therefore expect
that if God is perfectly knowing, he, too, knows of evil firsthand.
He lies, cheats and steals. God knows what it means to steal
because he steals, just as we know what it means to steal because
we steal. However, as Aquinas points out, knowledge of evil by
doing evil could not be available to the God of Christianity. The
Christian God is not merely omniscient. He is also perfectly kind
and loving. In technical terms, he is omnibenevolent. So, God
cannot lie, cheat or steal. Evil deeds would be unloving, and the
very thought of doing evil would be unkind.

Equally sadly, you and I know what suffering means since we
suffer. We are afflicted by disease, riddled with doubt and worry,
fearful of death and vulnerable to the whims of madmen (like
Hitler). However, the Christian God is not merely omniscient and
omnibenevolent, he is also perfectly powerful. In technical jargon,
he is omnipotent. So, it seems to many Christians, such as
Aquinas, that God is not susceptible to suffering. According to

Aquinas, susceptibility to suffering would be a sign of weakness; and the very possibility of weakness ill suits God.

Once perfect love and power are counted as attributes of God, there is reason to deny that God knows the evil which transpires in this world by doing or experiencing evil. On the other hand, denying that God knows evil by doing or experiencing evil risks denying that God knows evil *unless another route to knowledge* of evil can be found. But what route is available? If God does not know by doing or suffering, how does he know?

Ignoring the details of Aquinas's overall philosophy, he offers a solution to the dilemma of how God can both know evil and yet be perfectly powerful and loving; of how evil, deprivation and defect can enter into His mind without destroying his divinity. Aquinas's solution is to argue that in addition to knowing by doing or experiencing (practical knowledge), there is knowing by intuiting – by being aware. Knowing is then either practical knowing or intuitive ('speculative') knowing. God knows through awareness; he knows by intuiting the evil which transpires in the world. Since God performs and suffers no misdeeds, he remains loving and powerful; and, since he is aware of evil, he also remains altogether knowledgeable. Nothing undermines his goodness or power; nothing escapes his knowledge.

It is tempting to examine Aquinas's solution: his appeal to intuition. This would involve exploring several doctrines in his philosophy, including the simplicity of God, God's knowledge of his own essence, the non-discursiveness of divine knowledge and much else besides. These are complicated and technical ideas which are beyond the scope of this book. My purpose in mentioning Aquinas is not to set the stage for Thomas's theories. I want to extract a different and more general lesson.

There is a general lesson to be learned here, having to do with the mind of God and with the concepts of mind which can be applied to him. Because God has a certain stature and nature, because he *is* God, his mind has a special nature or character. Not just any mind concepts befit or suit him. In the case of Christianity, for instance, God is perfectly knowing, loving and powerful, so whatever inhabits or enters his mind – whatever he knows or thinks of – must be consistent with his perfection. If Aquinas is right, ascribing practical knowledge of evil to God does not befit him.

Once we recognize the general lesson, other examples of concepts of mind which could or could not apply to God reinforce it. I will mention two. I will develop an argument that the first does not apply to God. Then I will briefly sketch an argument that the second concept does apply to Him.

Belief

Should we speak of God as believing? Does God possess beliefs?

There is considerable debate in the philosophic literature over the nature of belief. What is belief? The most common answer goes something like this: to believe something is to mentally represent it as true. If, for instance, I believe that Descartes is a great philosopher, I represent him to myself as a great philosopher. Equivalently: I take it to be true that Descartes is a great philosopher.

Here is a short argument that God does not have beliefs. It turns on an essential feature of belief. The essential feature can be summarized in a single sentence: Beliefs are inherently capable of being true or false. I believe, for instance, that my name is George Graham and that I was born in Brooklyn, New York. Both these beliefs are true, but they could have been false, if I had a different name and birthplace. They are inherently capable of being true (for they *are* true) or false (for they would have been false had the relevant facts been different). Meanwhile, you believe (let's suppose for the sake of example) that I (the author of this book) am Christian. But the belief is false. I admire Christianity; but I am no Christian. Again, the belief is inherently capable of being true (had the fact been different) or false (for it *is* false).

Back to divinity. Suppose God is omniscient. He is perfectly knowing; never in error, never mistaken. He is incapable of falsehood. Hence, God does not have beliefs. If God had beliefs, he could be mistaken; but he cannot be mistaken, so he does not have beliefs.

In short, beliefs do not suit God. Of course, knowledge suits him: He is – we are supposing – omniscient. But this cannot be knowledge which involves belief. (Perhaps it is Aquinas's intuitive knowledge and perhaps intuitive knowledge is knowledge without belief.)

The idea that beliefs are inherently capable of being true or false requires defence. It's a tricky idea.[10] At the risk of complicating something which already is complex, what of it? As said, the term 'belief' stands for a certain type of mental representation; namely, beliefs represent things as true. Beliefs are not alone in being representational. Numerous sorts of things can be representational, some mental, some non-mental: a map, a gesture, the dance of a bee, a picture, a desire and so on. A map may represent Alabama; a gesture hello; a dance the location of flowers; a picture Winston Churchill; a desire ice cream. But beliefs are ways in which minds represent. And they are ways in which the mind represents when someone takes something to be true.

Without going into detail, the representationality of belief is connected with its Intentionality. Because a belief is about something, it represents it. My belief that Descartes is a great philosopher is about Descartes; it represents him as a great philosopher.

Some representations are better than others; some correctly represent, others incorrectly represent. My map represents Montgomery as the capital of the State of Alabama; Filbert's map represents Birmingham as the capital. My map is correct; Filbert's is incorrect. Montgomery is the capital; Birmingham is merely the State's largest city. Mine 'represents'; Filbert's misrepresents. In the case of belief, a belief which correctly or truly represents is called 'true'; a belief which incorrectly represents is called 'false'. (Maps which represent are 'accurate' or 'apt'; maps which misrepresent are 'inaccurate'.) If I believe that Montgomery is the capital of Alabama, this represents the capital correctly, for the capital is Montgomery. The belief is true; the representation 'represents'.

Beliefs are inherently capable of being true or false because beliefs are inherently capable of 'representing' or misrepresenting. They can be correct or incorrect. I can represent something as true when in actual fact (unbeknownst to me) it is false; I can endorse a falsehood. Just in themselves, therefore, beliefs afford no guarantee of truth. They are not inherently correct. Now let's return to the claim that God does not have beliefs.

We can schematize the argument that God does not possess beliefs as follows:

1 Whatever represents can also misrepresent.
2 Beliefs represent.

3 So, beliefs can also misrepresent.
4 A belief which misrepresents is false.
5 But God is incapable of falsehood and misrepresentation. He is omniscient.
6 So, he does not possess beliefs.

The above argument is not the only argument that God does not believe. Nor is the denial of divine belief some sort of heretical doctrine. A number of Christian philosophers have defended it, if not for the same reason.[11] True, there are various ways in which one might try to attack the argument. However, attack and counter-defence of the claim that God lacks beliefs lie beyond the scope of the present book.

The purpose behind my arguing that God does not possess beliefs is not to prove that God lacks beliefs. It is to reinforce the general lesson extracted from Aquinas. God's mind must be characterized in a manner which befits him. *If* because of omniscience, belief does not befit God, *he* lacks belief. If representation does not suit him, God does not represent.

By way of contrast with the argument that the concept of belief does not apply to God, let's examine a mind concept which arguably does apply to him. Can God suffer?

Suffering and love

'Perhaps,' says Marilyn McCord Adams in a recent paper, 'the inner life of God includes deep agony as well as ecstatic joy.'[12]

Deep agony? God? On the face of it, it seems incredible to say that God suffers; that he experiences deep agony. It is usually supposed that while human beings are caught up in the experience of suffering, of grief, depression and sorrow, God's life is altogether unperturbed and serene. He is devoid of passion, unfamiliar with pain, foreign to grief, depression or sorrow. But Adams gives the suffering of God a distinctive twist. There is, on her view, good reason for entertaining the idea that God suffers. God's perfect love comes into play here. God may not be content, she says, to be immutable and impassible, to witness the suffering of his creatures with the cool eye of unperturbed omniscience. He may instead prefer to unite himself to those whom he loves. If he does, then he himself will sympathetically feel their misery and pain. He will suffer.

What is Adams's thought here? What is her line of reasoning? She never quite develops it. But perhaps we can add a few details.[13] Why would God join with the suffering of his creatures? Why would he prefer to give up an unperturbed omniscience?

One answer may be that it is the very nature of love to suffer when its object suffers and that uninterrupted suffering-free serenity is incompatible with love. A person who shows no grief at the death of a friend or child or the rape of his wife is rightly described by us as unloving and uncaring. Similarly, a God who shows no grief or sorrow over the suffering of his creation is also rightly described as unloving and uncaring. To love another is to sorrow when they sorrow: to live in the solidarity of grieving (and rejoicing) with them. The possibility that God's knowledge of the world gives him no vexation at all, no unhappiness, no sorrow, therefore, is incompatible with the claim that God is perfectly loving. God's omniscience by itself may be compatible with freedom from suffering, but Divine Love is not. In loving God gives up the immutability and freedom from disturbance he might otherwise possess.

By connecting the divine mind with the idea of loving and suffering, Adams gives the mind of God psychological and emotional depth. Instead of a divine subject unfamiliar with longing, everlastingly content, she describes a God who knows what it is like to suffer. Rather than the suffering of his people leaving God untouched, he too undergoes suffering. What we finally think of her suggestion should depend on what we think of other attributes of God and whether the notion of a suffering God systematically fits or coheres with them. In the Christian tradition, for instance, God is said to be incorporeal (without embodiment).[14] How does the idea of a suffering God impact on the idea of an incorporeal God? When persons suffer they experience a disturbance in their nervous system; some philosophers even claim that physiological disturbance is essential for suffering. Well, clearly, if an incorporeal God suffers he is not physiologically disturbed. So is the body truly essential for suffering? Or might God (contrary to the Christian tradition) actually possess a body, so that when he suffers his body is disturbed? Perhaps (as some philosophers speculate) the whole wide world is God's body; hence when he suffers the world is physically disturbed. God is incorporeal in that he lacks a particular body or specific embodiment; but he is corporeal in that he is physically realized in everything, everywhere. Does *that* make sense?

A second difficulty – familiar from the discussion of St Thomas above – may even be more perplexing. It is an error, some philosophers charge, to hold that an omnipotent being can suffer, for suffering compromises power. Omnipotence, on this view, involves (in part) freedom from pain and grief. God is omnipotent; thus he does not suffer.

Perhaps the best response for Adams to make to the second difficulty is to argue that just as suffering is compatible with divine omniscience, it is consistent with divine power. The question now to be addressed is whether a concept of omnipotence can be found which enables us to say God suffers.

Perhaps the first step is to argue that God's perfections are not separable: His power is part of his love which is part of his knowledge, which in turn is part of his power, and so on. If God was *merely* omnipotent, perhaps he would not suffer. But he is not only omnipotent; he is also omnibenevolent. Thus, his love and power are intertwined. This means that rather than floating mysteriously like some potentate above the world, God's love brings him into communion with his creatures so that he suffers along with them. Unlike us, his power fortifies him when he suffers, so that suffering neither diminishes nor embitters him. But divine power does not insulate him from suffering, since it is inseparable from his love.

The concept of divine suffering and the issues surrounding it are difficult and perplexing; but Adams's tempting suggestion makes questions about divine suffering, power and love required thinking for the intelligent theist sympathetic to Christian themes. It also offers an alternative to Aquinas's view. Intuitive apprehension or speculative knowledge of suffering may seem too spectatorial and removed from the painful fray. Aquinas permits God to know evil but not to know 'what it is like' to suffer or to experience evil. By contrast, Adams suggests that God does know what suffering is like; he suffers. Does he? I shall leave the response to the reader.

5.4   Lessons about Computers and God

I launched the chapter with two questions. The first was whether computers could believe. The second was whether if we conceive of God as minded, there are limits on the very idea of the mind of God.

There are two lessons to be learned from the chapter. First, considered as candidates for the ascription of belief, computers are on a par with human and nonhuman animals. The real puzzle over whether computers possess intrinsic Intentionality and genuine beliefs is whether computer behaviour warrants the attribution of belief. Is computer behaviour sufficiently intelligent to warrant saying that a computer believes? Second, supposing that God exists and is minded, certainly the mind of God is not on a par with either animals or computers. This is because God's mind is conceptually unique and unlike any other mind. There are of course a variety of ways in which people construe the uniqueness of God's mind. One of these is expressed in the Christian notion that God is omnibenevolent, omniscient and omnipotent. Certainly no animal or computer is blessed with perfect traits. Any account of God's mind, then, if it is to stand a chance of describing what his mind really is like, must show how God's psychology is fixed or constituted by the overall character of his divinity. Since God is divine, his mind must be godly as well.

The story that the ancients considered elephants to have religion is contained in Plutarch's *The Cleverness of Animals*. A citizen of contemporary culture, a programmer of computers, may wonder of The Cleverness of Computers.

What happens to the elephant? Supplication does not rest in the position of its trunk. Religion is distinctively human. From the human point of view divine assistance is needed to plumb the The Cleverness of God.

NOTES

1   John Searle, 'Is the brain's mind a computer program?' in *Metaphysics*, eds. R.C. Hoy and L.N. Oaklander (Wadsworth, California, 1991), p.281; originally appeared in *Scientific American* (January 1990).

2 John Haugeland, 'Understanding natural language', in *Foundations of Cognitive Science*, ed. Jay Garfield (Paragon, New York, 1990), pp.398–410.

3 Alan M. Turing, 'Computing machinery and intelligence', *Mind*, 59 (1950), 433–60.

4 John Searle, 'Minds, brains, and programs', *Behavioral and Brain Sciences*, 3 (1980), 417–57 (including peer review).

5 John Tienson, 'An introduction to connectionism', in *Foundations of Cognitive Science*, ed. Jay L. Garfield (Paragon, New York, 1990), p.385.

6 On computers and parallel processing, see William Bechtel and Adele Abrahamson, *Connectionism and the Mind: An Introduction to Parallel Processing in Networks* (Basil Blackwell, Oxford, 1990).

7 Patricia S. Churchland and Paul M. Churchland, 'Functionalism, qualia, and Intentionality', in *A Neurocomputational Perspective*, ed. Paul M. Churchland (MIT Press, Cambridge, MA., 1989), pp.23–46; Daniel C. Dennett, 'Fast thinking', in *The Intentional Stance*, ed. Daniel C. Dennett (MIT Press, Cambridge, MA., 1987), pp.323–37.

8 Detailed analysis of the Churchlands and Dennett would reveal subtleties neglected here. See chapters 7, 8 and 9 for related discussion.

9 David Hume, *An Enquiry Concerning Human Understanding* (Oxford University Press, Oxford, 1955), p.114.

10 The claim that beliefs are inherently capable of being false needs qualification in the light of potential counter-examples, such as 'beliefs' in logical truths, which cannot be false. The topic of how to qualify or precisely formulate the claim is beyond the scope of the present discussion.

11 See, for example, William Alston, 'Does God have beliefs?', in *Divine Nature and Human Language*, ed. W. Alston (Cornell University Press, Ithaca, New York, 1989), pp.178–93.

12 Marilyn McCord Adams, 'Redemptive suffering: a Christian solution to the problem of evil', in *Rationality, Religious Belief, and Moral Commitment*, ed. Robert Audi and William Wainwright (Cornell University Press, Ithaca, New York, 1986), p.264.

13 Ideas along the following lines are explored in Nicholas Wolterstorff, 'Suffering love', in *Philosophy and the Christian Faith*, ed. Thomas V. Morris (University of Notre Dame Press, South Bend, Indiana, 1988), pp.196–237.

14 Within Christian theology, the idea of an incorporeal God is complicated by the doctrines of the Trinity and Incarnation; but I gloss over such complications here, since they would take us too far afield.

6

Rational Action

No characteristic of mind is more important than its role in bringing about behaviour. No behavioural role is more important than bringing about purposive behaviour or what philosophers call 'rational action'.

In this chapter I shall offer a definition of rational action, describing what makes action rational, distinguishing rational from irrational action and briefly examining some issues which typically come up when philosophers discuss rational action, viz., Is weakness of the will unreasonable? Are actions selfish because they are motivated by one's own reasons?

6.1 The Concept of 'Rational Action'

What is rational action? Rational action is behaviour done for reasons or purposes of the agent. To take a simple example, suppose it is a hot, steamy summer day in Birmingham, Alabama. You and I have just finished wresting weeds from my favourite patch of backyard okra. I ascend the porch and open the door to my home. I feel absolutely wretched. I want an ice-cold beer – very cold. Suppose, not to be left out in the heat, you, too, wish an ice-cold beer. However, while I walk to the refrigerator, you drive to the supermarket. Why do we travel in different directions? I walk to the fridge because I believe that cold beer is located there, whereas you drive to the market because you believe that, although the fridge is empty, the market stocks cold beer.

Walking to the fridge is something I do for a reason or on

purpose: wishing the beer expected there. It is rational action. Driving to the market is something you do for a reason. So it, too, is rational action.

Rational actions contrast with mere movements or non-rational behaviour, activities of the agent or their body which they undergo but which they do not perform for a reason. When I fall or stumble, for example, what happens is not something for which reason is responsible. True, I move when I stumble, but I do not produce the movement. I am not the stumble's agent, but only its anxious and perhaps embarrassed patient. Again, as a young boy when my body grew, its growth was not something brought about by me for a reason. I was not the growth's agent but only, so to speak, its subject or source.

What distinguishes rational action from mere movement or non-rational behaviour such as falling and growing? I assume the following partial division: rational action is performed for a reason, whereas mere movement happens because of a cause. Equivalently: Every rational action is explained by reference to the agent's reason for doing it, whereas movements are explained by reference to causes. My stumble – a mere movement – occurs because my foot, say, strikes a rock or sticks in the muddy pavement. The striking or sticking is causally responsible for the stumbling. By contrast, my walking – a rational action – happens for a reason. The reason includes the purpose or goal I seek to attain (a cold beer), and my beliefs about means for attaining it (going to the fridge). The rationality presupposed in rational action is agent-centred or subjective. It turns on whether I take the behaviour to be fitting or appropriate means for achieving my purpose given my beliefs and expectations.

If you believe that the fridge is empty, you no doubt believe that it offers zero prospects of containing cold beer. Then, you refrain from walking to the fridge, for there is no reason to walk. Then why do I venture to the fridge? I believe that it contains cold beer. Given my wish and expectation, it is rational for me to go to the fridge.

The distinction between cause and reason, though critical, is not mutually exclusive. Although no mere movement occurs for a reason, actions stem from reasons which causally contribute to action. We may put this by saying that reasons help to causally explain action. For instance, my walk to the fridge springs from my desire for beer, whereas your desire motivates your drive to the market.

Most philosophers favour what may be called a *network* or *holistic* theory of reasons as causes, in which mental events or occurrences mix together to produce an effect. According to network theory, a statement like 'desiring ice cold beer I walk to the fridge' means that the desire mixes together with my overall state of mind, perhaps including my conscious deliberation or calculation, to contribute to walking. For example, it would be implausible to suggest that I walk to the fridge just because I want beer. A full account of the manner in which reasons help to bring about action would recognize that reasons function in networks of psychological states and perceptual conditions which must prevail if action occurs.[1]

Consider, for instance, the action of flipping a light switch in order to illuminate a dark room. It takes more than reason to flip the switch. For starters, I must perceive the switch; and then monitor, perhaps non-deliberately or sub-personally, the position of my hand and the thrust of my finger, for I should not hit the switch too hard (it may break) or too soft (the electrical circuits may not engage).

Does *any* reason of a person cause or help to bring about action? Certainly not. Just because someone has reason for action does not mean that they will perform or even try to perform the action. Filbert wants a cold beer. Even more, however, he wants to avoid Temperance who is standing by the fridge. So, although Filbert believes that beer is in the fridge, he refrains from walking there.

Likewise, just because a person possesses reason for action and performs the action does not mean that they perform the action for that reason. Consider possessing reason for walking to the fridge and walking, but not for that reason. Albert wants cold beer. However, even more he wants to eat a piece of cake. So, although he believes that beer is in the fridge, and he struts to the fridge, Albert does not act for beer. He cakewalks.

The following three theses are widely held in recent philosophical discussion of rational action and have been employed above:

1   To act rationally is to behave for a reason.
2   Reasons make actions rational or appropriate from the agent's
    point of view.
3   Reasons help to produce action. They help to causally explain
    action.

The three theses (especially 3) are not problem-free; but, they will
be presupposed in the sections to follow.

6.2   Rationality versus Irrationality

In this section I want to discuss one of the most perplexing philosophic problems connected with the topic of rational action. How
should rational action be distinguished from irrational action?

Just as rational action contrasts with mere (non-rational) movement, it also contrasts with irrational action. People no doubt
act irrationally. What this means is that we act for reasons, but
the reasons themselves may be bad or irrational. When action is
performed for bad or irrational reasons, the action itself is irrational. Rational action, in contrast with irrational action, is done for
a good or rational reason.

The basic idea behind irrational action is hard to express without risk of linguistic confusion. The confusion is between (1)
'rational' in the sense of *for a reason* and (2) 'rational' in the sense
of *good* reason and thus 'irrational' in the sense of *bad* reason. One
and the same action can be both rational (performed for a reason)
and irrational (performed for a bad reason).

The two senses of 'rational' surely are not the same. As a young
boy, I sometimes feigned illness to escape going to school and
taking a tough exam. Unfortunately, because of absences, I fell
behind in schoolwork and had to feign still more illnesses to
escape more demanding exams. I feigned illness for a reason; so,
the feigning was rational. No illness moved me; reason did. But
the rationality of the reason should be doubted, since the success
of my efforts did not encourage schoolwork. If anything, the practice discouraged me academically. Hence, although feigning was
rational in that I feigned for a reason, it was irrational in that I
feigned for a bad reason.

Reasons can be bad or irrational from different perspectives and points of view.[2] They can be bad from the agent's point of view, that is, in terms of the agent's subjective conception of the goodness or badness of his or her reasons. Let us call actions performed for subjectively bad reasons *internally* or *subjectively irrational actions*. They can also be bad in terms of external standards or criteria which may or may not be part of the agent's subjective perspective. Let us call actions performed for externally bad reasons *externally irrational actions*.

External irrationality (and rationality) comes in many different forms. In the worst possible cases – instances of severe self-delusion, moral psychosis, mental illness – external irrationality not only expresses failure to act on good reasons, judged by external standards, but it can have tragic personal and social consequences as well. For example, in 1984 the *British Journal of Psychiatry* published an article with the fascinating title of 'Self shooting of phantom head'.[3] The article described the case of a mentally ill man who thought that he had two heads, one of which taunted him with hostile thoughts. He tried to rid himself of the alien head by shooting it off with a revolver. He survived but was seriously wounded, dying two years later of chronic infection caused by the shot. The deed was irrational, externally. However, the man performed the action for a reason. In fact, he acted for a subjectively good reason. He believed that he possessed an extra head and wished to terminate its taunting. What more appropriate means to terminate than to destroy? As he said, 'The other head kept trying to dominate my normal head, and I would not let it.'

Why was the man's action externally irrational? The shooting was externally irrational on two grounds. First, it stemmed from a grossly unhealthy or imprudent desire. The desire to shoot ticketed him for disaster. Second, it rested on a belief (that he had two heads) which was not merely false but plainly false and should have been plainly false to the man.

Internal or subjective irrationality (and rationality) also comes in different forms. Some internally irrational actions stem from beliefs and expectations which the agent admits are foolish or faulty; others reflect disvalues or unwelcome desires of the agent. To take a simple illustration, Temperance smokes. Indeed, she smokes for a reason; she likes it. But in her own mind this is a bad reason, for she knows that smoking is harmful to her health and she sincerely claims that she values health more than enjoyment. The expected harm undermines the internal rationality of smoking and makes it, in a certain sense, subjectively irrational for her to smoke.

We need a clear way in which to distinguish linguistically between actions done for reasons (and hence rational) and actions done for bad reasons (and hence irrational). One way is to claim that an action may be both rational *and* irrational – rational in one sense, irrational in another sense. But this way of speaking is both cumbersome and unclear. Rational *and* irrational? So, I propose speaking of actions which are rational and *unreasonable*, internally or externally, as the case may be. Temperance's smoking is both rational and unreasonable, judged from her own point of view. 'Rational' conveys the sense of smokes for a reason; 'unreasonable' identifies the reason as bad.

Note that in calling an action unreasonable, internally, we as outsiders are not condemning it. Internally bad reasons may be good or bad externally. The measure of internal badness (or goodness) is agent-centred, not outsider decided.

6.3 Is Weakness of Will Unreasonable?

The ancient texts combed most thoroughly for lessons about the rational and reasonable are, probably, the Old and New Testaments. One of the most intriguing Rationality Tales in the Old Testament is the story of how David, after Saul tried to kill him, sought refuge in Gath, the city from which Goliath had come. According to the version of the story reported in the Book of Samuel, fearful of the reception which he, a one-time enemy, would receive in Gath, especially from its king, Achish, David pretended that he was insane.

So he changed his behaviour before them [the Philistines of Gath] and feigned himself mad in their hands, and scrabbled on the doors of the gate, and let his spittle fall down upon his beard. Then said Achish to his servants, 'Lo, you see the man is mad; why then have you brought him to me? Have I need of mad men, that you have brought this fellow to play the madman in my presence?'

David gives us a glimpse of what it means to be a certain type of rational agent: a type much admired by philosophers. This is someone who is strong-willed or 'continent', to use a philosopher's term of art. What is a strong-willed agent? A strong-willed agent is someone who acts in terms of their better conscious judgement, that is, in terms of what they judge to be their best reasons. Even if it seems to outsiders as if they are unrestrained and un-controlled, they are self possessed and self-controlled. They are concerned with their reasons for action; they listen to the dictates of their deliberation; and, finally, they hold fast to those dictates. They do what they decide that they should do. In David's case, although his countenance was slovenly, for spittle ran down his face, his behaviour ingeniously expressed his strength of will and resolve: to enter the land of the enemy and by feigning madness to seek refuge.

Continence consists in abiding by one's better conscious judgement. If continence is a virtue or admirable feature of rational agency, the corresponding vice may be that of weakness of will or 'incontinence'.[4] A weak-willed or incontinent agent is someone who acts against his or her better conscious judgement; they knowingly fail to abide by the dictates of deliberation. Garden variety examples include: the over-eater who is incontinent in acting against his sincere intention to diet, the excessively critical parent who is weak-willed in acting against her judgement that children should be treated with patience and tolerance, and the kleptomaniac who is weak-willed in acting contrary to her resolve to respect other people's property.

Is incontinence subjectively unreasonable? Is one never weak-willed for a good (internal) reason but always only for a bad reason?

I will argue that in certain situations incontinence may actually be more reasonable than continence, internally. If incontinence is a vice it is a defeasible vice, which means that even if it is usually or typically unreasonable, people can be incontinent for good (internal) reasons.

First, let us examine the contrary view that incontinence is internally unreasonable. An argument that incontinence is intern-ally unreasonable finds its roots in Aristotle, who was (with Plato) one of the two greatest and most influential of the ancient Greek philosophers. Aristotle says that whereas the 'continent person seems to be the same as one who abides by his rational calculation ... the incontinent person seems to be the same as the one who abandons it' (*Nichomachean Ethics*, 1145b10–11). The terseness of Aristotle's remark contains a disarmingly subtle argument that incontinence is internally unreasonable. The argument may be reconstructed as follows:

> Good internal reasons are reasons consciously judged good by the agent. Incontinent agents knowingly act against reasons which they judge good. Hence, incontinence is internally unreasonable.

To take a simple illustration, suppose that Sam sells cars. His boss's business is doing poorly, so he urges Sam to unload some 'lemons'. Lemons are really bad cars and Sam has moral scruples about selling them. He deliberates and decides not to follow his boss's request. However, at the first sign of a customer, Sam abandons his resolve and asks 'Can I interest you in a premium car' – as he points to the worst lemon.

Sam is Aristotle's incontinent agent. Sam deliberates (calculates) and judges 'refraining from selling lemons' as the reasonable thing to do; but Sam then knowingly abandons his calculations and attempts to sell bad cars. For Aristotle, Sam's action is unreasonable, internally.

Aristotle operates with what may be called a *consistency with conscious judgement* model of internal reasonableness. His idea is that an action is reasonable, internally, just when it is consistent with the agent's judgement of the goodness or reasonableness of his reasons. In the case of Sam, if Sam had deliberated again and made a second judgement that he should sell lemons, then his action of selling would have been both continent and reasonable, internally.

Aristotle did not regard his argument about the unreasonableness of incontinence as a mere terminological nicety.[5] He stressed that incontinence was a blot against a person's character – 'to be avoided and blameworthy'. Is Aristotle's argument sound? Must incontinent action be unreasonable? Is there no room for reasonable incontinence?

Consider the case of Mark Twain's Huckleberry Finn.[6] In *The Adventures of Huckleberry Finn* Twain tells the tale of a young boy prior to the Civil War in the United States who takes a trip by makeshift raft down the Mississippi River with a runaway slave named Jim. Actually, Huck and Jim are both runaways: Jim from slavery, Huck from a brutal parent.

Some way into the trip, feeling what he describes as pangs of conscience for helping Jim escape from his owner, Huck judges that he should turn Jim in at the first opportunity. But when confronted unexpectedly with bounty hunters, Huck's resolve weakens. He lies to protect Jim and blames himself for his weakness.

From an external standpoint, especially from the moral point of view, it is eminently reasonable for Huck to act against his judgement by failing to turn Jim over to the slave hunters. Given the terrible immorality of slavery, Jim ought to remain free. However, such an assessment does not correspond to the reasons which ground Huck's judgement. To Huck Jim is stolen property and stolen property belongs with its owner. Remember internal rationality is agent-centred. It concerns the agent's own attitudes. Huck knowingly acts against what he judges he has best reason to do and responds to consciously unwelcome reasons leading him to protect Jim.

What would Aristotle say about Huck? Aristotle's emphasis on consistency with judgement means that Huck is both incontinent and unreasonable, since he knowingly acts against his judgement. But the contrary possibility that incontinence can be reasonable gains a powerful foothold in the example of Huck. Reasons figure prominently if not deliberately in his refusal to turn in Jim. Huck sympathizes with Jim's desire for freedom and is aware of Jim's trust and gratitude. And frankly, Huck seems to care much more for these – as he views them – morally irrelevant considerations than he does for moral rules about property.

Twain puts Huck's point of view after refusing to turn Jim over in prose:

Well, then, says I, what's the use you learning to do right, when it's troublesome to do right and ain't no trouble to do wrong, and the wages is just the same? I was stuck. I couldn't answer that. So I reckoned I wouldn't bother no more about it, but after this always do whichever come handiest at the time.

How should we interpret Huck? Arguably, we should say that Huck is reasonable, internally, in being weak-willed or knowingly acting against his 'better' judgement. This is because his judgement is out of kilter with his subjectively best reasons. What are those reasons? They are the reasons which matter most to him even though they do not ground his conscious assessment or calculations prior to being confronted with the slave hunters.

Aristotle imagines a standard of internal rationality imposed by the agent in calculation and judgement. But agents' points of view are multi-dimensional and complex. Sometimes, especially in cases of self-doubt, the so-called 'better' judgement is incompatible with what matters most to a person; it arises from less than the internally best reasons. On this broader conception of internal rationality – which I call *fidelity to the agent's overall internal perspective* – none of us makes all and only those judgements of better which in fact *are* (subjectively) better and which faithfully reflect our total point of view. If behaviour runs against the grain of one's most inclusive or personally important reasons, then, admittedly, it is unreasonable (internally) to act knowingly in such a fashion. However, if behaviour runs merely against the grain of one's judgement, then this may be reasonable if the judgement itself fails to reflect subjectively more important considerations.

On the analysis which pictures internal rationality in terms of fidelity to overall internal perspective, Huck's refusal is reasonable. More generally, it can be reasonable to be weak-willed.

The point I am making may be refined with a distinction and sharpened on another example. Talking of the goodness/reasonableness or badness/unreasonableness of an action or reason from the agent's internal perspective is ambiguous. It may suggest two things, which I shall call the 'judgementalist' and 'holist' approaches to the matter.

The judgementalist approach takes as its premise that an action to be reasonable (internally) must be judged reasonable by the agent. It concentrates on the agent's calculation. The holist approach, in contrast, factors the agent's judgement as just one among many factors in discovering whether an action is reasonable from the agent's point of view. It focuses instead on the richness, complexity and often unconscious elements in an agent's perspective.

On the judgementalist approach, Huck's failure to return Jim is unreasonable, internally. But what of the holist approach? Interpreted as an action which fits with what means most to Huck, it is hard to deny its reasonableness.

Let us consider another example. A promising young pianist's hands are injured in a motorcycle accident. Unless she allows the hands to heal she will no longer play the piano. She knows this, and resolves that she remain off her motorcycle for two months while the hands heal. Within a few weeks of formulating her resolve, however, in response to an invitation to participate in a race, she rides the motorcycle fully realizing that the ride contravenes her judgement.

To start with, note that she is not following her judgement or decision. She is incontinent. But does it follow that she races for bad reason, internally? As noted by many writers on weakness of will, there is something unfortunate when a decision is abandoned. On balance, it renders deliberation irrelevant. But must we say that her action is unreasonable? Riding in the race may, after all, express her deepest desires in an appropriate way. True, she risks a promising musical career; but, if one takes her overall point of view into account, and not just her judgement, motorcycling may mean more to her than music. Perhaps racing is a triumph of spontaneous enjoyment over a faulty judgement about a career she neither likes nor finds rewarding.

By distinguishing or disambiguating, as above, between the 'better' judgement which the agent makes – the conscious evaluation of reasons made by the agent – and reason's overall internal standing, we can allow for a broad range of incontinent though internally reasonable actions. All internal factors must receive their due place if we are to call an action unreasonable from the agent's point of view.

One philosopher who perceptively and subtly appreciates that internal rationality should be interpreted in terms of an agent's overall internal perspective is Robert Audi of the University of Nebraska. Audi writes:

It should be expected that where an action accords with those overall grounds... better than does a... judgement it contravenes, the action may be rational despite its incontinence. Here, incontinent action, far from a failure to do what is better or best, may be the best option, and may eventually be seen by the agent to be so.[7]

Of course, questions remain. If weakness of will is not always a vice, should it be reinforced and cultivated? Certainly no. Aristotle was correct to warn that incontinence must be uncharacteristic of rational agents, for habitual incontinence reflects impaired powers of deliberation and resolve. Aristotle quotes the proverb, 'If water chokes us, what must we drink to wash it down?' By this he means that if people are habitually incontinent, then they cannot be persuaded by reason to be guided by reason. Their chronic lack of resolution will prevent them from acting even when their judgement is reasonable in their own subjective terms.

What of situations in which the incontinent action is not the best option from the agent's point of view but a very bad option? Is that unreasonable? Certainly yes. Consider a seat-belt case. Suppose a person, say, Ned, judges the aggregate benefits of buckling up to outweigh the costs and inconvenience; he decides all things considered to buckle up. Suppose also that this decision accords with Ned's total subjective point of view. Ned is no Huck or motor-cyclist whose judgement is out of kilter with personally salient values, but someone who properly understands himself including what he most wants. However, on entering a car his resolve fails him. The modest comfort of not buckling up softens his will.

Given Ned's overall perspective, one must pronounce that his incontinent action is unreasonable, internally. Ned has a lot to cherish: a power of deliberation, knowledge of his deepest values and concerns and a judgement which springs from that self-knowledge. But sometimes personal assets fail to function as assets. In some cases they compete with motivational liabilities, and the assets lose. People act incontinently *and* unreasonably – in their own subjective terms.

6.4 Is Unselfish Action Impossible?

Thomas Hobbes said that 'of all voluntary acts, the object is to every man his own good.'[8] According to traditional interpretation, by this and other remarks Hobbes meant to claim that there is just one kind of reason ('object') which moves agents to act: selfish reason i.e. promotion of the agent's own welfare or well-being. People act to promote the welfare of others only when they believe that there is something good in it for themselves. Unselfishness is motivationally inert.

The doctrine that all human rational action (Hobbes's 'voluntary acts') is selfishly motivated and driven by selfish reasons is known as *psychological egoism*. The contrary doctrine that some human action is unselfishly motivated and driven by desire to promote the welfare or well-being of others is known as *psychological altruism*.

I cannot settle the question of whether Hobbes truly was an advocate of psychological egoism.[9] I wish to consider whether egoism is true. Is unselfish action impossible? Are the only reasons for which agents act selfish?

Notice how egoism presupposes a partition of reasons for action into two types: selfish or egoistic reasons and unselfish or altruistic reasons. A selfish reason concerns the agent's welfare and well-being, where this does not imply the welfare or well-being of others. An unselfish reason concerns another's welfare or well-being, where this does not imply the welfare or well-being of oneself.

It may be replied that *obviously* people act for unselfish reasons. A mother jumps in front of a car to save her child's life; Mother Theresa nurses the poor in the slums of Calcutta. However, egoism's counter-reply is that the only thing that is obvious is that people *seem* to act for unselfish reason. Meanwhile, things are not always as they seem. If egoism is correct, 'unselfish' actions really are selfish actions; 'altruistic' behaviour is psychologically egoistic behaviour in disguise. For instance, many people believe that Mother Theresa's reason for helping the poor is to make them better off; she is altruistic. However, if psychological egoism is correct, the nun's altruism is neither central nor genuine. When Mother Theresa helps the poor, she does so because her own well-being is advanced. Her helping behaviour springs from egoistic motives.

Suppose that Albert notices that Filbert has jammed his finger in the refrigerator door. Assume the egoist dichotomy between selfish and unselfish reasons. Filbert acts for a selfish reason if he tries to remove his own finger from the door; whereas Albert apparently acts for an unselfish reason when he helps Filbert to remove the finger. However, egoists deny that apparent unselfish actions really are unselfish; they take an agent's reasons to be a direct function of selfish reasons. So, for the egoist, acting to help another requires personal compensation. An agent is moved to protect or promote another's well-being only in case the agent expects to receive significant benefit in return (or he may fear losing significant benefit, such as companionship).

Consider the finger in the door. If Albert fails to help Filbert, Filbert may then neglect Albert when Albert needs assistance. The benefit to Albert in helping is that it may deliver Filbert's help if the tables/doors are turned.

Of course, judged from the perspective of psychological egoism, egoistic helpers are vulnerable when they assist. If Albert's helping Filbert is their single encounter, and they do not exchange services in a mutually beneficial way, Albert may be better off to refrain from helping Filbert. Doing for Filbert will do nothing for Albert; it may even harm him. However, this is only to allow that agents can harbour mistaken expectations. Social life is often unpredictable. Albert may help Filbert, expecting, subconsciously perhaps, that Filbert will help him in return; but Filbert's help may never arrive. This does not fault egoism so much as express human fragility and fallibility.

Is egoism warranted? Is psychological egoism supported by good argument?

The debate over psychological egoism is enormously complicated. I cannot here provide a full discussion of the issues. What interests me here is just one protracted worry about egoism. Producing a good argument for egoism is not as simple or easy as some people think. There are several popular but bad arguments for egoism.

Let's look briefly at three. In order to hasten discussion I shall coin names for each argument.

The ownership argument

All actions originate in reasons of the person. Reasons-of are selfish reasons. Because I act for *my* reasons I act selfishly.

The ownership argument is flawed. It assumes that simply because a person acts for their own reasons, the reasons themselves are selfish. However, this just does not follow, for it must be demonstrated that people possess only selfish reasons. Ownership doesn't make reasons selfish. If a person sincerely desires to help others, the desire is *her* desire, but it isn't selfish.

The fact that actions originate in reasons of the person means merely that reasons are not free-floating entities. Instead, reasons are possessed by real agents. Reasons are things *had*. Whether they are also selfish is another question entirely.

The satisfaction argument

People act only when they are dissatisfied; they act so as to be satisfied. Satisfaction is selfish; so, people act selfishly. To take a quick illustration, Mother Theresa's apparent objective in helping the poor is to promote their welfare, but ultimately she helps them because she expects that she herself will be satisfied and would be discontent if she refrained.

The satisfaction argument is flawed. In the first place, do people act only for satisfaction? David Hume, in *An Inquiry Concerning the Principles of Morals*, wrote: 'There is some benevolence, however small, infused into our bosom; some spark of friendship for human kind; some particle of the dove kneaded into our frame, along with the elements of the wolf and serpent.' Hume meant to say that people sometimes act even though they realize in advance that they will not be satisfied. They help others with no hope of satisfaction. They are moved by the 'dove' in themselves. The mother jumps in front of the car to save her child knowing she herself will be killed.

In the second place, egoism misunderstands the nature of satisfaction. Satisfaction is not inherently selfish. Someone who acts to be satisfied may actually be unselfish.

This is a crucial and subtle point. There are confusing ambiguities in the concept of satisfaction. The main ambiguity is between being satisfied *in* another's satisfaction and being satisfied *independent of* another's satisfaction. You should not be called 'selfish' just because you derive satisfaction in helping others. Mother Theresa finds satisfaction by nursing the poor. If she helps for fame and fortune, or to evoke their help should tables turn, her satisfaction is selfish. But if she helps because of sincere interest in their well-being, her satisfaction is unselfish. The nun is satisfied in their satisfaction.

A romantic way to make the same point is to consider what Harvard's Robert Nozick calls 'love's bond'.[10] According to Nozick a love bond exists between yourself and someone you love when your own satisfaction (or dissatisfaction) is derived from theirs. When something negative happens to the person you love, therein something negative also happens to you; you are dissatisfied in their dissatisfaction. When something positive happens to the person you love, therein something positive happens to you; you are satisfied in their satisfaction.

Consider one example. Your lover has lost his tuition money for college classes in the current term. He is disappointed and unhappy and this leaves you dissatisfied. So you loan him money to attend classes. Learning of your action, would we wish to describe it as selfish? Surely not. Selfish for what? For *his* college education? How would Nozick help us to describe the situation? Nozick would say that egoism misunderstands love's bond. The egoist pictures people as closed figures whose boundaries are self-centred; but love shapes or alters your boundaries to include the person you love. You centre on them. If the other is dissatisfied by losing his money, so (at least to some extent) are you. The removal of your own dissatisfaction is inseparably linked to the removal of theirs.

The core of the love relationship is how lovers take satisfaction in each other's satisfaction, how they respond with their partner. The core of egoism is how people use other people, how they get the other to respond to them. In love, your satisfaction consists in the other's satisfaction. By contrast, for egoism your satisfaction consists in what the other does for you if and when you satisfy them. The 'love' of egoism is reciprocal tit for tat; the love of love's bond is conjoined satisfaction.

The baby faced argument

Children enter the world with nothing but selfish needs and desires; acts motivated by needs for food, warmth and nurture are the first acts performed by the infant. Selfish reasons remain the only reasons for action, although their scope broadens to include desires for fame, fortune, power and social position.

Suppose we concede, for the sake of argument, that baby's first reasons are selfish. This is a controversial concession for two reasons. First, some psychologists contend that there are unselfish desires for which there is evolutionary selection in young children. Indeed, Charles Darwin, in chapter 4 of *The Descent of Man*, supports the idea that people are natively unselfish by saying that various nonhuman animals are capable of altruism. Second, describing an infant or young child as selfish may be far fetched since the very young do not mentally harbour a self/other distinction. Newborns do not conceive of themselves as one among 'other minds'. But let's make the concession and not question its infantile assumptions. May we still deny that selfish reasons remain the only reasons for action? Must Mother Theresa act within the imprint of her childhood selfishness?

Imagine that Filbert begins life as an egoist. He cares just for himself. But also imagine that he is often placed in situations in which he must help others to receive personal benefit. Might not the link or paired association between his benefit and the good of others change the character of his reasons? Whereas helping others at first occurs just because it helps Filbert, as a consequence of conditioned or paired association with benefiting himself Filbert comes to value the good of others independent of his own benefit. The means (benefit to others) becomes an end-in-itself: something he wishes for its own sake.[11]

To take a simple illustration, suppose that Baby Filbert wants above all to be fed, and that he believes that he must please his mother to be fed. But as years pass, bringing pleasure to his mother slides apart from the desire to be fed. Teenage Filbert looks into her eyes and feels guilty for not bringing pleasure to her, although his stomach is full.

The possibility of developing into altruists is psychologically natural and plausible.[12] Complex are the ways in which reasons develop over time. In general, one type of reason can be the sole motive at one stage of development, only to be displaced by other types at later stages. An analogy should help here: At thirteen years of age Filbert smokes cigarettes because of pressure from his peers, many of whom smoke and urge him to smoke. However, at forty-seven years old, peer pressure points in the opposite direction to stop smoking; yet Filbert still smokes. Whatever the new sorts of reasons (e.g. the desire to reduce anxiety, nicotine enjoyment), the old reasons are impotent. Reasons at one stage need not remain reasons at another stage. Likewise, a person might be an egoist in infancy or childhood, but an altruist in mid-life. When a child perhaps I helped others just to help myself, but now I help others for its own sake.

The dubious assumption behind the baby faced argument is that the reasons of childhood persist uncontested through the seasons of adulthood. The inference from being selfish as an infant to being selfish as an adult is unwarranted.

The above three popular arguments for egoism are nowhere near as powerful as first they may appear. As for positive warrant for altruism, there are a significant number of actions, both heroic and mundane, which seem to be motivated by unselfish reasons. Perhaps the amount of self-sacrifice is great; death is risked. Or there is significant personal unhappiness expected by the agent. Mahatma Gandhi, Desmond Tutu, the anonymous rescuers of Jews during the Holocaust, of Kuwaitis during Iraq's occupation, and of blacks during slavery in the southern United States; the list goes on.

Perhaps it is unusual for altruism to be deeply rooted in a human being; perhaps most people are predominantly egoistic, sacrificing for family and friends but rarely or never for strangers. It may even be that persons are inconsistent, exposing themselves to great risk for others in some situations, but failing to offer even minimally inconvenient help in other similar situations. However, even inconsistent altruism and predominant egoism imply that some actions are unselfish.

Readers should be aware that this chapter does little more than skim the surface of many critical topics connected with rational action. But certain conclusions can be drawn even on the basis of our brief discussion. We need not accept the gloomy picture of rational action as selfish; we need not accept the intellectualized picture of abandoned resolve as unreasonable. Rationality is not steering one's way through life, focused on self, settled in judgement. Rational agents can follow a zigzag path, earlier walking to the fridge, now mounting a motorcycle, later risking life and limb for a child's safety or success.

NOTES

1 The network may include a certain amount of elbow room or ideterminacy, if, for example, persons possess the dual power involved in free choice. See chapter 8 for discussion.

2 They can also be irrational (and rational) in different degrees, measuring up to bad (and good) to a different extent.

3 D. Ames, 'Self shooting of phantom head', *British Journal of Psychiatry*, 145 (1984), 193–4.

4 In talking of continence and incontinence, I trust readers will not be misled by visions of enuresis. I want to make clear which fish I am trying to fry: 'incontinence' and 'continence' are technical terms of philosopher's art.

5 My interpretation of Aristotle is controversial. Aristotle is sometimes read as addressing whether incontinence has any reason behind it, good or bad. I read him as presupposing that incontinence has reason behind it – that is, agents act incontinently for a reason. What I take him to address is the following question: Supposing incontinence occurs for a reason, must the reason be bad internally?

6 The first edition of *The Adventures of Huckleberry Finn* was published in London in 1884. Various philosophers have noticed the richness of the character of Huck for examples of the multiple components of rational agency. I am indebted in what follows to Jonathan Bennett, 'The conscience of Huckleberry Finn', *Philosophy*, 49 (1974), pp.123–34; Alison McIntyre, 'Is akratic action always irrational?', in *Identity, Character, and Morality*, eds. Owen Flanagan and A.O. Rorty (MIT, Cambridge, MA., 1990), pp.379–400.

7 Robert Audi, 'Weakness of will and rational action', *Australasian Journal of Philosophy*, 68 (1990), p.279.

8 Thomas Hobbes, *Leviathan* (Clarendon, Oxford, 1909), ch. 15.

9 For discussion of whether Hobbes was a psychological egoist, which also includes clear and useful reflections on egoism, see Gregory S. Kavka, *Hobbesian Moral and Political Theory* (Princeton University Press, Princeton, 1986).

10 Robert Nozick, *The Examined Life* (Simon & Schuster, New York), pp.68–86.

11 See Elliott Sober, 'What is psychological egoism?', *Behaviour and Philosophy*, 17 (1989), p.98.

12 See e.g. Michael Hoffman, 'Developmental synthesis of affect and cognition and its implications for altruistic motivation', *Developmental Psychology* 11 (1975), pp.607–22.

7

Does Mind Depend Upon Brain?

Spare no words: mind depends upon brain. Thanks largely to neuroscience, which is the branch of physical science concerned with the brain, we know a great deal about how damage or trauma to the brain can cripple or damage the mind. We know that impaired mathematical calculation is associated with damage to the posterior sectors of the left hemisphere and that the ability to read can be selectively impaired by cerebral lesions. We know of dozens of behaviour and emotion-controlling chemicals (lithium, chlorpromazine, cocaine and so on) and of the susceptibility of consciousness to caffeine, anesthetics and alcohol. We know, too, that degeneration of nerve tissue will cause senile dementia and other impairments of one's capacity for memory, including facts so plain and ordinary as recognition of one's husband, wife or home.

But what *exactly* is the dependence of mind on brain? How intimately does mind hinge upon brain? The dependence of mind upon brain, obvious in general though it is, is not clear in its specific character or nature. What sort of dependence is it?

7.1 Materialism

The theory of Materialism or Physicalism – which can be traced back at least to Thomas Hobbes in the seventeenth century – is the most popular contemporary view among philosophers of the nature or character of mind-brain dependence.[1] Materialism can be summarized in three theses:

1 *The identification thesis*. Mind is somehow nothing but matter. States and processes of mind are nothing more than physical

states and processes. Specifically, in the case of human persons and other vertebrates, the mind is the brain and central nervous system. Mental states or processes (for example, believing that ice is cold, or being sad) are neurophysiological.

2 *The explanation thesis*. Human and animal behaviour is best – fully and most deeply – explained by something physical: not, to be sure, in the seventeenth and eighteenth-century sense of cogs and pulleys, but in the more contemporary sense of neuro-chemistry and neurophysiology. Rational or intelligent action is the upshot of processes or activities physically internal to the brain.

3 *The exclusion thesis.* Human beings have no powers or pro-perties which no physical object or system can possess. For exam-ple, if the power of free choice – or what philosophers call 'free will' – is assumed to be mental, but no physical system is free, then there is no free will. Likewise, if it is built into the con-cept of the soul both that the soul is something mental and that the soul survives bodily death, whereas the brain fails to survive, then there is no such thing as the soul. The soul is excluded from existence. As the materialist D.M. Armstrong says in his book *A Materialist Theory of Mind*, 'Man is nothing but a material object having none but physical properties.'

Materialism advocates a maximally intimate dependence of mind upon brain. Indeed, strictly speaking, for the materialist the rela-tion between mind and brain is not dependence. One *thing* is not dependent upon *another* thing. Given the identification thesis, the relationship is identity. One just *is* the other.

What are Materialism's virtues? Materialists claim four main virtues for their doctrine.

The first virtue is the *economy* or *simplicity* achieved by assert-ing that anything mental or intelligent can be explained by some-thing which is material or physical. We do not have to account for human and animal behaviour by referring separately to mind and brain. We can and should refer only to brain.

Economy or simplicity is a feature whose nature and merit may be hard to grasp. What is simplicity? What does it mean to say that simplicity is a virtue? The nub of the first answer is that a theory or doctrine is simple or economical just when it fits neatly with things we already know. By contrast, when theories fail to fit neatly with background knowledge, they are complex and uneconomical, for adjustments must be made in our system of beliefs to make them fit. Then, assuming that neatness of fit with background knowledge is virtuous, if simplicity means neat fit, simplicity is a virtue.

The idea behind simplicity or neatness of fit is abstract, but it is also important, as may be suggested by the following illustrations. Learning, we know, involves lasting chemical changes in the brain; the materialist holds that such chemical changes are most neatly explained by presupposing that the psychological processes involved in learning are themselves physical/chemical processes. Some animals (e.g. dolphins), we know, are psychologically more complex than others (e.g. rabbits). The materialist proposes that this is most economically explained by identifying psychological complexity with neurological complexity. Mind is nothing more than brain. Since the dolphin brain is more complex than the rabbit brain, the mind of the dolphin is more complex than the mind of the rabbit.

The second and related virtue of Materialism is its *unified conception of the world*. Behind Materialism lies a conception of nature as consisting of objects and processes at different levels of organization and sophistication. A promising if partial description is that animals are made of organs, which are made of cells, which are made of molecules, which are made of atoms. The behaviour of these levels are described in terms of different concepts and terminology: those describing animal behaviour, cell behaviour and so on. Materialism downwardly unifies the different levels of organization. It understands the behaviour of higher levels of organization (e.g. those of animals) in terms of lower-level units (e.g. the biochemistry of the brain).

The third virtue is that Materialism *expels superstition* from our understanding of human behaviour. Let's look briefly at one example: Witches. Religious madness (or what today psychologists call 'religious hysteria') is a fairly common affliction among humans, and in earlier centuries its victims were often described as cases of devil possession, in which Satan himself occupied the mind of the hysteric.[2] The opening page of what perhaps is the first autobiography in the English language – transcribed because the woman, Margery Kempe, was illiterate – presents an account of a woman born around 1373 whose contemporaries thought her possessed by the devil.

Because of the dread she had of damnation on the one hand, and [Satan's] sharp reproving of her on the other, this creature went out of her mind and was amazingly disturbed and tormented with spirits for half a year, eight weeks and odd days.

A materialist can point to the success of modern brain-centred theories of mental illness which have helped to eliminate reference to witches and possessed people from our understanding of religious hysteria. Today, instead of diabolical possession, Margery Kempe would likely be diagnosed as suffering from an organic deficiency or chemical disorder in her central nervous system. For instance, one of the most telling signs of demonic possession was thought to be spontaneous and erratic bodily movements: bumps and jerks believed associated with invasion by Satan's spirit. A significant finding in brain-centred psychological science was the demonstration in the mid-1960s that movement disorders (spontaneous bumps and jerks) result from a loss of a neurotransmitter substance (dopamine) in the brain. Modern theories of movement disorder have dismissed reference to immaterial spirits from serious psychology.

Materialism exorcises witch-hunts. It substitutes material neurons for spiritual demons.

The fourth and final if less dramatic virtue of Materialism is that it positions the mind so that it can be *studied by physical science*. Materialism puts the study of mind within the scope of physical science. This means that, where mind is concerned, the study of mind is no different from the study of brain. Mental or psychological science is not autonomous. It does not have its own methods and its own standards of truth and validity. It has the same methods and standards as physical science. Thus, we can and should use what we know about the brain from sciences such as neurophysiology and neurochemistry to understand mental states and processes.

7.2   Is Materialism Correct?

Materialism has been enormously attractive to philosophers. Paul Teller sums up popular attitudes when we writes: 'Most of us take ourselves to be hard-headed materialists: Everything, we take it, is at bottom physical.'[3] And it has spun approximately a dozen currently or once fashionable variations, ranging from *type/type identity theories* to *eliminative materialisms*. However, Materialism is not without problems and puzzles. The appeal of Materialism should not obscure its difficult or objectionable features. Indeed, the history of Materialism consists largely of attempts to rebut objections by clarifying and reformulating the claims and virtues of the doctrine. Consider a historically influential case.

Appeal to the aspectual

A common objection to Materialism, which I shall call *the access objection*, holds that the mind cannot be the brain because we know mind and brain in different ways. We have what is termed 'direct' access or knowledge of our minds, but we find out about our brains only indirectly if at all. Since we have direct access to our minds but lack direct knowledge of brains, mind and brain cannot be one and the same.

Suppose, for example, a neurophysiologist comes up with a complete physical-chemical description of the pain system of the brain. An illiterate peasant may well be able to describe their pains without knowing of their physical-chemical description. They may, like the man described in the last chapter, even believe themselves to possess two heads, without any failure in ability to make true claims about their pains.

The access objection relies on an implicit premise. The premise is that if mind is brain, then the knowledge which each person has of their mind should be the same in kind or expressed in the same terms as the knowledge they have of their brain. Defenders of materialism, like U.T. Place and J.J.C. Smart in the 1950s, reject this premise.[4] They hold that one and the same thing can be known or accessed in different ways. I can know something in one way even though I know nothing of it another way.

There is a basic reason why I can know something in one way although I know nothing about it another way. Knowledge is aspectual. Consider a famous example from Frege (1848–1925): I may know the planet Venus as the Morning Star without knowing it as the Evening Star, although they are the same entity (Venus).

Appearing in the morning is one of its aspects; appearing in the evening is another. In knowing Venus under the first aspect I know it as the Morning Star; in failing to know it under the second I fail to know it as the Evening Star.

Other examples are obvious and numerous. Mark Twain and Samuel Clemens are one and the same person; but many people know the author of *The Adventures of Huckleberry Finn* as Mark Twain without knowing him as Samuel Clemens. Water is two parts hydrogen and one part oxygen. This is the case even though illiterate peasants who are very good at identifying water may know nothing of chemistry. If Materialism is true, we should be able to give a general account of pain in physical-chemical terms. However, even when this project is complete there could still be people who do not describe pain in material terms. They may know when they are in pain without knowing whether pain is physical. They may describe their pain as, for example, sharp and stabbing without describing it as a neurochemical condition.

The reply of Place and Smart exploits the fact that knowledge is aspectual. (Equivalently: Knowledge is knowledge 'under a description'.) I can know of Twain without describing him as Clemens. I can know my mind without recognizing that I know my brain. As we will discover in the next section, criticisms of Materialism do not stop with the objection that brain access differs from mind access; but the proposition that knowledge is aspectual and related propositions have become fixtures of every version of Materialism developed since Place and Smart. They are invoked to fend off many anti-materialist criticisms. Consider one more example.

The example is sometimes referred to as 'Descartes' first argument for Dualism' and is due to René Descartes (1596–1650).[5] It goes roughly as follows:

> I can conceive of myself as lacking a brain, but I cannot conceive of myself as lacking a mind. If I try to doubt that I have a mind, I will discover myself with thoughts like 'I doubt I have a mind', and so must admit that I have a mind – for the activity of doubting is mental. Hence, brain and mind must be distinct.

Here is a second application of the idea of the aspectual character of access to mind. The psychological concept Conceive like the concept Know is aspectual. Descartes says that he cannot conceive of himself as lacking a mind but can conceive of himself as brainless. However, from this it does not follow that mind and brain are distinct. Just because 'two' things are conceived of in different terms does not mean that they really are two things.

Consider by way of analogy the mythic tale in ancient Greece of a man named Oedipus condemned by the gods to marry his mother. Oedipus of course did not want to marry his mother. If you asked him if he wished to marry his mother, he might have said something like this: 'The very idea disgusts me. I find it inconceivable that I will marry my mother.'

Despite inconceivability, Oedipus met a woman by the name of Jocasta whom be wished to marry; and, without learning until after the marriage that Jocasta was his mother, Oedipus married her. If you asked Oedipus before marriage if he wished to marry Jocasta, he might have said something like this: 'The very idea pleases me. I find it eminently conceivable.'

Now consider the following argument placed on the tongue of Oedipus: 'I can conceive of myself as marrying Jocasta, but I cannot conceive of myself as marrying my mother; so, Jocasta must be different from my mother.'

Obviously something is wrong with the argument because Oedipus's wife (Jocasta) *is* his mother. The crucial mistake is failing to appreciate that conceiving, like knowing, is aspectual. Consequently, just because Oedipus cannot conceive of his mother as his wife but can conceive of Jocasta as his wife does not mean that Jocasta is not his mother. Analogously: If I can conceive of myself as brainless but cannot conceive of myself as mindless, it does not follow that brain and mind are distinct.

One might quarrel with particular applications of the materialist appeal to aspectuality, but the main idea is highly plausible. Unless we have other reasons to attribute distinctness to mind and brain, the mere fact that we know or conceive of them in different terms does not mean that they are distinct. They can be one and the same. But are they?

7.3   Brentano's Thesis

Many states of mind are characterized by *aboutness* or what Franz Brentano (1838–1917) called the *intentional in-existence of objects* and what we have called earlier in the book Intentionality. Brentano also said that Intentionality distinguishes the mental from the physical. He held the thesis – which I shall call *Brentano's thesis* – that aboutness is exclusively a feature of mental phenomena. No physical phenomenon possesses anything similar.

How aboutness or Intentionality distinguishes the mental from the physical may be understood by the illustration of a mental attitude like believing. Take, for instance, six-year old Carl and his belief that his Uncle Roderick is bald.

Believing is a mental activity that is about an object or state of affairs. In Carl's case, the belief that his uncle is bald is about the uncle. One could say that it aims or is directed at its object. It mentally points towards Roderick.

Why is mental aiming or pointing different from physical aiming, as when Carl's toy dart gun accidentally points in the direction of Roderick? Why is mental aiming or aboutness nothing physical? There are three differences:

1   One difference is that physically the dart gun points at Roderick only if Roderick really exists. If there is no Roderick, there is no pointing at Roderick. By contrast, Carl can entertain beliefs about Roderick even if Roderick doesn't exist and never did or will exist, but just is a figment of Carl's youthful imagination.

2   Even when belief aims at something which does exist, mental aiming or aboutness still is distinct from physical processes or relationships. Mental aiming possesses a specificity or aspectuality which physical aiming lacks.

Suppose the following propositions are true:

> Carl's dart gun points at his Uncle Roderick.
> Uncle Roderick graduated from Yale.

It follows,

> Carl's dart gun points at a Yale graduate.

On the other hand, suppose the following propositions are true:

> Carl believes that his Uncle Roderick is bald.
> Uncle Roderick graduated from Yale.

It does not follow,

> Carl believes that his bald-headed uncle is a Yale graduate.

Why? This conclusion does not follow because Carl may not realize that Roderick attended college. Suppose Carl knows Roderick only as his bald uncle, not under the aspect or description of being a college graduate.

The physical process of aiming is not aspectual. If the dart gun points at Roderick, it does not point at Roderick as bald or as having graduated from Yale; it points at Roderick full stop – whether he is bald, from Yale or whatever. By contrast, Intentionality or aboutness is aspectual. Carl entertains beliefs about Roderick under this or that aspect rather than another; not Roderick whatever he is, but Roderick as bald, as his uncle and so on.

The same point can be made with a small stone. Suppose Roderick is standing under a cliff wall and a stone drops off the cliff and lands on his head. When the stone traces a trajectory to Roderick, it does not fall on him *as* bald or *as* Carl's uncle or as anything else. It falls on him no matter his aspects. Even if Roderick were nephew-less and hairy, the stone would still have struck him. But when Carl entertains a belief about his uncle, this belief may very well specify Roderick only under the aspect of being bald. The stone hits Roderick full stop; whereas Carl's belief 'strikes' Roderick just insofar as the boy thinks of the man as bald.

3   A third and related feature of Intentionality is that whatever is Intentional can misrepresent or misinterpret. Intentional phenomena represent something (their objects) as being a certain way. For instance, Carl's belief that Uncle Roderick is bald is not just a mental state with an object. It also has Roderick characterized in some manner, for instance, as his uncle and as bald.

The representational character of Intentional phenomena helps to explain why there can be false beliefs. False beliefs misrepresent. Suppose Carl believes that his uncle graduated from Columbia. Carl misrepresents Roderick. It is false that Roderick is a Columbia graduate.

The physical process of pointing or aiming cannot misrepresent. If the dart gun points (just) at Roderick, who is a Yale graduate, then the dart gun does not point at someone who graduated from Columbia. Meanwhile, Carl can (falsely) believe that Roderick graduated from Columbia, even if Roderick does not fit the description.

The third point is only a stone's fall away from another example. When the stone falls in the direction of Roderick, there is a physical relationship between Roderick and the stone. It has a Roderick trajectory. In falling towards Roderick it could strike a Columbia graduate only if Roderick himself graduated from that New York university. But Carl can entertain a belief about Roderick's graduating from Columbia even if Roderick has never stepped off the Yale campus.

Taken together, the above distinctions form an impressive argument for Brentano's thesis that Intentionality is a unique phenomenon and that nothing which is both mental and possesses aboutness is physical. Brentano certainly seems to have proven that there are mental phenomena which are not physical and that mind (with aboutness) is not brain (without aboutness).

7.4   Aboutness and Materialism

Brentano's thesis constitutes one of the most serious fault lines in Materialism. It threatens to crack open the doctrine. In order to patch up the doctrine, some materialists argue that contrary to Brentano physical states or processes can possess Intentionality. D.M. Armstrong, for instance, explicitly admits that Intentionality is a pervasive and critical feature of the mental and he says that the materialist theory of mind must account for it. 'No materialist can claim that intentionality is a unique, unanalysable property of mental processes and still be consistent with his Materialism. A materialist is forced to attempt an *analysis* of intentionality.'[6]

A materialist analysis of Intentionality would account for aboutness in material terms. It would show that even though a process (such as brain activity) is physical it can possess aboutness. Let us briefly look at two candidate materialist analyses of aboutness/Intentionality. One is in terms of resemblance; the other is in terms of causality.

The resemblance analysis

An old idea, dating back to Aristotle (384–322 BC) and found also in David Hume (1711–76), is that one thing is about something else when it *resembles* it. A map, for example, is about a city if it resembles or is like the city. In the case of mind it has been argued that the mind is about objects or states of affairs when it contains mental images or pictures of those objects or states of affairs. A materialist form of this view (neither Aristotle nor Hume were materialists) holds that the assumed images or pictures are physical or material – perhaps geometrical patterns of electrical activity in the brain. So, for instance, believing that Uncle Roderick is bald means having a physical picture or pattern in the brain which resembles the believed Roderick. The pattern projects onto Roderick: it matches the uncle in some physical way. Therein the pattern is about Roderick.

The resemblance analysis works only if resemblance really can achieve or constitute aboutness. But the anti-materialist should not admit this, for resemblance is radically different from aboutness. Whereas resemblance is 'symmetrical', aboutness is 'asymmetrical'. For instance, a picture of Uncle Roderick resembles Roderick as much as Roderick resembles the picture but Roderick is not about the picture. Aboutness moves in one direction: from the picture to Roderick – in essence, that's asymmetry. By contrast resemblance moves forth and back: from the picture to Roderick and from Roderick to the picture – in essence, that's symmetry. Hence, even if physical resemblances of objects are housed in the brain, the essential difficulty is that the mere fact that two things resemble each other does not mean that one is about the other.

A second difficulty with the resemblance analysis is that aboutness can occur in the absence of resemblance. The word 'George' refers to me, but it does not resemble me in any interesting way at all. It certainly does not look like me. Since aboutness can occur in the absence of resemblance, aboutness cannot be understood in terms of resemblance.

The third and final troublesome feature of the resemblance analysis pivots on the presumption that there are physical pictures or patterns in the brain which resemble things outside the brain. What does *that* mean? The brain is helter-skelter with neurological activity. In devising a materialist criterion of brain pictures, the task is to specify precisely the features or configurations of brain activity which constitute a picture, leaving the remainder as pictorially irrelevant. For instance, in the case of Carl's belief about Roderick, what specifies the outline of the face, the constellation of eyes, mouth and bald head? At what level of abstraction or embedded detail does the brain resemble Roderick? We need a materialist criterion for resemblance which interprets the human brain as the seat for resemblances of objects. But no one – neither scientist nor philosopher – has a clear idea of how to develop the criterion.

The causal analysis

Few materialists are attracted to the resemblance analysis. Most favour the causal analysis. The causal analysis has been championed by Jerry Fodor, Fred Dretske and several other philosophers.[7] There is no shortage of versions of the causal analysis and some offer links with biology and other natural sciences as arguments in their favour.

In simplest form, according to the causal analysis something physically internal to the brain is about some object when the object causes that internal activity. For instance, believing that Uncle Roderick is bald means entertaining a brain state or process produced by Roderick and his bald pate. Since Roderick's baldness causes the brain activity, the activity is about the uncle.

One virtue of using the concept of causality in the analysis of aboutness is that causality respects the asymmetry of aboutness. Causality – like aboutness – is asymmetrical. If **A** causes **B**, **B** does not cause **A**. If flipping the light switch causes the illumination of the room, the illumination does not cause the flip. Analogously: just because X is about Y does not mean that Y is about X. Just because Carl's belief is about his uncle certainly does not mean that his uncle is about Carl's belief.

The importance of respecting asymmetry fades, however, when we focus on difficulties for the causal analysis. What about the features of aboutness mentioned by Brentano?

The causal analysis does not account for objects of mental phenomena ((1) above) which really do not exist, since a non-existing object or state of affairs cannot cause anything. If Roderick does not exist, there is no Roderick-cause for Carl to entertain beliefs about Roderick.

Misrepresentation ((3) above) also is left out. Suppose that bald-headed Roderick is causally responsible for a photograph of him-self. The photo was taken of Roderick. He is the causal spring of the picture. According to the causal analysis, the picture is of him because it is caused by him. But imagine that the image somehow appears as not bald but hairy. Suppose it misrepresents Roderick. Perhaps shadows fell upon him which to the uninformed viewer's eyes appear as hair on Roderick's head. Note that if mis-representation just is a causal process it would be impossible for the photo to misrepresent. This is because the photo would still represent bald Roderick, since bald Roderick causes the 'hairy' image in the photograph.

Causally speaking, the 'hairy' photo represents Roderick equally to the 'bald' photo because bald Roderick is responsible for both photos. Similarly, a (false) belief that Roderick is hairy represents Roderick as much or as well as the (true) belief that Roderick is bald, once again, if bald Roderick is the causal source of both beliefs and representation consists in causality. In terms of repre-sentation, however, the 'hairy' photo or belief does not represent Roderick equally to the bald. Strictly speaking, 'hairy' misrepre-sents. So, although Roderick is causally responsible for both 'bald' and 'hairy' photos or beliefs, 'bald' represents, 'hairy' misrepre-sents. Causality does not account for the difference between them.

The most serious unfulfilled project for the materialist causal analysis of aboutness is to provide a satisfactory account of mis-representation. In whatever detail materialists formulate the account, the objection can always be raised: It does not explain the difference between representation and misrepresentation: between true belief and false belief: between accurate photo and inaccurate photo. To illustrate, let us quickly consider the plight of the most popular variation in the causal analysis, which has been adopted in response to the misrepresentation criticism.

Some materialists try to counter-reply to the charge that appeal to causality cannot account for misrepresentation by distinguishing two major causal axes along which representation/misrepresentation can occur. They take as their primary target the idea that misrepresentation does not have the same cause as representation. Misrepresentation occurs along an improper or wayward axis, whereas representation occurs along a proper axis. So, for example, a photo depicting (or belief about) Roderick as hairy is not caused by Roderick properly. Had Roderick been properly photographed (e.g. without shadows) his depiction would be bald. Analogously, roughly speaking, a brain state represents some entity or state of affairs when the entity or state of affairs properly causes the brain state; it misrepresents if causation is wayward or improper.

Appeal to propriety or waywardness works only if proper and improper causes can be distinguished. This proves immensely difficult. It makes no sense, for example, to say that an improper (misrepresenting) cause of a Roderick photo is one with shadows upon Roderick's head. Suppose we know that Roderick is bald and has been photographed in shadows. Those with such background knowledge might interpret or see the photograph taken under such 'wayward' conditions as accurately depicting Roderick as bald. Meanwhile, only those without background knowledge might see the photo as that of a hairy man.

There is no principled manner in which to exclude background knowledge from the interpretation of a representation. The 'improper' cause can always produce a proper representation for someone who extrapolates the right interpretation. For this and other related and more complicated reasons, the distinction between proper and improper causality is like a talented prize-fighter, perpetually bobbing and weaving. It forms an elusive target. No sooner does the causal theorist fix on how to define the distinction, when the target shifts and has to be sought in another direction.

When it is attacked as severely as this, the causal theory seems doomed. So why are materialists attracted to it? I should mention that one reason why causality provides an appealing account of aboutness for the materialist is that materialists take causality to be part of the sticks and stones – or better: cement and glue – of the physical world: to be part of the material processes of the world. If causation is physical and aboutness can be analysed in terms of causation, then aboutness, at bottom, is physical.

Where does all this leave us? Whether an appropriately materialist account of Intentionality can be provided is very much a hotly-debated question. I suggest we draw the following conclusion: Materialism must surmount the Brentano thesis with an account of Intentionality in physical terms. Without offering the account, the doctrine should be resisted. However, if we reject materialism, what happens to the dependence of mind upon brain?

7.5   Supervenience and Melancholia *or* Why Did Robert Schumann Starve Himself to Death?

To all informed ears Robert Schumann (1810–56) is one of the finest composers of classical music of the mid-nineteenth century. The great Romantic composer Johannes Brahms, who had visited Schumann two weeks before his death, believed it and his wife, the accomplished pianist Clara Wieck, predicated her marriage on its assumption. Schumann, however, characterized himself as haunted by 'loathsome dreams' and frequent feel. ₃s of dread. In his prime, he was the victim of dramatic mood swings. For instance, after Clara's concert tour in Russia in 1844, he was abysmally depressed and admitted to being envious of her success. He developed phobias about being poisoned and became withdrawn.

On 27 February 1854, Schumann threw himself into the Rhine River. One biographer describes the scene as follows:

Just past noon... a hulking figure suddenly emerged from a house on Bilkerstrasse and turned left on the cobbled street. Although it was a cold, rainy day in Dusseldorf, the man wore only a thin robe and slippers. His face was pasty, his eyes were downcast, and he was sobbing. Walking unsteadily, as if on tiptoe, he headed for the Rhine River, only four blocks away. There, on the Rathaus Ufer overlooking the west bank he stopped. A narrow pontoon bridge led to the other side, and to get across it one had to pass a tollgate. Absentmindedly he searched in his pocket for money. Finding none, he smiled apologetically and offered his silk handkerchief as a token fee. Then, before anyone could stop him, he rushed down the incline leading to the bridge, ran part way across, paused briefly, and threw himself headlong into the icy torrent.[8]

On rescue, Schumann confessed to being shamed and humiliated by his suicide attempt: 'O Clara, I am not worth your love.' He insisted on being placed in a lunatic asylum. After more than two years in the asylum he again tried to take his life. This time he succeeded: he starved himself to death. He died, alone, on 29 July 1856.

How is this sad event to be explained? Why did Schumann starve himself to death?

Imagine that in Schumann's case or situation you get to play resident asylum psychiatrist and try to discover why he starved himself to death. To organize your search for the explanation you distinguish between two sets of facts which pertain to Schumann. The first you call mental or Mind facts; and the second you call neurophysiological or Brain facts. The point of this pattern of organization will become clear when we examine a candidate instance of explanation.

The Mind set of facts includes the following: Schumann was clinically depressed. He was, to use Robert Burton's seventeenth-century but still apt term, severely 'melancholic'.[9]

The Brain set of facts includes the following: Schumann had depleted biogenic amines. These are special chemicals in the brain which help transmit nerve impulses across the gaps (synapses) between nerve cells (neurons).[10]

It is possible to both vary and complement the Mind facts and Brain facts. As resident psychiatrist you might add fine-grained brainy detail concerning such things as molecular structure, location, synthesis, re-uptake, and breakdown of biogenic amines. And you could complement the Brain facts by, for example, describing in neurophysiological detail how things were at some much earlier time before Schumann's suicide. The complementary details might look something like this:

> Susceptibility to depleted biogenic amines is a genetic inheritance. The following factors in such depletion are heritable

traits: abnormalities of biogenic amine metabolism, disturbances of cortisol circadian rhythms and, finally, deficiencies in the brain-thyroid axis. Several lines of evidence converge in Schumann's case on saying that he inherited such traits and thus his susceptibility to depletion. Depleted biogenic amines were widespread among his family. During maturation these fundamental biological factors interwove with specific neurotransmitter depletion brought about by heightened neuronal excitability; and in Schumann they caused the neurochemical condition of depleted biogenic amines.

Susceptibility and other esoteric complementary details aside, however, the central question is: How are the two sets of Brain and Mind facts related? How do Brain and Mind facts fit together to form a unified explanation of Schumann's suicide?

(1)   One response is that they do not fit together. Brain facts have absolutely nothing to do with Mind facts. Brain and mind are wholly independent. As far as mind is concerned the brain just is a stone.

This response of course is outlandishly ill-advised. If there is an absolute misfit between brain and mind, then we should expect mind to be invulnerable to direct control or pathology by damage to the brain. In fact, however, as mentioned in the paragraph which started this chapter, just the opposite is true. Consider, for example, not depression, Schumann's malady, but apoplexy or stroke. The mental consequences of apoplexy can include aphasia (loss of understanding of language), amnesia (loss of memory) and agnosia (loss of perceptual powers). From the case of apoplexy and many others it follows that there is a close relation between Mind facts and Brain facts; brain imparts a special vulnerability to mind.

(2)   But how intimate? How tight the fit? How vulnerable? Materialists argue for the most tight fit. Materialism combines both sets of facts into one set: Mind facts are identical to Brain facts. This is because materialists identify mind with brain. Thus the following hypothesis may be offered by a materialist:

> The Mind fact of severe depression just is identical to the Brain fact of depleted biogenic amines. To be severely depressed is to have depleted biogenic amines.

It is no easy task to winnow through competing explanations of Schumann's suicide. However, suppose you eventually come to endorse the following explanatory sketch couched in Mind fact terms:

> Schumann committed suicide because he was severely depressed. A self-destructive response in depression was not alien to Schumann. He had attempted suicide in 1854.

According to Materialism, supposing severe depression is depleted biogenic amines, this would mean that you should also endorse the following explanation of Schumann's suicide, which is expressed in terms of Brain facts:

> Schumann committed suicide because he had depleted biogenic amines. In other words: 'Schumann committed suicide because he was severely depressed' just means 'because he had depleted biogenic amines.'

However, the materialist explanation is also (assuming Brentano's thesis) in its own way poorly advised. The materialist locates depression altogether physically in the brain. However, Intentionality permeates many sorts of depression. Intentionality occurs, for example, in Schumann's depression. The central ingredients in Schumann's mental illness include such aboutness states as his jealousy over Clara's success as a pianist, his desire for recognition as a composer, his feeling of personal worthlessness, his despondency over his failed suicide attempt and so forth. All such states possess Intentionality. Matters are far from final; but it certainly appears that the current inability of materialists to provide a physical analysis of aboutness means that attitudes such as those of Schumann are not physical states or conditions.[11] Schumann's depression harboured characteristics his neurochemicals lacked. So there is no neat materialist fit between Mind and Brain Schumann facts. Schumann's depression should not be viewed as a neurochemical deficiency. The explanation of his suicide, therefore, cannot occur strictly within the confines of Materialism.

(3) However, aren't Mind facts vulnerable to Brain facts? Perhaps Mind facts are vulnerable to Brain facts without being identical to them. This is the view of a number of philosophers who have described the relationship between mind and brain as one of mind/brain *supervenience*.[12] The primary idea behind mind/brain supervenience can be stated quite simply by means of an illustrative thought experiment.

Suppose we (or God or Mother Nature) create an exact neurophysiological replica of Robert Schumann, exactly like him cell for cell, molecule for molecule, biogenic amine for biogenic amine. For a mnemonic think of the replica as Replica Schumann. Given that Robert and Replica are exactly alike neurophysically, will the respective Schumanns also share their psychological life? Will Replica be depressed and commit suicide?

If you answer yes, then you should be sympathetic with the concept of mind/brain supervenience. The core idea behind mind/brain supervenience is that there is no psychological difference between two persons (or the same person at different times) unless there is a neurophysiological difference between them. Robert Schumann, therefore, cannot be said to be depressed unless his replica is depressed. This is because the replica is perfectly like him neurophysiologically.

The mind/brain supervenience idea can be generalized by means of the following description using the notions of Brain and Mind facts employed above. Briefly, Mind facts are said to *supervene* on Brain facts, and Brain facts are said to constitute the supervenience *base* of Mind facts, just in the sense that any two persons who share all the same Brain facts cannot diverge with respect to any Mind facts. Only if the Brain facts differ can the Mind facts differ. In short, the brain anchors the mind. It is the 'embodiment' or 'jacket' of mind.

What, then, of the third or supervenience way of understanding the connection between Mind and Brain facts? Construed as an admonition to respect physical similarities and differences between people, it is difficult to challenge. But supervenience is capable of many different interpretations and has raised questions in the minds of philosophers.[13]

Some puzzlement over supervenience is explanatory in nature. If mind supervenes on brain, then does reference to brain suffice to explain behaviour? If and when we discover the supervenience base of Schumann's depression, do we thereby explain his suicide? In addition, in acknowledging supervenience bases, aren't we presupposing the truth of Materialism? If the supervenience base of Schumann's depression is depleted biogenic amines, aren't we saying that the depression itself is biogenic amine deficiency?

Consider the query about Materialism first. Things would certainly be neat for Materialism if minds have brainy supervenience bases, for then, even if Brentano's problem could not be solved, Materialism might be defended by defending supervenience. However, advocacy of supervenience is not sufficient to make one a materialist. A philosopher can advocate supervenience without advocating Materialism.

If mind/brain supervenience holds, Materialism can be false. Consider the following analogy. Imagine that you own a beautiful recording of Schumann's *Carnaval*, Opus 9 (*Carnaval* is one of his most successful compositions for the piano). Suppose beauty/*Carnaval* material supervenience holds. That is, suppose that facts about the beauty of the recording supervene on facts about its material makeup, so that any recording which is just like yours in all physical respects must of necessity be a beautiful *Carnaval* recording.

No matter how we ultimately analyse the notion of beautiful recording, it seems clear that the beauty of the recording cannot be identified with its material makeup. Other recordings, some made on CD, some on magnetic tape, still others on LP records, might be equally beautiful *Carnaval* recordings. There are many, perhaps endlessly many, ways to make a beautiful recording of the piece. And thus arises the possibility that even if the beauty of the recording supervenes on physical features, the beauty itself should not be identified with those features. Beauty conceptually surpasses the material base on which it may supervene.

Now reconsider mind/brain supervenience. An analogous point obtains for mind/brain supervenience. However we ultimately understand depression, there may be many, perhaps endlessly many, ways to make a depressed person: some with depleted amines; others with disordered neurochemicals of other sorts. And thus arises the possibility that even if Schumann's depression supervenes on amine deficiency, depression itself should not be equated with the deficiency. Depression conceptually surpasses the material base on which it may supervene. Indeed, in the words of three scientific researchers on depression: 'Depression cannot be equated with imbalance in one or another class of neurotransmitters, endocrine messengers, or disordered electrolyte metabolism.'[14]

Hence, supervenience is compatible with non-materialism. Supervenience does not presuppose Materialism. What of the other (explanatory) question above about supervenience?

Our explanatory question about supervenience was this: If supervenience holds, does reference to brain suffice to explain behaviour? I shall end the chapter by answering the question.

7.6 Explanation and Mind/Brain Supervenience

A number of friends of supervenience claim that if mind supervenes on brain, then this means that all psychological phenomena or facts are best – most fully – explained by theories of their neurophysiological supervenience i.e. by reference to Brain facts. Supposing mind/brain supervenience, Schumann's suicide is sufficiently accounted for just by reference to Brain facts such as amine depletion. We can and should dispense with explanation by reference to Mind facts.

I cannot here provide a systematic discussion of this bold and complex explanatory claim. Yet, in the end, I believe, along with a number of other philosophers, that it is unjustified.[15] This is because reference to supervenience bases cannot handle numerous questions we need to ask about the mental phenomena to be explained. The power or ability to answer questions is a hallmark of good explanation.[16] There are numerous questions about Schumann's suicide for which supervenience explanation is a failure and for which reference to Mind facts is required.

Consider the diverse phenomena surrounding the suicide: Schumann suffered from severe, recurring depressive episodes throughout his life. Often he was sleepless, hopeless and agitated. Imaginary voices would tell him he was worthless and that his compositions were dreadful. Both his parents were occasionally severely depressed. A sister had committed suicide. His social behaviour alternated between isolation and intimacy. Schumann's marriage was beset with financial problems, the responsibilities of many children and the conflicts between his compositional career and his wife's ambitions as a pianist. Schumann was emotionally and quite occasionally financially dependent on his wife. A persistent source of stress was Clara's father, who strongly disliked Schumann and had become in the words of one biographer 'his bitter enemy'.[17] The list of troubles goes on.

Schumann was a genius but also a mess. I am reminded of a remark of Carl Jung: 'Great gifts are the fairest, and often the most dangerous fruits on the tree of humanity. They hang on the weakest branches, which easily break.' Schumann's branch broke.

What sense can be made of the surrounding facts about Schumann? Are some of them explanatorily relevant to his suicide? And how can we know?

A common tactic for criticizing explanatory hypotheses is to brand hypotheses as 'superficial' and 'unrevealing'. The suggestion that Schumann's suicide was caused by depleted amines – by the alleged supervenience base of his depression – would be attacked as a shallow explanation, which touches on merely a fragment of the questions which should be asked of his suicide, and then only superficially. Individually it has little explanatory impact.

Consider, by way of illustration, two questions asked of the suicide:

Q1 Why did Schumann starve himself rather than commit suicide some other way?
Q2 Why did Schumann starve himself after two years in the asylum rather than at some earlier time – say soon after admission?

Obviously the supervenience base for depression most likely did not fix the manner of suicide, for whereas in 1854 Schumann threw himself into the Rhine, in 1856 he starved himself to death. If we assumme that his amines were depleted in both cases, his mode of attempt differed. So, something other than deficiency must help to account for the suicide. If so, what? Nor does such a base answer why Schumann resorted to self-starvation in 1856 rather than earlier, when his neurochemicals were perhaps equally or even more seriously depleted. The purported relevant supervenience base is unable to answer key questions about the event. So it is explanatorily deficient.

To make the inadequacy even clearer, consider by comparison how reference to Mind facts helps to answer those two questions.

A1   Schumann committed suicide through starvation rather than by other means because he knew he was closely guarded by asylum staff and death by starvation was the only form of suicide the staff could not prevent.

A2   Schumann starved himself in 1856 rather than earlier because prolonged isolation in the asylum made him believe that he would never recover his status as a composer or musician, and confirmed his deepest fear that he was insane. The asylum became, with time, the exact opposite of everything which Schumann hoped for when he volunteered for admission, which, in brief, was a cure for his depression and a restoration of his creative powers. Hence, it took the passage of time to evoke the desire for suicide even if the passage did not markedly increase the depression or deplete its neurochemical base.

Given the illuminating and apparently necessary assistance which reference to Mind facts provides in accounting for the suicide, it is difficult to imagine that any explanation couched exclusively in supervenience terms would be superior to an account which includes reference to Mind facts. True, the criticism of supervenience as best explanation might be deflected if it is argued that such Mind facts as Schumann's knowledge of asylum life and desire for suicide also have supervenience bases, and that reference to those bases as well as to the bases of other relevant surrounding Mind facts can explain the suicide. But surrounding supervenience bases are likely to be horrendously variable and complicated. As we expand the supervenience base from such local biographical facts as the depression of 1856 to such global facts as family psychological history, knowledge of asylum life and so on, we will soon get something much more complicated and elusive than we gambled for or anticipated: a perplexing and bewildering list of Brain facts effectively useless for purposes of accounting for the suicide.

It is no wonder, therefore, that explanation exclusively in terms of brainy supervenience does not figure much in contemporary psychological theorizing about depression and other mood disorders or mental illnesses. Some explanations are of the supervenience sort but most are not. Most are 'mixed' or Brain fact/ Mind fact explanations. Many authorities have drawn attention to the complexities involved in trying to establish an explanatory framework for understanding depression. They have argued that depression is best accounted for in terms of Mind facts, including facts about the family history and environment of the depressed person, supplemented but surely not displaced by reference to Brain facts.[18]

Note that the conclusion that supervenience is explanatorily inadequate does not mean that reference to supervenience is irrelevant for explanation. Supervenience facts may be germane to some questions without being relevant to all questions. For instance, they might suggest neurochemical treatments for conditions like depression. Once the identification of a supervenience base is made, the hypothesis that naturally suggests itself is this: zero in on the base to block or dampen the depression. This may be accomplished by drugs which alter neurochemical levels. True, matters could be, and likely are, tremendously complicated. Probably no single drug neatly parcels out to block just the depression without having other and possibly unwanted side-effects.[19] One reason for this is that one and the same Brain fact may serve as the supervenience base for many Mind facts and play a role in supporting other and perhaps even antagonistic mental states. However, the point being urged here is that, supposing supervenience bases for mind, supervenience facts can be germane to various questions even if they are not relevant to all questions.

Supervenience has come to occupy an increasingly influential role in the philosophy of mind, reaching its height of appeal in the thesis that supervenience explanations should displace Mind fact explanations. I am reminded of a line from Shakespeare: 'I'll put a girdle round about the earth' (*A Midsummer Night's Dream*, Act II, Sc 1). Supervenience puts the girdle of brain round about mind. On the other hand, it seems that reference just to supervenience bases is inadequate to answer many questions about behaviour and mental phenomena. These questions require reference to mind.

To return for a postscript and moral to Schumann. Clara viewed the body of her emaciated husband within an hour of his death: 'I stood by his corpse... And as I knelt at his bed... it seemed as if a magnificent spirit was hovering over me – ah, if only he had taken me along.'[20] To Clara her husband's death was a sad mystery; she knew only that she wished to be with him.

It may be all too easy for the champion of supervenience to pronounce that the brain is all that is relevant to the psychological twists and turns of a person like Schumann. However, Brain facts hardly exhaust the mind of this or any other man or woman. Careful inspection of the conceptual and explanatory complexities involved in supervenience offers a different diagnosis. 'There are more things in heaven and earth, Horatio, Than are dreamt of in your philosophy' (*Hamlet*, Act 1, Sc 5).

NOTES

1 William Bechtel, *Philosphy of Mind: An Overview for Cognitive Science* (Erlbaum, New Jersey, 1988), p.94.
2 Herschel Prins, *Pizarre Behaviours: Boundaries of Psychiatric Disorder* (Routledge, Chapman & Hall, London, 1990), pp.23–41.
3 Paul Teller, 'A poor man's guide to supervenience and determination', *Southern Journal of Philosophy*, 22, Supplement (1983), p.147.
4 U.T. Place, 'Is consciousness a brain process?', *The British Journal of Psychology*, 47 (1956), pp.42–51; J.J.C. Smart, 'Sensations and brain processes' *Philosophical Review* 68 (1959), pp.141–56.
5 See, for instance, Elliott Sober, *Core Questions of Philosophy* (Macmillan, New York 1991), Lecture 18; Owen Flanagan, *The Science of Mind*, 2nd edition (MIT, Cambridge, MA., 1991). I owe the example of Oedipus (to follow) to Sober. To keep things simple, I formulate Descartes' argument differently than does Sober (and most commentators on Descartes). Sober's formulation is in terms of the concept of propertyhood and the principle of the indiscernibility of identicals; mine is in terms of the notion of conceiving-as. There are important differences in these formulations, but discussing them would take us too far afield in this context.

6   D.M. Armstrong, *A Materialist Theory of Mind* (Routledge Kegan & Paul, London, 1968), p.57.

7   Jerry Foder, *Psychosemantics: The Problem of Meaning in the Philosophy of Mind* (MIT, Cambridge, MA., 1987); Fred Dretske, *Explaining Behaviour: Reasons in A World of Causes* (MIT, Cambridge, MA., 1988).

8   Peter Ostwald, *Schumann: The Inner Voices of a Musical Genius* (Northeastern University Press, Boston, 1985), p.1.

9   Robert Burton, *The Anatomy of Melancholy* (Vintage, New York, 1621/1977).

10 Why include facts about amines among the brain facts which might be explanatorily relevant to Schumann's suicide? The answer is because one of the most popular neurochemical explanations of depression attributes depression to biogenic amine deficiency. See, for example, David Rosenhan and Martin Seligman, *Abnormal Psychology* (Norton, New York, 1984), p.323f. Just such an explanation will be examined later in the chapter.

11 At least, they are not *wholly* physical states or processes. There may be elements in depressed attitudes which are physical.

12 See Teller, 'A poor man's guide', for relevant discussion.

13 One interpretation is to construe Mind facts as supervening not just on Brain facts but on facts about a person's natural and social environment. See, for discussion, Jaegwon Kim, 'Psychophysical supervenience', *Philosophical Studies* 41 (1982), pp.51–70. The suggestion that the natural and social environment helps to constitute Mind facts seems to have originated, in contemporary philosophy, with Hilary Putnam, 'The meaning of "meaning" ', in K. Gunderson ed., *Minnesota Studies in the Philosophy of Science, VII* (University of Minnesota, Minneapolis, 1975). The topic is beyond the scope of the present book.

14 Peter Whybrow, Hagop Akiskal and William McKinney, *Mood Disorders: Toward a New Psychobiology* (Plenum, New York, 1984), p.195.

15 See, especially, Harold Kincaid, 'Supervenience and explanation', *Synthese*, 77 (1988), pp.251–81.

16 See C.B. Cross, 'Explanation and the theory of questions', *Erkenntnis*, 34 (1991), pp.237–60. Cross refers to an interesting discussion by W.M. Runyan of an incident in the life of Vincent Van Gogh, which, like incidents in Schumann's life, raises multiple questions about the explanatory relevance of Mind facts. See W.M. Runyan, 'Why did Van Gogh cut off his ear?: The problem of alternative explanations in psychobiography', *Journal of Personality and Social Psychology*, 40 (1981), pp.1070–77.

17 See Ostwald, *Schumann*, p.306; see also Roy Porter, *A Social History of Madness: The World Through the Eyes of the Insane* (Weidenfeld & Nicholson, New York, 1987), pp.65–71.

18 See Whybrow, et al., *Mood Disorders*.

19 See, for example, J.F.W. Deakin, 'The clinical relevance of animal models of depression' in *Behavioural Models in Psychopharmacology*, ed. Paul Wilner (Cambridge University Press, Cambridge, 1991), p.157.

20 Quoted in Ostwald, *Schumann*, p.293.

8

Inside Persons

8.1 A Question of Gender

What is it like to be a person of the opposite sex? Presumably, there is something it is like to be a man and something it is like to be a woman. But can a woman understand the inner life of a man or a man that of a woman? What it is like to be a woman may be at least partially closed off to me: to know a woman's pain, pleasure, happiness, misery – certainly her sensations in childbirth. For I am a man.

Among the various thought experiments and fantasies available in science fiction, one of the most captivating concerns an account of what a society of human androgynies might be like. (An androgyne is a sexually intermediate or indeterminate individual.) In *The Left Hand of Darkness* (1969) Ursula Le Guin describes a cold planet named Winter, which has been inhabited by a race of persons who are androgynous. Once monthly each person – otherwise neither male nor female – enters 'kemmer', a biological period in which they become sexually fertile and aroused as either a male or female. Lovers, for example, may enter kemmer at the same time, but neither will know in advance whether they will become male or female, although one will emerge male, the other female. Any person may either beget ('father') or bear ('mother') a child, and many individuals do both, although at different periods in life.

Le Guin describes the androgynous world of the planet as follows:

There is no unconsenting sex, no rape. As with most mammals other than man, coitus can be performed only by mutual invitation and consent... There is no division of humanity into strong and weak halves, protective/protected, dominant/submissive, owner/chattel, active/passive. In fact the whole tendency to Dualism that pervades human thinking may be found to be lessened, or changed, on Winter.

Le Guin's attempt to describe a social world around essentially genderless people and to identify the experiential benefits to both 'men' and 'women' alike which would attach to such a world is described by one commentator as representing 'the fulfillment of an ancient human dream: the dream of bridging the gap which separates male and female experience, confining each of us to just half of the human experience.'[1]

In a world of kemmering, people would still bear distinct personalities, but they would know what it is like to be male as well as what it is like to be female. Or at least they would know what certain experiences are like from male and female subjective points of view. Even if persons turned out to be stereotypically masculine or feminine in interests, nothing would follow about one being unable to grasp, capture or directly experience female or male pains, pleasures, experiences or sensations. The persons in Le Guin's imaginary world would grasp much better than people do in our world the inner feelings of both men and women.

8.2   What Is It Like to Be a Person?

Suppose you could 'super-kemmer', as it were, and experience life just as a person – a pure person – abstracted from all the particularities of your own situation, not just the particularities of sex and gender. Is there a general way experience appears which all individual persons share beneath, as Owen Flanagan puts it, 'the noise and clatter of their own particularity'?[2]

The move from genderlessness to generality would be a move from understanding male and female experience to understanding some still more universal way of experiencing things: not what it is like to be a man, woman, African philosopher, Irish hockey player, twenty or ninety year old but what it is like to be a person. If there is something it is like to be a person, it is something for each and every reader of this book – and the author too – no matter what otherwise distinguishes and divides us.

In this section of the chapter, we will look at two candidate components in what it is like to be a person. The main idea behind each candidate is that it is supposed to be universal in the inner life of persons. Individuals stripped of either or both components are subtracted in personhood. They are stripped of the sorts of thoughts, feelings, sensations and attitudes otherwise deeply ingrained in our own – your own, my own – sense of ourselves as persons. Psychologically stripped individuals may partially share in the inner life of personhood, if their deficits are partial, but they are precluded from fully participating in that life.

1 Memory

Is there a general way experience seems to persons? The first truly great British empiricist, John Locke (1632–1704) thought there is. Locke argued that the inner life of persons feels continuous; a person's subjective sense of identity, of direction, of their own intelligence, happiness and misery are all grounded in the person's autobiographical memory or the connections they take themselves to have to their past. Locke puts the point as follows: 'As far as consciousness can be extended backwards to any past action or thought, so far reaches the... person.'[3] From an inner point of view, a person is who they remember themselves being.

Oliver Sacks, an American neuropsychologist, in 'The Lost Mariner' in *The Man Who Mistook His Wife for a Hat* (1987), tells the tale of Jimmie, who lost his autobiographical memory to Korsakoff's disease (the classical Korsakoff's syndrome is a destruction of memory caused by alcoholism). Whatever was said or done to Jimmie was likely to be forgotten in a few moments' time. Sacks asks, 'What sort of world, what sort of self, can be preserved in a man who has lost the greater part of his memory and, with this, his past, and his moorings in time?' (p.23). Jimmie impressed Sacks as, 'isolated in a single moment of being...[a] man without a past (or future), stuck in a constantly changing, meaningless moment' (p.29).

Jimmie's story, and those of others like him, reveal how within persons the continuities of autobiographical memory are necessary for a wide variety of thoughts and experiences. The necessity can be made vivid by considering, by way of illustration, a connection between intending and acting.

A person intends an action only if the person wants to perform the action. For someone to have the intention to, say, play chess, they must want that they themself play chess. Sacks takes it as given that Jimmie's connections between intending and acting were severed. He could form plans or intentions but of only a few moments duration. Carrying out complex intentions and tasks was beyond him; he would forget his goals. 'He was superb at calculations, but only if they could be done at lightening speed' (p.27). If there were many steps, and too much time involved, he forgot what he intended, and where he was in the process. His intelligent behaviour was fragmented and dislocated. Chess, for instance, was beyond him. It was beyond him not because he was unintelligent; he was bright. It was beyond him because in chess there is an ongoing need to remember one's previous intentions, moves, strategies and wants. Stripped of that memory one is stripped of capacity for the game.

Guilt and pride were also impossible for Jimmie. For someone to feel guilty for, say, stealing a piece of cake or to take pride in accomplishing a task, say, writing a poem, one must remember the theft and the task. Guilt and pride are bound by contentful autobiographical memories, whereas Jimmie lived in an often surprising succession of unrecollected impressions and events. 'Clearly, passionately, he wanted something to do; he wanted to do, to be, to feel – and could not; he wanted sense, he wanted purpose' (p.37). Jimmie wanted purpose, but his present could not provide purpose without reference to the past.

If Locke is right, autobiographical memory is an essential and universal element in the inner life of persons. In cases like Jimmie's, victims of Korsakoff's syndrome, acute schizophrenia, advanced Alzheimer's disease and others like them, when individuals cannot extend their consciousness from one moment to the next, cannot consciously integrate personal past with present, people are 'condemned to a sort of... froth, a meaningless fluttering on the surface of life' (p.39). Living on the surface, individuals are occluded from the inner life, the 'what it is like' of personhood. Theirs is a life without aspiration, without remembered achievement, without the backward stretch of recoverable hope.

2   The conviction of freedom

Locke is not alone in believing that there are universal elements in personal experience (I will return to Locke's emphasis on memory much later in the chapter in discussing happiness). In *Minds, Brains, and Science* (1984), John Searle argues that a 'conviction of freedom' is built into what it is like to be a person. By 'conviction of freedom' Searle means that 'though we did one thing, we feel we know perfectly well that we could have done something else' (p.87). The conviction is the belief that one has *dual power*, that is, the power to choose or do something or to choose or do something else (including refrain).[4] Searle writes:

Reflect. . . on the character of the experiences you have as you engage in normal, everyday ordinary. . . actions. You will sense the possibility of alternative courses of action built into those experiences. Raise your arm or walk across the room or take a drink of water, and you will see that at any point in the experience you have a sense of alternative courses of action open to you (p.95).

New York University's Thomas Nagel makes a similar point when he writes: 'From the inside, when we act, alternative possibilities seem to lie open before us: to turn to the right or left, to order this dish or that, to vote for one candidate or the other – and one of the possibilities is made actual by what we do.'[5] The thesis that intentional action includes a subjective sense of freedom or dual power may be illustrated by means of an imaginary example. The example involves two prototypical antecedents of conscious intentional action: deliberation and decision.

Suppose Beth, a college student, is deliberating whether to pay her tuition. She weighs the reasons on both sides. For instance, on one side, she remembers that the university did not permit her to take the course she needed in physics; the course over-enrolled. She remembers that she could not park her car near the dormitory where she lived. She recognizes that she has not yet picked a major and worries whether she truly belongs in college without a major. On the other side, Beth remembers that the philosophy course in which ultimately she did enroll (when physics closed) was unexpectedly enjoyable. She recollects with enthusiasm the instructor's explanation of the concept of kemmer. She suspects that finding a major is less important than getting a good general education; and she recalls that some of her happiest moments have been in college. So, after considering pros and cons, she finally makes up her mind. She decides, all things considered, to pay her tuition. If Beth is a conscientious ('continent') agent, she will then pay her tuition.

In trying to decide whether to pay it is important to note that Beth believes that she can either pay or not pay. She believes she possesses dual power. If we revise the story so that she believes that her cash reserves are empty and that she cannot secure money, then she could not properly decide whether to pay. To see herself deciding it must seem to her as if it is up to her how she decides. The buck stops (tuition starts) here because dual power subjectively rests here.

Searle and Nagel are not alone in claiming that the inner life of persons contains the conviction of freedom and that in acting intentionally persons believe themselves to possess dual power. It is one of the primary ideas which has fuelled traditional debate over the issue of *freedom of will* or *free choice*. To possess free will or the power of free choice is to possess dual power: the power to choose one way or the other. Failure to possess dual power spells absence of free will. Searle and Nagel, however, are almost alone among philosophers who write on free will to say candidly that the conviction, although essential or unavoidable, is also unreasonable or unwarranted. No genuine decision or action can take place without the conviction but, alas, no person truly is entitled to it.

Nagel's candour is more opaque than Searle's. So I will focus on the reasoning behind Searle's claim.

According to Searle we cannot abandon the conviction of freedom since 'that conviction is built into every normal, conscious intelligent action' (p.97). To be an agent is to seem to oneself 'dually' powerful. Why then assert that the conviction is unreasonable or unwarranted? Searle claims that the conviction is unreasonable because it is inconsistent with what we know from science. Science's 'conception of. . . reality simply does not allow for. . . freedom' (p.98).

8.3 Freedom and Explanation

Searle assumes that if the conviction of freedom is warranted it must be consistent with science. If dual power is incompatible with science, then the conviction is unreasonable and must be abandoned.

It is instructive to distinguish two ways in which the conviction of freedom may be inconsistent or incompatible with science. It may be inconsistent either locally or globally. Local inconsistency means that a particular agent is mistaken that they possess dual power, given what science says or implies about them or people of their type. To be incompatible globally means that any agent is mistaken in the conviction, given what science says, full stop.

Consider Arthur, an advanced alcoholic. Suppose for the sake of argument that medical science shows that alcoholism is a disease.[6] The classic disease concept of alcoholism includes the following element: 'Those inflicted with the disease eventually progress to uncontrolled drinking because the disease produces a distinctive disability: loss of dual power in the matter of drinking.'

Arthur enters a bar and wonders whether to order a drink. If Searle is right, and Arthur is otherwise normal, he will seem to himself to have the (dual) power to order or to not order. Suppose he weighs reasons on both sides. For instance, he remembers the pleasant drink he had earlier in the day, and he feels acute discomfort associated with not drinking. On the other side, he is beginning to notice negative personal and social consequences of heavy drinking: the depletion of his bank account, the strain on his marriage, insomnia and fatigue. After weighing reasons, he makes a choice. He decides, all things considered, to drink.

Now the question is does Arthur truly possess dual power in ordering? The locally relevant facts in the case – that he is an advanced alcoholic and that alcoholism is a disease – mean that although Arthur *feels* 'dually' powerful, he is not. According to science, he is in the grip of a disease. He lacks the ability to refrain.

Supposition of Arthur's disease means that Arthur is unfree, although he feels free. The scientific facts about alcoholism are locally incompatible with his freedom of choice in deciding whether to order. However, not everyone, fortunately, suffers from alcoholism or is beset with disease-like disability. So local incompatibility is not the source of Searle's claim that the conviction of freedom is unwarranted.

Searle's charge that the conviction is unreasonable has a different source. Global incompatibility is the source. On Searle's view of science, no one – neither alcoholic, nor you, nor me – possesses dual power in any situation. Each and every one of our decisions and actions is unfree.

Why is each and every one of our decisions and actions unfree? If we consider science, what is there in science that excludes dual power?

According to Searle, an assumption underlies science which is globally incompatible with the claim that persons possess dual power. Searle never states the assumption explicitly, but it lies behind his argument as well as behind many other philosophers' writings on free will. This is the assumption, which I shall call the *externalist explanation assumption*, that each and every decision or action has a sufficient cause or explanation altogether outside itself. We decide to act in the manner that we do because our decisions and actions follow the heels of conditions which rest entirely outside those decisions and actions.

Advocates of the externalist explanation assumption develop the assumption in different ways, depending upon what is contained in the notion of explanation being outside the event or decision explained. Two kinds of externality or 'outsideness' may be distinguished. The first kind, which I shall call *sub-personal or vertical externality*, has two salient features: (1) it denies that the psychology or mind of a person has any real effect on the person's choice or action; and (2) it also asserts that explanation of behaviour must be given in sub-personal neurophysiological or (to use the language of the last chapter) Brain fact terms. An advocate of sub-personal externality may endorse a version of the thesis (discussed in the previous chapter) that behavior is best explained by reference to brainy supervenience bases of mental states. Searle is attracted to sub-personal externalist explanation; however, the previous chapter, by raising doubts about the explanatory significance of supervenience, suggests that sub-personal externalist explanation of psychological phenomena (decision, action) should be resisted.

In any case there is another kind of explanatory externalism, *horizontal* or *backtracking* externalism, which lacks (1) and (2) but asserts (3) that events in the agent's past suffice to explain the person's choices and actions – and hence they are wholly outside the circumstances of decision itself. In order to accommodate the previous chapter's misgivings about neurophysiological explanation, I shall couch Searle's claim that science is incompatible with dual power in backtracking externalist terms.

Imagine that you and I enroll as medical students. For me, in the light of my heretofore disappointing academic career, enrolling is a fragile gamble. I have not been a good student; but, somehow, perhaps through my parents' political connections, I am admitted and enroll. For you, in the light of your stunning record of academic success, it is a natural step. You graduated near the top of our college class.

Suppose I take my first exam, do poorly, and decide to give up. You take your first exam, do equally poorly, but decide to persist. The question is: Why do I decide to give up, whereas you choose to persist?

Consider a sample scientific explanation which is couched in backtracking externalist terms. In 1975 Martin Seligman, a professor of psychology at the University of Pennsylvania, conducted scientific inquiries into the sources of quitting and persistence, and reported these in a book with the fascinating title of *Helplessness: On Depression, Development, and Death*. Although Seligman's theory, the so-called learned helplessness model of depression, has had to be refined and reformulated, it remains, almost 20 years later, a primary contender for the title of Best Explanation of Quitting and Persistence in the scientific literature.[7] The gist of Seligman's explanation of the difference between the two sorts of decisions and behavior goes like this:

> Imagine someone (like me, above) with a history of failure; when such a person receives disappointment in spite of their efforts, the person learns that it is pointless to persevere. Impediments are perceived as insurmountable barriers to success. Such a person learns to be helpless. By contrast, imagine someone (you above) with a history of success; when such a person achieves positive results because of their

efforts, they learn that it is purposeful to persevere. Impediments stimulate effort. Such a person learns to be industrious.

Within the learned helplessness model, the following explanation may be offered of why I gave up and you persisted:

I have learned to be helpless. You have learned to be industrious. Failure on my first exam reinforced my history of academic disappointment and my expectation that nothing I can do is likely to bring success. Failure on your first exam inspired your effort. You believe that future success still is under your control despite a temporary setback.

My point in mentioning Seligman's model is not to suggest that it is correct or to agree that frustrated history is helpless destiny. I want to make a different point. The point is that the model explains certain decisions in terms of circumstances wholly outside the decisions themselves. The decisions are accounted for by backtracking: by explanatory reference to past events and personal history. Moreover, Seligman's model illustrates Searle's contention that science leaves no elbow room for dual power, not just for alcoholics, but even for medical students.

8.4 The Consequence Argument, Folk Psychology and Free Will

If decisions are explained in terms of circumstances wholly outside or before themselves, then agents lack dual power. This is the conclusion of the so-called consequence argument defended in the free will literature by Peter Van Inwagen and others.[8] The main idea behind the consequence argument goes like this:

1 If persons possess dual power, then we can decide to do something or decide to do something else (such as refrain).
2 If science sufficiently explains decisions and actions in terms of circumstances or events wholly before their occurrence, then we possess dual power only if we can control those past events.

Only if we can change the past do we have the power to choose differently now.

3 However, we cannot change the past. What is done cannot be undone. Indeed, ultimately, the past stretches through childhood and before birth. And we certainly cannot change events before birth.

4 Therefore, if science sufficiently explains our decisions in terms of wholly prior events, we do not possess dual power.

The consequence argument is based on the notion that dual power is incompatible with the assumption that decision and action are sufficiently explained by wholly past circumstances. What is a sufficient explanation? A sufficient explanation is an explanation which shows that what is explained is inevitable; under the circumstances it could not have been otherwise. Thus, to take a brief nonhuman illustration, if the breaking of a dam sufficiently explains the flooding of the valley, and the dam breaks, then the valley must be flooded. We can't correctly say that the dam broke but the valley could have been spared. The break suffices.

It is also important for the consequence argument that the events cited in a sufficient explanation occur wholly in the past. We may wish that the flood could have been avoided. However, if sufficient explanation rests in the burst dam, then the flood could have been avoided only if the dam did not burst. Hence, to avoid the flood, one would have to travel backwards in time, which presumably is impossible, and somehow prevent the break.

The consequence argument hinges on prior occurrences which suffice for explanation. Past breaks determine current floods.

What about the human case? Is failing the first test sufficient to make a person give up medical school? Not necessarily: it depends on personal history. According to the learned helplessness model, it depends on whether I have a record of disappointment and frustration. If I have a disappointing history, then the history explains why I gave up after the first exam. We can't correctly say I failed the test but could have persisted. Giving up follows the determining heels of history.

Of course, I may feel in deciding to give up as if the future contains the possibility of persistence, and that, despite my past record, I have the (dual) power to give up or to persist. However, since history is past, and suffices to quit, then I could persist only if the personal history were otherwise.

The consequence argument makes it easy to see why Searle asserts that science is inconsistent with dual power. Science, for Searle, is committed to explanatory externalism and externalism is incompatible with dual power.

Explanatory externalism (sub-personal or backtracking) is capable of different variations or formulations. Some are versions of what philosophers call *strict determinism*; others are not. An externalism is strictly deterministic if it is committed to a highly rigid form of scientific explanation, according to which events are and must be explained by reference to iron-clad and exceptionless laws. Searle is not committed to strict determinism, but I shall bypass Searle's discussion of strict determinism, for it does not affect the points which I wish to make here, and move directly to a troublesome dilemma with which Searle says we are confronted.

Searle (and Nagel, too) leaves us in a nasty dilemma. The dilemma is as follows. According to Searle, when we act – at least, consciously and deliberately – we believe we possess dual power, but the belief is an embarrassing scientifically-misbegotten false-hood. Something we cannot abandon when we act (the conviction of freedom), we should abandon (because it conflicts with a key global assumption of science). Searle lodges us between the pro-verbial rock and hard place.

It is instructive to note that the Searlean dilemma arises only if (a) science really presupposes the externalist explanation assumption or (b) we must decide and act with a conviction of dual power. If science is not committed to explanatory externalism or if we can decide without believing ourselves free, then we can escape the dilemma.

Some philosophers sympathetic to free will reject (a). They try to offer a general theory of dual power compatible with science. In offering a general theory of dual power, they contend that at least some events or occurrences are not sufficiently explained by refer-ence to circumstances altogether outside themselves; explanatory externalism is incorrect. The contrary view is explanatory interna-lism: at least at certain key junctures in people's lives their choices and decisions are *partially self-explaining* or have *sufficient reasons partly within themselves*. In fact, one of the most penetrating and systematic attempts to defend the conviction of freedom, Robert Kane's *Free Will and Values* (1985), describes explanation in just this way. According to Kane, decisions do not spring from nothing, but neither do they always stem exclusively from past or external factors; instead, they stem partially from us as autonomous rational agents. Kane also contends that explanatory internalism fits with science.

Other philosophers opposed to free will reject (b). They argue that people can decide and act without believing themselves possessed of dual power. A paradigm decision, on this view, is one in which I weigh pros and cons but suppress any presumption that my decision really is up to me; perhaps I see myself as ignorant of the real springs of my behavior. I admit that alternate possibilities may seem dependent upon me. I believe, however, that this impression is woefully incorrect. The present is determined; the future is closed. In fact, one of the most penetrating and systematic attempts to displace the conviction of freedom with another presupposition, Daniel Dennett's *Elbow Room: The Varieties of Free Will Worth Wanting* (1984), describes decision in just that way. Decisions do not require a conviction of dual power, although they do require a commitment to a policy of weighing pros and cons.

Much can be learned by systematically exploring the nature and merits of rejecting either (a) or (b). However, we have neither time nor conceptual resources to conduct a systematic exploration here. So, let us learn what we can from a quick and unsystematic discussion. I shall return to Searle's dilemma later.

The manifest image and the scientific image

In framing a discussion of whether (a) or (b) should be rejected, I want first to consider a distinction introduced into the philosophical literature by Wilfred Sellars.[9] Sellars draws a distinction which has become standard in philosophic writings on personhood. This is the distinction between the world as it *manifestly appears* and the world as conceived in the *scientific image*. Roughly, the manifest image is the world of ordinary experience; the world as conceived by ordinary folk. It is the world of such familiar objects as tables and chairs. It is the world that contains all the qualities and sensations we experience: of colour, size, motion, taste, pleasure, pain and so on. The scientific image is the world of scientific entities – atoms, protons, electrons, velocity, force and so on; the world of theoretical scientists and especially of physicists.

In comparing and contrasting the two images, some characteristics of the manifest image survive in the scientific image. Others, however, find no place in science. Size and motion, for example, survive. Colours and chairs, for instance, do not. Red chairs play a certain role in everyday life; they are for sitting and ornamenting perhaps with yellow pillows. However, all the stuff we call 'chairs' really is – to Sellars' physical scientists – clouds of colourless molecules. Granny's rocker is bits of matter off which light bounces. The red colour of her chair is replaced in the scientific image by frequencies of light waves, for instance, and channels of retinal stimulation.

There is at best limited agreement among philosophers as to just what the manifest image says or implies about persons, but a common theme in recent discussions is that the manifest image includes a psychology of persons. It includes a 'theory' of what personhood is and of how and why persons decide and act.[10] Arguably, at the heart of the theory or psychology, sometimes called *folk psychology*, is the assumption that a person is a free and rational agent. To be a person and to decide and act is to possess dual power as well as to exercise this power in a rational manner.[11]

What does rational agency involve? Rational agents perform rational actions and make rational decisions. As readers familiar with chapter 6 may recall, to the extent that an action (or decision) is rational it occurs for reasons of the agent. Rational actions are intended to contribute to the purposes and goals for which the person decides and acts. To take two simple illustrations, Beth's decision to pay tuition fees contributes to her goal of a college education. Your persistence in medical school contributes to your purpose to become a doctor.

Folk psychology is a controversial theory. Philosophers are divided on whether folk psychology is sacrosanct or should and will be displaced by scientific psychology: the psychology of the scientific image. An *eliminative materialist* approach to folk psychology rejects everything about folk psychology. Eliminative

Materialism says that the manifest image of persons can and should be flouted; not just the idea that persons possess dual power, but the idea that persons are rational agents and act for reasons.[12]

Most philosophers of mind, however, disagree with eliminativists that science should or will displace folk psychology. They contend that 'folk psychology is here to stay' and that it can be integrated with science.[13] There are two main models or views of the staying power of folk psychology. The first model, which I shall call *the anti-freewill model*, is that the overall framework of folk psychology must be refined and revised in the light of science; in particular, the idea that persons possess dual power must be jettisoned or displaced. Persons undergo beliefs and desires and make rational decisions, but the decisions are unfree. They are sufficiently explained by reference to outside events.

The second, *freewill model*, is ecumenical: dual power is acceptable from a scientific point of view. A paradigm of decision on this model is one in which a person harbours the reasonable conviction that the decision is not sufficiently explained by events lying wholly in the past. The scientific image allows events to occur whose sufficient explanations rest partly within themselves.

Each model – the freewill and the anti-freewill – has its troublesome aspect. Neither inspires universal assent among philosophers. Let me elaborate briefly.

The freewill model has difficulty explaining how a decision which is not sufficiently explained by events wholly external can avoid being inexplicable and unexplainable *full stop*. Rejecting externalist explanation seems tantamount to rejecting explanation.

To return to an earlier illustration, when I decide to give up medical school, as a rational agent I am supposed to be able to explain why I did so by describing or citing my reasons. If the choice is free and I possess dual power, I could equally have chosen to persist. However, if I was rational in choosing to persist, I also am supposed to be able to explain why I persist by citing my reasons for persisting. Either way, as rational agent my reasons for choosing are supposed to explain my choosing. Free choice is not just dual power; for a person (rational agent) it is dual rational power. If I am free, I am rationally free. My free decisions are rational either way.

Why is this troublesome? Why should we not rest content with the idea that no sufficient explanation in terms of wholly past events can be given of free choice?

The reason we cannot reject externalism, at least not without more careful defence of free will, is that without externalism there seems no way to explain why I decided one way rather than some alternative way which apparently was equally and rationally open to me. If I am able to explain why I gave up by citing reasons for giving up, and would have been able to explain why I persisted by citing reasons for persisting, then why did I quit rather than persist? Deciding one way rather than the other seems to be something for which there is no explanation – at least, no explanation by reference to reasons. Asked why I stopped rather than persisted, or why I responded to reasons for giving up rather than to reasons for persisting, it seems I can only say 'I just did'.

By contrast, by couching explanation in terms of wholly past events the choice can be explained. Why did I give up rather than persist? True, I had reasons for giving up and reasons for persisting. However, I was moved by reasons for giving up rather than for persisting because of my history: I am a product of learned helplessness. Had I been a product of learned hopefulness or industriousness, I would have been moved by reasons for persisting and persisted instead. Of course, externalist explanation renders unwarranted the claim that my choice was free. My decision is no longer assignable to me as its source, but instead becomes a link in a history which suffices for the decision. Externalism – as noted in the consequence argument – eliminates freedom.

If the freewill/internalist model has trouble making free choice intelligible and explainable, the anti-freewill/externalist model has trouble explaining how I can legitimately view myself as an agent without believing myself to possess dual power. An agent *does* something; he or she deliberates, decides and acts. That which is not an agent does nothing; it is patient (perhaps acted upon). Thus, for example, we talk of rain falling, but it would be more scientifically accurate to say that past events (e.g. rising barometric pressure) bring about rain. Rain is not the agent of falling; it does not *do* anything. By contrast, when Beth pays her tuition fees, that is something she does; she acts. She is not acted upon.

Suppose we look from an anti-freewill/externalist point of view at Beth's decision to pay her tuition fees. We imagine the entire flow of Beth's personal history available before us. We see that right at the edge of that flow sits Beth, in the student accounting office, debating whether to pay tuition fees. We also see, although Beth does not grasp this yet, that circumstances wholly other than the decision suffice for her decision. If she believes, with a conviction of freedom, that she has dual power, she is mistaken. She cannot change the past; she cannot change what she is fated to decide. 'Deciding' is something that happens to her, not something she does. Just as barometric pressure makes rain fall, past circumstances make Beth pay her tuition fees. The decision is all sparkle, glitter and noise; her past does all the necessary work.[14]

Externalism seems to throw the baby (agency, action) out with the bathwater (free will, dual power). Thomas Nagel sums up the main trouble with the anti-freewill/externalist position as follows: 'Something peculiar happens when we view action from an... external standpoint. Some of its most important features seem to vanish under the... gaze. Actions seem no longer assignable to individual agents as sources, but become instead components of the flux of events in the world of which the agent is a part.'[15]

I shall not try to adjudicate between the freewill model and the anti-freewill model or between internalism and externalism concerning explanation with which the debate over free will is connected. In part, I confess, this is because for me there is something inescapable about the conviction of freedom. The conviction seems utterly essential to some of my decisions. In them, my past seems a kind of inheritance limiting but allowing me to make some fresh decision in the present. So rather than conceding that the conviction is unreasonable or unwarranted, and asserting that it should be displaced (although I cannot imagine how to eradicate it), I favour instead a different and agnostic approach. This is to remain open and receptive to philosophers who champion free will: to learn if free will can be illuminated and ultimately both vindicated and made compatible with science.

Now I realize that not all readers will give the same preference to 'saving how the author's decisions seem to him'. I wish I had a decisive argument for free will, but unfortunately I do not. However in my judgement, philosophers are far from the last word on free will. True, Searle's dilemma is pressing and genuine, but patient waiting and receptivity to further contributions may dull one of its horns.

To sum up, whether persons possess free will depends on whether explanatory externalism is required of decisions and actions. It also depends on whether the scientific image of persons will or should displace the view of persons offered by folk psychology of free and rational agents. The idea that we have a power of free choice is not without profound and vexing complexities.

8.5 A Happy Ending

No discussion of what it is like to be a person is complete without mention of happiness. Three hundred years before the birth of Christ, Aristotle concluded one of the most famous passages in the history of philosophy with the thesis that, more than anything else, persons want to be happy.[16] While some people may doubt whether happiness is so singly important, none can doubt that happiness *is* important. Given the opportunity for happiness or unhappiness, no person would willingly (rationally, freely?) choose unhappiness.

However, it does not take observational genius to realize that happiness is hard to achieve. The world is not designed with the happiness of people in mind. It is filled with hardship of all sorts. Millions of people lead lives of brutal misery and suffering. Some philosophers, such as the philosophical pessimist, Arthur Schopenhauer (1788–1860), have even gone so far as to say that given the evils of the world happiness is not possible. No person of sane or sound mind could be happy. Only a fool or a madman can be happy. Others, such as Bertrand Russell (1872–1970) in his book *The Conquest of Happiness* (1930), admit that life is often unhappy, but contend that many people are unhappy simply because they do not know what happiness is. Sensitive, intelligent people can be happy if they set their minds to it, although before seeking happiness, people should ponder what they seek.

What is happiness? My dictionary defines 'happiness' as a feeling of pleasure or contentment, in short happiness is identified with 'happy feeling'. To be happy is to feel happy. However, philosophers and psychologists often distinguish happy feeling from happy person. Georg Henrik Von Wright in *The Varieties of Goodness* (1963), says that a happy person is someone who in judging or assessing the circumstances of his or her life derives pleasure or satisfaction from those circumstances. 'Happiness is not in the circumstances' but 'springs into being' because of the judgement or assessment of the circumstances.

Perhaps no psychologist has spent more time or energy in the investigation of happiness than Mihaly Csikszentmihalyi, professor and former chairperson of the Department of Psychology at the University of Chicago. In his *Flow: The Psychology of Optimal Experience* (1990), he claims that a happy person is someone who derives satisfaction from reflection on his 'life themes' – the overall character and structure of his life. He writes: 'The tide of rising expectations is stilled; unfulfilled needs no longer trouble the mind'.

What is the difference between happiness as feeling (of pleasure or contentment) and happiness over circumstances or themes of one's life, that is, a happy person? The difference is twofold. One is that we cannot assume that just because a person feels unhappy that they are unhappy as a person. To be a happy person is to be in a certain positive relationship to one's life; and someone can be in a happy relationship to their life even though unpleasant things happen and even though they are sad at the present time. Perhaps they have a severe headache or have just discovered that their car needs an expensive repair. They feel unhappy at the moment, but otherwise are pleased with the gist or thrust of their life. If, by contrast, news of repair makes them an unhappy person, we should be pinpointing not only, or perhaps not at all, current unhappy feelings, but discouragement and regret over their life itself – its themes and circumstances. Perhaps news of the bad car infects their assessment of life and turns it sour and negative.

Similar observations can be made about happy feelings and unhappy persons. As Von Wright notes: 'A piece of news, say of an unexpected inheritance, can make a man jump with joy. But whether it makes him happy. . . can only be seen from effects of a longer lasting and less obvious showing on his subsequent life'. Happy feelings – pleasure, contentment, gladness – may make essential or important contributions toward being a happy person, but they can occur in a person without making them happy *as a person*. To be a happy person they must pass positive judgement on their life; perhaps not each and every moment of that life, but on the living of it itself and on whether they are satisfied with the course and character of life.

Another – the second – significant difference between happiness as a feeling and in one's person can be described as follows: Happy people are not crushed or degraded by negativity. Someone engulfed by negativity, such as a severely guilt-ridden person, may still experience (albeit occasional) happy feelings. They may be pleased to see their children, take delight in an ice-cold beer and even appreciate that on balance their days are not filled with suffering. But they are unhappy given the judgement they pass on their 'circumstances of life'. They may judge that they do not deserve to live or that they should be punished or that they are not worthy of their children's visit. Unhappy judgments may insinuate themselves into their daily routine making them feel afflicted in their person, although not for this reason precluded from pleasurable (happy) feelings.

Manic depressives are persons notoriously capable of happy feelings but unhappy as persons.[17] Robert Schumann, the composer discussed in the last chapter, seems to have been a manic depressive. Schumann felt elevated, expansive, glad, for periods of weeks or even months, all the while harbouring, in some sense, attitudes of inadequacy and self-reproach, and unable to function effectively or prudently socially and occupationally. His life was at loose ends and lacked positive self-assessment despite his expansive efforts to positively reconstitute it.

In a different way, nonhuman animals help to show that happy feelings are possible without being happy as a person. There are profound differences between the attitudes and capacities of animals and human beings. For instance, we human beings are capable of passing judgement on the overall circumstances of life. We can write autobiographies, keep diaries, appreciate the course of life and so on. At the same time, nonhuman animals cannot do these things. There are limited if difficult to precisely define horizons within which animals think. Life *as a whole* cannot be a source of happiness for them. Life on balance may be pleasant for them, but they cannot reflect upon and appreciate that balance.

So, although there seem to be situations in which an animal (a dolphin, chimp, whatever) has positive or 'happy' feelings, there are no situations in which it is happy by virtue of assessing the circumstances of life. People, by contrast, can be happy both in the balance and over the balance; they can possess happy feelings as well as happiness over the circumstances of life.

To sum up, when Russell asks, 'What is happiness?' we must distinguish happiness in one's person from happy feeling. The hypothesis I offer is that although happiness comes in many forms, and has many distinguishable elements or ingredients, some of which no doubt include happy feelings, a happy person is someone who in judging the circumstances of their life and its themes is pleased and satisfied. There is in them a conviction that their life is worth living.

The thesis that happiness in one's person does not rest on mere feeling can be developed in a number of ways. One line of development consists in identifying components of happiness other than feeling.

I propose that an essential component is self-respect or self-worth. Self-respect is necessary if one is to avoid becoming defeated and helpless in the face of life's disappointments and obstacles. At some point, especially during sustained and un-relieved blows to hopes and expectations, people may begin to give up. Disappointed medical students lose enthusiasm and become alienated from medical school; famous composers (like Schumann) whose lives are littered with marital discord, financial debt and unachieved ambition become apathetic and depressed. Defeat, Bertrand Russell remarks, 'makes people feel that nothing is worth doing'. Kierkegaard writes that a person who is consist-ently disappointed may feel that life is 'like a series of consonants only' and be rendered 'dumb'.[18] Such an individual may suffer from 'despair of necessity due to lack of possibility' (unhappiness over efforts which seem ineffectual and useless).

A person who respects themselves, by contrast, and who values themselves despite faults and failures, may be able to swing free of unhappiness over disappointment and defeat. Indeed, self-respecting people often seem able to press forward with renewed efforts invigorated by otherwise negative occurrences.

Another and related essential component in happiness is

autobiographical memory. Without autobiographical memory an individual may experience happy feelings but cannot be happy as a person. Even if such a subject may somehow qualify as a person they cannot count as a happy person.

Memory and recollection are necessities of the happy person, providing awareness of life themes and a perspective on the present – a broad sense of what life means to the person in the way of achievement and defeat. Only in the light of memories can a person's life assume its proper depth and meaning, for in that light a person can distinguish between the conditions of life which matter to them and those which are hollow and unimportant.

Amos Tversky is a professor of psychology at Stanford University and a recipient of the prestigious MacArthur Prize in 1984. Dale Griffen is a psychologist at the University of Waterloo in Canada. Together they contend that there are two components in happiness: one is 'endowment' (roughly, how a person feels, their current experience), and the other is 'contrast'; in particular, the contrast between a person's current condition and remembered past experience.[19] Tversky and Griffen claim that a person who cannot contrast current with past experience cannot be happy as a person. For instance, they cannot be relieved when a dreaded event does not happen or cheered when a hoped for event does occur.

Here we should agree. For victims of Korsakoff's syndrome, and others unable to reappropriate their past, the capacity for happiness as a person is stolen. They cannot make intelligent, informed assessments of their life (its circumstances and themes), because they do not recall what for them is at stake. Personal perspective is lost. Sacks' Jimmie, and others like him, lack perspective on their life.

The inability to remember and thereby evaluate life does not mean that the memory-less are unable to experience happy feelings of pleasure and contentment. Sacks reports how Jimmie liked gardening and would show rapt attention in 'following' simple music or dramas. Here, for a few short minutes or (in the case of gardening) hours Jimmie seemed to find a way of, 'transcending the incoherence of his. . . disease'. His spirits rose and he seemed elated in the moment. Conscious connections with his past were cut off; he could pass no judgement on his life themes: he could not plan, self-scrutinize, sense the connectivity of his life. But neither could he judge his life worthless or himself a miserable wretch. He would get satisfyingly lost in the moment.

Jimmie impressed Sacks as like a young child with a cheerful heart. So, perhaps Jimmie's freedom from unhappiness was merciful compensation for not having his consciousness, in Locke's terms, reach back into the past. Unhappiness is woven into the fabric of many people's lives. Jimmie's loss of memory liberates him from that net.

However, lacking a capacity for happiness as a person perhaps is the most tragic part of the destruction of autobiographical memory. Minds occluded from unhappiness are cut off from happiness as well. Their inner life as persons is mutilated or truncated. 'If the gods give any gift at all to human beings, it is reasonable for them to give happiness also; indeed, it is reasonable to give happiness more than any other human [good], in so far as it is the best of human [goods]' [Aristotle, *Nichomachean Ethics*, Bk. 1, Ch. 1.

NOTES

1 Mary Anne Warren, *Gendercide: The Implications of Sex Selection* (Rowman & Allanheld, New Jersey, 1985), p.70.

2 Owen Flanagan, *Consciousness Reconsidered* (MIT, Cambridge, MA., 1992).

3 John Locke, *An Essay Concerning Human Understanding* (Oxford University Press, Oxford, 1690/1969), Book II, Chapter XXVII, Section 9.

4 The notion of dual power has been explored by a number of philosophers, whose ideas influence the discussion to follow, foremost Robert Kane in 'Two kinds of incompatibilism', *Philosophy and Phenomenological Research* (December 1989), pp.219–54; *Free Will and Values* (SUNY, Albany, 1985).

5 Thomas Nagel, *The View From Nowhere* (Oxford University Press, Oxford, 1986), p.113.

6 Herbert Fingarette's *Heavy Drinking* (University of California, Berkeley, California, 1988) is a provocative attack on the thesis that alcoholism is a disease. The supposition that alcoholism is a disease is controversial. However, the points I am about to make can be made by reference to other sorts of local incompatibilities: brainwashing, kleptomania and numerous other disabling conditions.

7 For the reformulation, see Lyn Y. Abramson, Martin Seligman and John Teasdale, 'Learned helplessness in humans: citique and reformulation', *Journal of Abnormal Psychology*, 87 (1978), pp.50–70. Seligman's theory has been found relevant to debate over free will by Bruce Waller, *Freedom Without Responsibility* (Temple University Press, Philadelphia, 1990).

8   Peter Van Inwagen, *An Essay On Free Will* (Oxford University Press, Oxford, 1983).

9   Wilfred Sellers, 'Philosophy and the scientific image of man' in *Science, Perception and Reality* (Routledge & Kegan Paul, London, 1963).

10 'Theory' may be too sophisticated a word to describe the status of manifest image psychology. Perhaps it would be better to call it a network of concepts or principles.

11 See, for example, Frederick Ferré, 'Self-determination', *American Philosophical Quarterly*, 10 (1973), pp.165–76.

12 See, for instance, Paul Churchland, 'Eliminative materialism and propositional attitudes', *Journal of Philosophy*, 78 (1981), pp.67–90.

13 Terence Horgan and James Woodward, 'Folk psychology is here to stay' in *Mind and Cognition*, ed. William Lycan (Basil Blackwell, Oxford, 1990), p.390. This paper first appeared in *The Philosophical Review*, XCIV (1985), pp.197–225. See also Terence Horgan and George Graham, 'In defense of southern fundamentalism', *Philosophical Studies*, 62 (1991), pp.107–34.

14 The marvellous expression 'sparkle, glitter and noise' I owe to Owen Flanagan.

15 Thomas Nagel, *The View From Nowhere*, p.110.

16 Aristotle, *Nichomachean Ethics* 1097b.

17 See, for example, *Diagnostic and Statistical Manual of Mental Disorders* (Third Edition – Revised) (American Psychiatric Association, Washington, D.C., 1987), p.214ff.

18 S. Kierkegaard, *Fear and Trembling and The Sickness Unto Death*. Trans. with introduction by W. Lowrie. (Princeton University Press, Princeton, 1969), p.171.

19 A. Tversky and D. Griffen, 'Endowment and contrast in judgments of well-being' in *Strategy and Choice*, ed. R. Zechauser (MIT, Cambridge, MA., 1991), pp.297–318.

9

Consciousness and Morality

'I have led you through a very sandy desert,' remarked William James, explaining: 'But now, if I may be allowed so vulgar an expression, we begin to taste the milk in the coconut.' From the perspective of the reader of this book, the irony in James's remark should be transparent, for I hope that the earlier chapters have been neither dry nor sandy. It is also true, though, that we have not yet 'tasted' the milk in the coconut or discussed the way red looks or pain feels. We have not yet focused on one major and challenging topic in the philosophy of mind: consciousness. True, the topic of consciousness surfaced in chapters on other minds and inside persons. But it has not yet had a chapter to call its own.

9.1 Consciousness Defined

What is consciousness? Let me answer this question by asking and answering another question. What do we know about consciousness, not as a professor of philosophy or student of neurophysiology, but simply in our capacity as subjects of conscious experience?

We know the following:

> It is like something to be conscious; by contrast, it is not like anything not to be conscious. Conscious states appear like something from the inside; they seem a certain way to those in them. Being nonconscious does not seem any way at all.

To someone in pain pain hurts. Perceiving a ripe tomato may mean one visually experiences red; coconut milk may offer a sweet taste. These kinds of conscious states differ in ways connected with how they appear on the inside. The look of red is not like the look of green. Sweet taste is not like bitter taste. Pains are unpleasant.

Philosophers refer to the appearances or seemings of consciousness as 'phenomenal qualia' or 'conscious qualities' ('qualia' for short). Thus, red looks, sweet tastes and the painfulness of pains are qualia.

In saying that the appearances are interior I do not mean that if a brain surgeon took off the top of your skull and peered into your brain while you savoured coconut milk, they would see sweet qualia. Evidently, all they would see, in the words of Thomas Nagel, 'is a grey mass of neurons.'[1] I mean that the qualia are interior with a type of interiority that is different from the way that your neurons are inside your head. Qualia are inside in the sense that there is something it is like to experience sweet tastes, and there is no obvious reason to think that this inside experience can be altogether open to public inspection.

By contrast, there is nothing it is like not to be conscious: to be a stone, ocean wave or pencil. Things do not appear to them in any way at all. The interior of a stone can be wholly open for public inspection. A surfer may relish a wave's qualities, but there are no qualia in waves. Relish is in the eye of the beholder and not in the wave itself. Should you accidentally stab a school friend with a pencil and he retort 'It hurts', he does not mean that the pencil is in pain. He means of course he is.

9.2 Five Roles of Consciousness

Consciousness plays five major roles in philosophy. Each poses problems and excites controversy. Some roles should be familiar to readers of earlier chapters. The fifth and last will occupy the closing sections of the present chapter.

First, the qualitative character – the subjective appearance – of consciousness is a *troubling impediment* to the physical scientific understanding of consciousness. There seem to be two very different kinds of things occurring in the world: the physical goings on that can be studied by science and exposed to public inspection, and those other things – qualia – that belong in consciousness and which must be experienced from the inside. There are brains; and then there are looks, tastes and pains.

Second, conceptions of consciousness serve *to orient and justify scepticism* about other minds. The person who consciously doubts whether other minds exist cannot doubt whether they themselves are conscious. The one and only consciousness of which they can and should be sure is their own.

Third, the concept of consciousness is the foundation of *explanations* of human behaviour. I withdraw my hand from the flame because it induces pain; you emulate another person's behaviour because you experience envy over their popularity and success. Without feeling envy, you would not emulate. Without pain, I would not withdraw.

The fourth role played by consciousness is as the alleged bearer of *personal identity*. John Locke is probably the most notable exponent of the view that the historical identity of a person hinges on the backward or retrospective stretch of their consciousness. If I should happen to remember experiencing the things that four-year-old Georgie Graham experienced on the streets of Brooklyn, New York, in 1949, then I am one and the same person as that boy. He grew up to be me. The chain of identity is as strong and expansive as connections provided by the autobiographical memory of the person.

Fifth, and finally, consciousness plays a *moral* role. A number of moral philosophers contend that all and only conscious creatures morally count. Non-conscious things (waves, stones, pencils, etc.) do not count, morally.

William James (1842–1910) the great Harvard philosopher and psychologist of the turn of the last century, whose words began the chapter, writes: 'Neither moral relations nor the moral law can swing *in vacuo*. Their only habitat can be a mind which feels them.'[2] The Australian philosopher Peter Singer, a powerful voice in the animal liberation movement, writes: 'The only acceptable limit to our moral concern is the point at which there is no awareness... no conscious preference, and hence no capacity to experience.'[3] James and Singer believe that the fact that a creature is conscious means that it counts, morally. Conscious creatures possess moral standing. This is not to say that every animal has moral standing. (What about worms and paramecia? It is doubtful whether they are conscious.) But it is to say that if things seem a certain way to animals, if they feel, sense and perceive, then such animals possess moral standing.

What does it mean to possess moral standing or to morally count? To possess moral standing is to be the sort of thing which deserves respect and ought to be given consideration by fair-minded moral agents. A person, for instance, can be treated fairly or unfairly; a stone cannot. A person can be wronged or disrespected; a wave cannot. Persons possess moral standing; stones and waves do not.

Suppose on a hot day I dig a hole. To take a rest I sit on a stone. If the stone is owned, the owner may protest, but the stone itself is indifferent to what happens. For the sake of the owner I may refrain from sitting, but I show no disrespect to the stone by sitting upon it.

At the base of the hole I set a trap to kill a rabbit for my private collection of stuffed animals. The rabbit is not indifferent to what happens; it strongly prefers not to be trapped. Do I wrong the rabbit in trapping it?

According to James and Singer, the answer is yes. Take any form of consciousness, James exclaims, 'however slight', which any creature may have, and this form of consciousness makes its own moral demands, carries its own moral imperative.[4] The rabbit 'asks' that I not trap it and, to be fair-minded – given that I wish the poor creature for no more serious purpose than my collection – I must refrain.

The five basic roles played by consciousness rotate in the centre of several controversies. Here are two examples.

1   Consciousness and Materialism

The most intense controversy concerning consciousness is whether consciousness is material or physical. Is consciousness something physical or something apart from the physical? Materialists contend that being conscious is one and the same as being a particular sort of physical state of the brain. Red looks, sweet tastes and pains are nothing more than particular sorts of neural conditions.

It should be noted that if being conscious is one and the same as being a particular sort of brain state, consciousness poses no stumbling block or impediment to its physical scientific study. Consciousness can be exposed to physical science, since with proper technology the brain can be exposed. A scientist familiar with relevant neural conditions can understand how a ripe tomato looks to you: they can determine whether you visually experience red. They also can discover the quality of your taste sensation on tasting coconut milk.

2 Consciousness and explanation

There is a connected though distinct controversy over whether reference to consciousness truly explains behaviour. Some philosophers charge that the idea that consciousness has an explanatory role in human behaviour is obsolete because we are on the verge of a neuroscientific revolution which will result in a genuinely physical-scientific understanding of human behaviour. In this new understanding – so the story goes – there will be no need for reference to consciousness. Pain does not cause me to withdraw my hand from a flame. Instead, the neural condition which realizes or underlies my pain is responsible for the withdrawal. Pain is an *epiphenomenon* ('epi' is Greek meaning 'above') which is not part of the physical phenomena in the brain which determine withdrawal. It has no impact on behaviour.

9.3 Consciousness, Materialism and Explanation

No philosopher of mind should be without opinions concerning the controversies surrounding consciousness. As readers familiar with the seventh chapter will recall, my own view of Materialism is that Franz Brentano showed, over a hundred years ago, that Materialism should be resisted. Brentano argued that Materialism runs foul of the Intentionality or aboutness of the mental, including the Intentionality of various forms of conscious mentality. To take a simple illustration, suppose that I consciously envy your success; the envy is about your success. If one takes the arguments of the seventh chapter seriously, nothing neural can be envious, for nothing neural can possess envy's Intentionality.

A second difficulty for Materialism, unmentioned in the seventh chapter, consists in a problem posed just by consciousness and is independent of Intentionality. There are several ways in which to characterize the problem. One goes as follows.

If Materialism is true, then two people exactly alike physically should also be exactly alike in terms of how things appear to them. Absolutely identical physical twins – molecule for molecule duplicates – should be consciousness or qualia twins. This is because being conscious is supposed to be one and the same as being a particular sort of brain state. Hence, persons in the same brain state should be the same in their conscious interior. But is this really correct? Must physical twins be qualia twins?

Imagine that a molecule for molecule duplicate of me, Physical Twin-me, looks at a ripe tomato. Can't we coherently suppose that he sees green when I see red, although we both perceive the same tomato (in the same lighting conditions)? Can't he, my physical double, see the tomato as green even though I see it as red? Is that possible? If such qualia inversion (green for red) is possible, then the putative identity of being conscious with being a particular sort of neurological condition fails to hold.

The possibility is bizarre, you will object. If Twin and me are exactly alike physically, we should be exactly alike consciously as well. That was my first reaction on imagining my physical twin too. Qualia, on this reaction, 'fit' the underlying physiology. Same physiology spells same consciousness. But if we set aside the first reaction and reflect more carefully, the possibility is intelligible and coherent.

What warrants saying that qualia inversion is possible? A tale reveals the answer. Once upon a time there was a famous neuro-scientist, Mary. She opened up my brain and insisted that the tomato looks green to me, although I sincerely insisted that it looks red. Mary gave much thought to how she could prove that it looks green to me, my protestations to the contrary. She discovered my absolutely identical physical twin and he sincerely asserted that it looks green. Must I be moved by my twin? Must I announce, like him, that the tomato looks green – to me?

Notice that this is not a disagreement over whether the tomato really *is* green, whatever that may mean. It is a conflict over the tomato's subjective appearance. Can I be mistaken in how the tomato looks to me?

It should be noted that, if I must maintain that the tomato looks green because my twin insists that it looks green, then I am abdicating authority over how things appear to me. I am admitting that I earlier mistook how the tomato looks, for I am allowing myself to be corrected by the report of my twin. Something like this materialists regard as inevitable if Materialism is true. Materialism requires abandoning the idea that we each are the final or ultimate judge of how things appear to us.

The principle that each and every person is the final or ultimate judge of how things appear to him or her I shall call a *subjective authority model of consciousness*. The opposing model would be (roughly) that a person's judgement or sense of how things seem to them must be consistent with evidence taken from outside the person (from their molecular twin perhaps) or from physical science.

Common sense or folk psychology presupposes a subjective authority model. I am the authority on how things seem to me; you are the expert on how things seem to you. If you try to inform me that I don't know how things seem to me, I would regard you as rude, uninformed or otherwise disposed to ruin the very idea that I have my own conscious point of view. Your judgements express your point of view – your consciousness; my judgements express my point of view – my consciousness. To me the tomato appears red, even if to you it looks green. The moment your judgements defeat mine is the moment I no longer possess an authority and perhaps even a consciousness of my own.

Much can be learned from examining the subjective authority model. I would speculate that the authority is limited and that the model is most plausible in cases of simple sensations and perceptions (pains, red looks and so on) and not complex emotions or feelings (jealousy, envy and so on). But my concern here is not to examine the model but to combat the suspicion that qualia inversion is bizarre and incoherent. I have done so by posting a consequence of Materialism: namely, Materialism overthrows my entitlement to sincerely disagree with my molecule for molecule twin. More generally, Materialism subverts my authoritative role as reporter of how things seem to me. But can that authority be subverted? Can't I be right that the tomato looks red to me, even though it looks green to my twin? Preserving my subjective point of view opens up the possibility and coherence of qualia inversion.

It also helps to block the door to Materialism. It permits me to differ from my duplicate; it blocks Mary from determining how things look or taste to me without asking me first.

As mentioned, recent controversy surrounding consciousness also challenges whether our behaviour hinges on what happens inside us, consciously. Do I avoid the open flame because it causes me pain? Or do I avoid it because of physical properties of my brain such that pain is irrelevant?

Here I will say only that I find epiphenomenalism, the position which denies causal power to consciousness, so grossly implausible that I cannot imagine how anyone could embrace it. My own opinion on this matter is independently shared and expressed by the philosopher Terence Horgan: 'Denying the causal efficacy of qualia is, I submit, just too much. Epiphenomenalism. . . should be an utter last resort, to be embraced only if all viable alternatives prove to be. . . paradoxical and untenable.' Horgan also remarks: 'I find myself utterly incapable of believing that the phenomenal quality of my experience never affects my behaviour, and I suspect that you do too. The qualitative content of various pleasures and pains, for instance, seems undeniably to have an effect upon our subsequent behaviour in pursuit of such pleasures and in avoidance of such pains.'[5] Painful qualia (feelings) naturally trigger psychological mechanisms or overt actions to eliminate the qualia or their causes. I avoid the flame because it hurts. Consciousness is one of the most salient sources of human behaviour.

I have, as you may guess, left out a lot of details and rebuttals supplied both by fans of Materialism and especially by friends of the causal irrelevance of consciousness.[6] However, I have said enough to indicate the general character of current controversies surrounding consciousness. Consciousness is inseparable from controversy.

The two main points I wish to extract from the above sections of the chapter are as follows:

1   There is something it is like to be conscious, whereas there is nothing it is like not to be conscious. Thus, for example, there is something it is like to be a person, horse or hen, for such creatures are conscious, but nothing it is like to be a stone, tree or wave, for such things are not conscious.

2   The topic of consciousness inspires several difficult problems for philosophers and motivates controversy.

I have now completed a quick survey of the nature of consciousness and its important roles in philosophy. In the remainder of this chapter, I wish to examine the significance of the topic of consciousness for moral philosophy. The examination shows that philosophy of mind can have important practical consequences. In the case to be discussed below, philosophical analysis of consciousness has immediate relevance to the treatment of nonhuman animals.

9.4   Animal Liberation

No philosophical debate has stirred more attention in moral philosophy and the popular press in recent years than the debate inspired by the publication in 1975 of Peter Singer's *Animal Liberation*. In that book Singer argued that human treatment of nonhuman animals is fundamentally morally objectionable. He argued that we should be forced

to make radical changes in our treatment of animals that would involve our diet, the farming methods we use, experimental procedures in many fields of science, our approach to wildlife and to hunting, trapping and the wearing of furs, and areas of entertainment like circuses, rodeos, and zoos. As a result, a vast amount of suffering would be avoided.[7]

As rarely happens with a philosophy book, people sat up and took notice. Some made deep changes in their lives, by dropping meat from their diets and animal products from their lifestyles. Here is how one reader described his reaction.

I have most of my adult life paid people to axe-murder and bludgeon to death a considerable variety of creatures, some of whom were babies, so that I might eat them; they were, in fact, tasty. That this description applied to my actions or that there were moral questions about those practices is something to which I was largely oblivious until reading [Singer].[8]

I have three objectives in the rest of this chapter. First, I want to discuss the idea that nonhuman animals count or matter, morally, just because they are conscious. Second, I want to explore, and ultimately to criticize, the moral weight which Singer says attaches to different forms or types of conscious life. Third, I would also like to suggest the importance for moral philosophy of having a philosophy of consciousness.

Philosophers have long felt that there is something inescapable but also elusive about the moral status of animals or at least those which are conscious. Assuming that conscious animals possess moral standing, how do we know whether animal A, who might be a member of a very different species from our own, counts more heavily, or less heavily, than creature B, another animal or perhaps a human person? To take a popular illustration, when used in medical research, nonhuman animals often suffer. Are we morally justified in imposing burdens on animals by using them in research? Suppose suffering animals count. Do they count more (or less) than the gains or benefits primarily to humans of research?

One of the chief problems facing the idea that conscious animals count is how moral consideration ought to be distributed or parcelled to all conscious creatures. It is useful to distinguish between *unscaled* and *scaled* ways of distributing moral concern. To the unscaling distributor the brilliant physicist Albert Einstein counts no more (or less) than a frog. Killing Einstein is equally evil to killing a frog. The scaling advocate, in contrast, acknowledges morally relevant differences between Einstein and frogs. The scaling distributor asserts that some forms of consciousness are inherently superior to other forms. The death of Einstein is much worse than the death of a frog.

There are two main approaches to scaling moral concern for conscious creatures. One approach scales or differentiates by species: members of the human species count more than members of nonhuman species. Einstein counts more than a frog because Einstein is human. The other approach scales by judgements about the superiority of some individual conscious lives over others. Einstein matters more than a frog because *his* conscious life is superior to the frog's. Einstein's life matters more, not because he is human, but because his consciousness is superior as consciousness. If contrary to fact Einstein really was not human, his life would still matter more.

Of course, superiority according to the second approach is not absolutely unrelated to superiority according to the first approach. The conscious life of a human being may often be judged superior to the conscious life of a member of another species. Human consciousness may typically come out on top. But that is not incompatible with the second approach. The point of the second approach is to resist rote application of species preference and to consider each and every conscious creature in its own terms.

Here I will not consider unscaled distribution, but will concentrate only on distributing in the manner recommended by Singer, who favours a version of the second form of scaled distribution. Happily for science in the twentieth century, Einstein's mother did not distribute her moral sympathies without differentiating between her son and his pet frogs. (Did Einstein have pet frogs?) Singer's proposal for attaching different moral weights to different forms of conscious life goes as follows.

Some conscious lives are inherently superior to others. Those which are inherently superior count more, morally, than those which are inferior. Meanwhile, the inherent superiority (inferiority) of a conscious life is a function of whether the life would be chosen or preferred, in contrast to other lives, by a neutral or impartial imaginative participant in that life. Creatures whose lives would be preferred from such a standpoint are superior and carry more moral weight than creatures whose lives would not be chosen.

In short, if A's conscious life is preferred – compared on the inside – to B's, A counts more heavily than B. Let's illustrate.

Suppose that I have suddenly been placed in a situation where I have a choice of saving one of two creatures from a fire. One is a barnyard hen; the other is a mentally handicapped human infant. According to Singer, then I must try to imagine myself as living the conscious lives of both hen and handicapped child. I must consider what existence is like to the child and I must 'do my best to grasp what it is like to be a hen'.[9] I do not then discount the hen just because it is a hen. The point is that once we grasp hen and handicapped infant consciousness, we can understand which form of consciousness – whose conscious life – is preferable. If we as impartial imaginative participants prefer to be the hen, despite the difference in species, then the hen carries more moral weight than the handicapped infant. Between saving the hen or infant, morally, I ought to save the hen.

I shall call Singer's idea for scaling or ascertaining the relative moral weight of different forms of conscious life, the *principle of imaginative interior impartial comparison*. The principle is a verbal mouthful because the idea behind it is a conceptual mindful. It may be abbreviated as the *inner comparison principle*.

The principle of imaginative interior impartial comparison, or the inner comparison principle, plays an important part in Singer's moral scheme. Singer rejects preference for species membership as the bench mark of moral weight. Mere difference in species between child and hen is morally irrelevant. He dubs species preference 'speciesism', which means that, in his moral universe, it is a moral evil similar to sexism or racism. In order to avoid speciesism, he appeals to the principle; it says avoid pegging the moral weight of a creature on species. Peg moral weight on the subjective character of the creature's conscious life. The principle also tells us to factor out externalities in determining the value of a life. Singer would urge that to be fair to the infant, I cannot save the hen just because it is my pet; and to be fair to the hen I cannot save the infant just because it is my child. A creature's relation to me (or to us) cannot be what makes its life superior or weighty, morally. The superior form of conscious life must be fixed by internal considerations: by what it is like on the inside. In comparing horses and humans, for instance, Singer says, one must decide, in effect, 'between the value of the life of a horse to the horse, and the value of the life of a human to the human.'[10]

Singer admits that the principle imposes conceptual strains, but he fails to appreciate the gross difficulties which actually undermine the principle. Some difficulties are familiar to students of moral philosophy. Singer's principle is a version of what moral philosophers call 'the choice criterion of value'. The key idea behind the choice criterion is that the value of something (in this case, a conscious life) rests on whether it would be chosen by a certain type of chooser (in this case, an impartial imaginative and comparative participant).

Certain moral difficulties are built into the choice criterion. These are neatly summed up by Vinit Haksar in his book *Equality, Liberty, and Perfectionism*: 'To be fair between different forms of life requires a choice from some sort of neutral value-free standpoint, but such an idea is not a coherent one.'[11]

For the principle to work comparison has to be made by choosers who are not biased. If we assume people can project themselves into genuinely different forms of conscious life (an implausible assumption as it turns out), which types of consciousness actually end up being preferred may depend partly on background moral beliefs or values which the projectors possess. Anti-speciesists like Singer may prefer being a hen; whereas speciesists may select the existence of the handicapped child. What constitutes impartiality or neutrality in choosing between different forms of consciousness? Is anti-speciesism necessarily the only impartial position? How much influence should background moral beliefs have in choosing a form? Are only certain sorts of background beliefs morally acceptable?

The principle says that the moral agent's project is to choose among various forms of conscious life. But what moral attitudes may they carry into their imaginative projections? Is it speciesist to judge that human life is always better than animal life even after one has imaginatively tasted animal existence?

In addition to moral questions, there is another set of problems for the principle. These are problems associated with imaginative projection – or 'imaginative reconstruction' as Singer calls the task. The most troublesome question is whether we really can grasp the consciousness of a member of another species and experience life, albeit vicariously, from the creature's point of view. What is it like to be a hen, eagle or horse? Is this even a coherent question? How would we discover the right answer?

In the words of Colin McGinn, a philosopher of mind at Rutgers University, 'apprehending animals as they are in themselves' should enable us to give them their proper due, morally.[12] Singer requires extraordinary imaginative feats in the apprehension of animals as they are in themselves. Singer's moral outlook is shaped by adherence to a comparison principle which requires grasping what it is like to be an animal – or as he also puts it, the value of the animal's existence to the animal.

9.5 An Impossible Consciousness

It is clear from Singer's description of how to distribute moral concern among different creatures that he intends to make the following *imagination requirement*: Between any two individuals of any species, to determine whose life is superior and carries the most moral weight, it is necessary to grasp their lives from the inside. One must imagine oneself as 'living the lives of... those affected... by my decision.'[13] One must turn one's consciousness temporarily and imaginatively into another's consciousness. One must imagine being them.

Let us suppose that one can imaginatively project oneself inside another human person's consciousness. I can know what it is like to be you; you can know what it is like to be me. The supposition may be worth questioning, especially in cases of projection into severely handicapped and pathological human beings, but I shall not question it here. Here I wish to explore the case of animals. What about animals? Can I grasp what it is like to be an animal? Singer says yes. The answer is no.

It is not obvious why Singer says yes. I suspect that this is because he assumes that grasping what it is like to be an animal is essentially analogous to grasping what it is like to be another human being. Just as I can imagine what it is like to be you, I can imagine what it is like to be a horse or hen. But can I?

The correct answer is no. Human beings do not have and never can acquire the sorts of conceptual equipment, the perceptual endowment, to imagine what it is like to be an animal. We are just *too different* from them. Hence, we cannot grasp what it is like to be them. Moreover, this also means that we are barred from using Singer's inner comparison principle.

The charge is not that we cannot grasp what certain animal experiences are like. If a ripe tomato appears red to me, perhaps it looks red to a horse as well; hence, I may imagine how a horse visually experiences the tomato. But imagining an equine colour experience is not the same as imagining being equine. Some animal experiences may be imagined; but then, it takes more than imagining some experiences to imagine being animal – namely, it takes imagining a full range of experiences from the animal's point of view. It requires being able to extensively and vicariously place oneself into the animal's form of conscious life.

My charge is that even if we can imagine certain animal experiences, we cannot grasp what it is like to be an animal. We are just too different from animals to project ourselves into a full range of their experiences. To penetrate to deep or extensive levels or forms of animal consciousness is impossible.

The basis for my charge may be made vivid by considering a description offered by Kathleen Akins, a philosopher and neuro-scientist at the University of Illinois, of trying to imagine what it is like to be an eagle as it spots its prey and dives at fantastic speeds. Here one is faced with not just imagining eagle colour experiences, but imagining what it is like to *be* an eagle embodied in its unique physiology, possessing its special visual acuities and cued to salient features of its environment.

How does a bird of prey 'attend to' a scene, look at the world? What does that mean and, more interestingly, what would that be like? Here, in my mind's eye, I imagined myself perched high in the top of a dead tree sporting a pair of very peculiar bifocal glasses. More precisely, I pictured myself in a pair of *quadra*focals, with different lenses corresponding to the horizontal band, foveal and peripheral regions of the eagle's eye. I wonder whether it is just like that, I thought, like peering successively through each lens, watching the world move in and out of focus de-pending on whether I look. First I stare through the horizontal section and scan the horizon for other predators; then I switch to my left central lens and make sure no one is approaching from behind; then I use the high-powered temporal lens to scrutinize the water below for shadows of some dinner. Is that how the eagle sees the world, I wondered? Is that what it is like to have [eagle eyes]?[14]

We will never know. Our eyes anatomically are very unlike those of an eagle. We also don't have the habits of perching, predation and flight which eagles possess. And they don't have the conceptual sophistication which we possess. An eagle, for instance, not only can't remember whether it's lunchtime, it can't even appreciate that it is an eagle. There is absolutely no evidence that eagles possess self-concepts or ideas of themselves as predators. The path into the conscious point of view of this predator is blocked by the differences between us.

Even animals (notably the higher mammals) which seem very like us are actually most unlike us – on the inside. Today's most fashionable type of animal theorizing, cognitive ethology, has pro-vided several elegant studies of the conceptual equipment and perceptual capacities of animals. One of the most detailed is a study by Dorothy Cheney and Robert Seyfarth, two professors at the University of Pennsylvania, of the minds of East African vervet monkeys. Here is how they summarize the results of their study in *How Monkeys See the World*: 'There are... many ways in which a vervet's view of her world is very different from our own... Her mental states are not accessible to her: she does not know that she knows. Further, monkeys seem unable to attribute mental states to others or to recognize that other's behaviour is also caused by motives, beliefs, and desires.' Again, the scientists say: 'The inability to examine one's own mental states or to attribute mentality to others severely constrains the ability of monkeys to transmit information, to deceive, to feel empathy with one another ... *We* attribute motives, plans, and strategies to the animals, but they... do not.'[15]

The conclusion to be drawn from this is that vervet monkeys fail to grasp that they themselves are conscious; they don't know what it is like to be them. Their consciousness exists in a kind of self-comprehending vacuum.

Suppose you try, Singerlike, to grasp what it is like to be a vervet. You say to yourself, 'Despite the strain, I have a pretty good idea what it is like to be a vervet'. Do you? How can you? If Cheney and Seyfarth are right, *you* cannot grasp what it is like to be a vervet because vervets themselves don't know what it is like. They don't think of themselves as being conscious; they fail to recognize that there is anything it is like to be them. And you can't know what it is like to be X when X itself can't know what it is like to be X.

Let us call a person who tries to grasp what it is like to be a vervet 'Vervette'. Vervette is a perfectly normal human being except for the fact that having read *Animal Liberation* she is deeply morally concerned for animals. Suppose that Vervette is suddenly placed in a situation where she has to choose between saving one of two creatures from a fire. Suppose one is a normal four-year-old human child and the other is a monkey.

Vervette wants to grasp what it is like to be a monkey as well as what it is like to be a child so that she can allocate her moral concern according to the impartially preferred or superior form of consciousness. Suppose that she completes grasping child consciousness. Her second task, then, is:

(1) Imagine myself to be a monkey

She then strains her imagination and projects herself into the mind of a monkey. What happens there? What is monkey consciousness like? What does it seem, feel or appear like? It would grossly violate the discoveries of Cheney and Seyfarth for Vervette to think:

(2) I have achieved the desired imaginative reconstruction. I am now simulating monkey consciousness. I am living a monkey's life, albeit projectively.

For monkeys lack that degree of conscious reflexivity. Although conscious, they have no reflective appreciation of the consciousness they possess; thus, Vervette cannot picture herself living (or recollecting having lived) monkey life.

To make the bar to monkey life still more vivid and impenetrable imagine that Vervette tries to imagine herself as a monkey terrified by the fire. Will she be able to imagine herself as such a monkey? She can't think:

(3) I am now terrified by the fire, monkey-like, imaginatively

because monkeys may feel terror but they do not know that it is terror which they feel.

To the question of what it is like to be an animal (hen, eagle, horse) we can only plead ignorance. It is futile to frame a human-to-animal imagination requirement because animals possess a subjectively alien form of conscious life. No matter how resolute and sympathetically disposed a person is, they cannot bring about the desired projection into the animal mind. There are profound differences between us and every other species.[16]

Once more, I am not charging that nothing can be known of what animal experience is like. Alien subjective worlds can overlap, perhaps permitting partial or fragmentary projection. What does the horse visually experience when it sees the tomato? Perhaps red like me. I am also not charging that we are unwarranted in attributing consciousness to animals. Attribution of conscious feelings, attitudes and other states of mind to animals is warranted by careful and systematic observation of animal behaviour, as readers familiar with the fourth chapter will recall. However, it is one thing to know whether an eagle is hungry; it is another to know how it feels to be a hungry eagle. Nothing known about overlap can reveal how life seems to an animal. Nothing can tell us, as Singer wants us to fathom, the import of animal existence to an animal.

Aware that people may have difficulty projecting themselves into animal lives, Singer says, 'Nevertheless I think I can make some sense of the idea of choosing. . . and I am fairly confident that. . . some forms of life would be seen as preferable to others.'[17] Perhaps. But perhaps this is only because some forms of life could not be seen *at all*. If human/animal comparisons are impossible, humans might prefer humanity by default. If Vervette is occluded from monkey life, Vervette inevitably will prefer any human life to which she may gain imaginative admission.

Singer's motives for making the imagination requirement, of course, may be morally commendable. For people like him who assume that animals count, morally, there needs to be a method by which to determine how much they count. Generally speaking, people know on which side their toast is buttered, and will prefer that side unless they can be shown that something is to be said for the other side. What counts as a benefit to humans which would be defeated by a burden to animals? We need answers to questions about experimenting on nonhuman animals, whether we should refrain from eating them, hunting and slaughtering them, and so forth. Singer's suggestion, even if intuitively appealing, is ultimately implausible: take their conscious standpoint, and feel what is, from their subjective point of view, their mode of existence; then make an intrinsic comparison. Is it worse to be a factory-farmed chicken or a person without cheap eggs? Is it worse to be a rabbit caught in a trap or a collector with a gap in his collection? Is it better to be an eagle spotting its prey or a human hunter spotting an eagle as its prey?

In this comparative interior our role as Singeresque moral agents is to compare and contrast how life is to creatures affected by our actions. Animals are looked at not in terms of their real or potential usefulness to us, but as apprehensible in themselves. We discover them in themselves by vicariously living their lives.

Singer's principle would be exciting if it worked. But alas, theoretically, it fails. There is no inter-species comparative interior. Nothing can enable us to know what it is like to be an animal.[18]

Human being is our mode of consciousness-in-the-world, insulating us, as well as isolating us from them.

NOTES

1   Thomas Nagel, *What Does It All Mean?* (Oxford University Press, Oxford, 1987), p.29.
2   William James, *Essays in Pragmatism*, ed. A. Castell (Hafner, New York, 1948), p.69.
3   Peter Singer, 'The significance of animal suffering', *Behavioural and Brain Sciences*, 13 (1990), p.12.
4   William James, *Essays in Pragmatism*, p.73.
5   Terence Horgan, 'Supervenient qualia', *Philosophical Review*, XCVI (1987), p.504.
6   Horgan observes that the possibility of qualia inversion conflicts with mind/brain supervenience (see chapter 7, section 5 of this book). Is this grounds for rejecting inversion?
7   Peter Singer, *Animal Liberation* (Avon Books, New York, 1975), p.17.
8   Donald VanDeVeer, 'Interspecific justice', *Inquiry*, 22 (1979), p.55.
9   Peter Singer, 'The significance of animal suffering', p.12. The quote is adapted from another example of Singer's, but it helps to capture the essence of his position.
10   Peter Singer, *Practical Ethics* (Cambridge University Press, Cambridge, 1979), p.89.
11   Vinit Haksar, *Equality, Liberty, and Perfectionism* (Clarendon, Oxford, 1979), p.211.
12   Colin McGinn, 'Evolution, animals, and the basis of equality', *Inquiry*, 22 (1979), p.95.
13   Peter Singer, 'The significance of animal suffering', p.11.
14   Kathleen Akins, 'Science and our inner lives' in Marc Bekoff and Dale Jamieson, eds., *Interpretation and Explanation in the Study of Animal Behaviour* (Westview, Boulder, 1990), p.415.
15   Dorothy L. Cheney and Robert M. Seyfarth, *How Monkeys See The World* (University of Chicago, Chicago, 1990), p.312.
16   Perhaps I should say 'almost every other species'. See discussion of Gordon Gallup's work on self-conception in the chimpanzee in chapter 4.
17   Peter Singer, *Practical Ethics*, p.90.
18   This sceptical conclusion should not, of course, be mistaken for endorsement of moral indifference to animals. The choice is not, mercifully for animals, between Singer's principle of inner comparison and moral irrelevance. There is a third alternative: any successful post-Singer defence of animal liberation will have to thread its way through issues of animal mentality and other issues in the philosophy of mind.

A Philosophy of Mind Bookshelf

The notes and citations in each chapter offer suggested readings for term papers and other projects on a topic by topic basis. The following section gives the titles of books, some mentioned in the text, which may serve as a foundation for a personal library or reading list in philosophy of mind.

You have just read a book which introduces the philosophy of mind by covering virtually the whole broad subject. There are other types of introductions to the field. *Matter and Consciousness*, by Paul Churchland (MIT, Cambridge, 1984, revised 1988), is a well-written introduction that approaches the subject through both the mind/body problem and the problem of other minds. Churchland also offers a surprisingly clear presentation of the brand of Materialism – eliminative materialism – which he favours. William Bechtel's *Philosophy of Mind: An Overview for Cognitive Science* (Erlbaum, New Jersey, 1988) is recommended as an introduction orientated around mind/body as well as Intentionality.

The century's classic philosophy of mind book is Gilbert Ryle's *The Concept of Mind* (University of Chicago, Chicago, 1949/1984). It is delightfully written though hobbled by reliance on a form of logical behaviourism. Another important book is D.M. Armstrong's *A Materialist Theory of the Mind* (Routledge & Kegan Paul, London, 1968). Much has been written since Armstrong defending Materialism, but no book does a more comprehensive, systematic job.

Every student of philosophy of mind should have a book written by Daniel Dennett on his or her bookshelf. Dennett is particularly good at exploring the links between folk psychological and subpersonal, neurological explanations of behaviour, although his own overall position, a mixture of Materialism and evolutionary biology, is enigmatic and elusive to his professional peers. I recommend *Brainstorms* (MIT, Cambridge, MA., 1978), since it contains some of his best and most accessible essays, including the brilliant 'Why You Can't Make a Computer that Feels Pain'.

Recommending more specialized treatments, one of the most heated debates in contemporary philosophy of mind is the debate over computer minds. The literature is, of course, huge. But John Haugeland's *Artificial Intelligence: The Very Idea* (MIT, Cambridge, MA., 1985) and William Bechtel and Adele Abrahamson's *Connectionism and the Mind: An Introduction to Parallel Processing in Networks* (Basil Blackwell, Oxford, 1990) offer lucid and informed discussions of various topics in the debate. Each has the virtue of explaining the rudiments of computer science without esoteric jargon.

On the free will issue, many positions are available, with so-called 'compatibilism' attempting conceptions of freedom compatible with the rejection of dual power. Usually compatibilist freedom is called 'free action' rather than 'free will', although some compatibilists prefer describing an unimpeded will as free even when it lacks dual power. A clear, readable presentation of issues surrounding compatibilism, which also considers connections between freedom and moral responsibility, is Bruce Waller's *Freedom Without Responsibility* (Temple University Press, Philadelphia, 1990).

Owen Flanagan's *Consciousness Reconsidered* (MIT, Cambridge, MA., 1992) is a synoptic and sensitively conceived view of the place of consciousness in the material world. J. Christopher Maloney's *The Mundane Matter of the Mental Language* (Cambridge University Press, Cambridge, 1989) contains an informative introduction to the language of thought hypothesis, a significant contemporary hypothesis in philosophy of mind, which has been neglected in the present book only because of my own reluctance to expose novices to its subtle nuances. The key claim behind the language of thought hypothesis is that people cannot learn to speak a natural language (like English) without having an innate language of thought or system of mental representations with linguistic structure.

Some of the best work in contemporary philosophy of mind

takes place in journal articles. Two useful collections are *Mind and Cognition*, edited by William Lycan (Basil Blackwell, Oxford, 1991) and *The Nature of Mind*, edited by David Rosenthal (Oxford University Press, Oxford, 1991). Owen Flanagan's *The Science of Mind* (MIT, Cambridge, MA., 1991) places much contemporary philosophy of mind in proper historical perspective and contains illuminating discussion of the interdependence of psychology and philosophy of mind. For the historical roots of many contemporary issues in the philosophy of mind, including selections from thinkers such as Plato, Aristotle, Aquinas, Locke and Hume, a good resource is *The Philosophy of Mind: Classical Problems and Contemporary Issues*, edited by Brian Beakley and Peter Ludlow (MIT, Cambridge, MA., 1992).

Index